ESSENTIAL
STATISTIC
APPLIE
LINGUISTICS

ESSENTIAL STATISTICS FOR APPLIED LINGUISTICS

Using R or JASP

HANNEKE LOERTS,
WANDER LOWIE AND
BREGTJE SETON

macmillan
international
HIGHER EDUCATION

RED GLOBE
PRESS

This edition published 2020 by
RED GLOBE PRESS

Previous editions published under the imprint PALGRAVE

Red Globe Press in the UK is an imprint of Macmillan Education Limited, registered in England, company number 01755588, of 4 Crinan Street, London, N1 9XW.

Red Globe Press® is a registered trademark in the United States, the United Kingdom, Europe and other countries.

ISBN 978–1–352–00781–7 paperback

This book is printed on paper suitable for recycling and made from fully managed and sustained forest sources. Logging, pulping and manufacturing processes are expected to conform to the environmental regulations of the country of origin.

A catalogue record for this book is available from the British Library.

A catalog record for this book is available from the Library of Congress.

CONTENTS

PREFACE: HOW TO USE THIS BOOK

This book is an adapted version of *Essential Statistics for Applied Linguistics* (Lowie & Seton, 2013). The original book has been used successfully for several years, first as a reader and then in its published form, to provide students of linguistics with a practical introduction to research methodology, focused on Applied Linguistics. It is the reflection of an introductory course to statistics and methodology that we have taught since 2005, first with SPSS and later with R.

Although the book could also be used for self-study, it was designed to support a research methodology and basic statistics course. After studying the material described here, you will not have reached an expert level of statistics and methodology. The course is rather intended to serve as a First Aid kit for students enrolling in an MA of Linguistics or Applied Linguistics and who have no or very little background in this area. Nevertheless, starting from scratch, you will develop a sufficient working knowledge of statistics, so that you will be able to understand Method and Result sections in articles and be able to set up and analyse your own empirical investigations in the field of linguistics. Moreover, after this course you will be able to extend your knowledge by searching for additional resources independently and adequately.

This book takes an activity-based approach. This means that you will first be asked to consider a problem and to try to solve it with the knowledge you have before the problem will be worked out and discussed in terms of conventional methodology. It may be tempting to skip the activities, but then the learning effect may be minimized. Therefore, we advise you to seriously consider all problems and activities in the book before reading on, even if you think the answers are obvious or trivial. Only then can you achieve the maximum result of the approach.

The main, though not the only, difference between the 2013 version and the current edition of the book is that we have chosen to use open source software, that is JASP (JASP team, 2018) and R/RStudio (R Core Team, 2018; RStudio Team, 2016), instead of SPSS. R is becoming more and more popular among linguists to process and analyse data as well as to create graphics. Many analyses that can be done in R can also be done in SPSS, but many linguistic researchers have struggled with SPSS, especially when using large datasets and when more advanced statistics are required. Despite all its advantages (also see 'Getting ready to start using R and RStudio'), the R program might trigger some anxiety among students as it also requires the use of codes or syntax. This might initially cause frustration, especially for students who are unfamiliar with scripts or programming languages. The practicals in Part 2 of this book are, however, also designed for those who have no programming or statistical experience whatsoever. The structure of the practical assignments is built up in such a way that you are first taken by the hand in a step-by-step procedure and after that will be asked to apply the newly developed skills on your own. Again, following this procedure will give you the biggest chance of success. R might have a steep learning curve, but is invaluable for most students and PhD students in Linguistics and especially those who would like to conduct quantitative research using larger datasets. JASP is a program that bears more resemblance to SPSS in the sense that it has a user interface and buttons you can press, without having to use any code. An advantage of JASP compared to SPSS, apart from that it is free, is that it is much more user-friendly, that it also allows for so-called Bayesian analyses, and that the program is based on R, which leads to R-like graphs and tables. The disadvantage of JASP is that it has diminished functionality in relation to R. However, for basic analyses, JASP is a very useful program. In addition to the theoretical part (Part 1) and the practical assignments (Part 2), the companion website (macmillanihe. com/loerts-esfal) contains How To units for both JASP and R/RStudio including step-by-step explanations of how to perform the various tests discussed.

In our own research methodology course we always try to show that everyone can learn to understand and apply basic statistics. In the past thirteen years, every single student who made a serious effort to acquire statistical knowledge and skills has managed to do so using this approach, even students who had initially considered themselves as 'hopeless cases' in this respect! So there is hope, but a serious effort is required. For students who really like the topic or who need to learn more about more advanced techniques, we will offer opportunities to broaden their horizon with references to advanced statistics, so that this group will be sufficiently challenged.

The preparation of this new edition of *Essential Statistics for Applied Linguistics* would not have been possible without the valuable feedback from our students (from the MA Linguistics and the Research Master in Language and Cognition in Groningen) on several draft versions of the book. We are particularly grateful to the patient and constructive student assistants who helped us in setting up and testing the practicals and the How To units, and their editorial assistance: Marith Assen and Mara van der Ploeg. Thank you very much!

It may be obvious, but the data that are used as examples throughout the book, in the practical assignments (Part 2) and in the How To units online, are mostly made-up data to illustrate a point. The authors will not accept any claims based on these data.

Hanneke Loerts
Wander Lowie
Bregtje Seton

PART
1

1 TYPES OF RESEARCH

1.1 Introduction

The field of Applied Linguistics (AL) is a large one and this means that applied linguists are interested in many issues. Here is a random list showing a variety of topics:

- The effectiveness of early bilingual education: how effective is an early start?

- The relation between characteristics of linguistic input and language development in early bilingual children.

- Assessment of problems of elderly migrants learning Swedish.

- The lag in development in language proficiency of migrant children or children in deprived areas where a local dialect is spoken.

- The storage of multiple languages in our head: language selection and language separation (How do we keep our languages apart?).

- Can you 'block' a language while listening the way you do while speaking?

- The impact of learning a third language on skills in the first language (L1) and the second language (L2).

- The role of interaction in the language classroom: who is talking, what is the input?

- What is the impact of ICT on language learning?

- How can a threatened language be protected?

- Are Dutch people better at learning English than, for example, German learners?

- Why are prepositions in an L2 so difficult to learn?

- How can a forgotten language be reactivated?

This list could be extended for pages. A quick look at the Current Contents list of journals in Arts and Humanities, which shows the tables of contents of over 1000 journals, will make clear that the creativity has no limits and that even for journals focusing on second language development, the range of issues is breathtaking.

ACTIVITY 1.1

- If you were to categorize the list of research topics into three or four categories according to the type of research required, how would you do that? On what grounds would you put a specific topic in a category?

- How would you label your categories?

- For four of these topics, briefly work out how you would go about investigating it.

There are many topics of research, but the range of types of research in AL is much more limited. In this chapter we want to give a systematic overview of different types of research: what are relevant distinctions and how are different types related? There will be no single optimal method for all research topics, since each topic can be worked out in different ways. For your understanding of the research literature, it may be useful to become acquainted with the major categories, so you know what to expect and how to evaluate the use of a particular design. Also, some familiarity with research terminology and categorization will be helpful in finding relevant research on your own topic.

For clarity's sake, we will make use of contrasting pairs of types of research, but it should be stressed from the outset that these contrasts are actually far ends on a continuum rather than distinct categories, and that the contrasts are all dimensions that may partly overlap.

1.2 Hypothesis generating vs. hypothesis testing

Testing and theory formation is a circular process. Theory must be based on empirical findings, and empirical studies can be used to test the theories formulated. One of the issues related to theory formation is to what extent a theory can be tested; that is, to what extent the theory can be used to set up hypotheses that can be tested empirically. Quite often, though, this is not a matter of either–or, but a sequential process. Often, theories have not been developed yet to the point that real, testable hypotheses have been generated. A current example could be the relation between the use of hand gestures and L2 development. We are only now beginning to see the importance of that type of research, and we are still looking for theories that may help us explain why people gesture the way they do (see for instance De Bot & Gullberg, 2010). So before we can test what explains cross-linguistic influence from L1 to L2 in gesturing, we first need to find out whether there are actually differences in gesturing between the two languages. Once we have established that, we can proceed to think about specific aspects, such as the use of gestures with motion verbs. This means that for relatively unexplored topics, we may first have to run some exploratory studies to generate hypotheses that can be tested in subsequent research.

The next step in the research cycle is to test the hypotheses we have generated. In research reports, we often see phrases like 'In this study, we test the hypothesis that …'. However, the formulation of appropriate hypotheses is not always obvious. For instance, if someone claims to 'test the hypothesis that after puberty a native level of proficiency can no longer be attained', then we may wonder what that actually means: is that true for every learner, no matter what? If only one single individual can be found who can achieve this, is the hypothesis then falsified? A hypothesis needs to be narrowed down as far as possible to show what will be tested and what outcomes count as support or counter evidence.

 **ACTIVITY 1.2**

Formulating a research hypothesis

It is not easy to formulate a research hypothesis that is not too broad and not too narrow. The more specific the hypothesis is, the better the chance to test it successfully. The development of a research hypothesis typically goes in stages. Consider a hypothesis like the following:

'Elderly people forget their second languages easily.'

The above sentence is not really a hypothesis, but rather a statement. Which elderly people? Compared to what other groups? Do younger people not forget their second languages? What does 'easily' mean here? So we need to narrow that down:

'Elderly people forget their second languages more quickly than middle-aged people.'

Still, this is rather broad and some concepts are not clear, such as the definition of 'elderly' and 'middle-aged'. For the hypothesis this will do, but in the description of the population the age range will have to be made clear. Likewise, do you also want to include elderly people suffering from dementia or other diseases? And do you want to test every part of the language system? Maybe it is better to limit the study to syntax, morphology, lexicon, or fluency. And do you want to look at all second languages? How about the level of education, which is likely to play a role? Narrowing the hypothesis down further could result in something like:

'Healthy elderly people forget words in their first second language more quickly than education-matched middle-aged people.'

'More quickly' is still a bit underdefined, but probably clear enough. Sometimes it may help to break the larger hypothesis down into a number of smaller ones in which more details can be provided.

■ For three of the topics of the list in Activity 1.1, formulate a clear and specific research hypothesis.

As we will see in Chapter 4, the careful formulation of hypotheses is crucial to our ability to find evidence for our observations. An important principle in finding evidence is the *principle of falsification*. Since it is logically impossible to prove that something is right, we will always try to prove that our hypothesis is wrong. In other words, the conventional common practice in research is to try and falsify hypotheses. When the formulation of a hypothesis is ambiguous, unclear, or too broad, it will not be possible to falsify a hypothesis.

The discussion of hypothesis testing inevitably leads to the issue of generalizability. *Generalizability* refers to the extent to which findings in a study can be generalized to a population that is larger than the samples tested. In most cases it is unimaginable that all individuals of a given group can be included in a study. No study of Chinese learners of English will include all those millions of people. What is typically done is that we draw a sample from that larger population. There are different methods to do so; we will get back to these later (in Section 4.9). The most desirable approach is to have a so-called 'representative' sample, which means that all the variation in the larger population is represented in the sample tested. This ideal is hardly ever fully achieved, because it is very difficult to assess what makes a sample representative; we need to know all the traits that may be relevant and should be included in the sampling. No data will tell us exactly what the relevant traits are to draw a sample from the large population of Chinese learners of English. The best we can do is to guess and use common sense (and all the relevant research there is, of course) to define the sample.

Statistics will help us in assessing how representative a sample is and how reliable it is to make generalizations of the findings of a sample to a larger population. Several factors will play a role in this, but one of the most important ones is the size of the sample. Here too, we can use common sense. Observations about a sample of ten participants can barely lead to valid conclusions about a population of a million people. But fortunately, we can also apply statistics to help us decide on the most appropriate sample size for a study, as we will see later on in this book.

Hypothesis testing and generalization of the findings to a larger population form the core of statistical studies. Many scientists believe that no serious research can be done outside this framework. However, not all studies use groups to understand or explain observations.

1.3 Case studies vs. group studies

Our discussion about hypothesis testing seems to lead to the conclusion that research should always be done with groups of people that make up representative samples, and that the larger the sample, the better it is. However, the comparison of groups of people is certainly not the only way to do research. In group studies, the similarity within the group is crucial. A group is selected with specific characteristics, for example Turkish undergraduate students doing a course on Academic Writing in English, and other differences are either ignored or controlled for by using background questionnaires and specific statistical techniques to cancel out such differences. But in many cases the grouping factor can be problematic, as there are more differences than similarities between the individuals within the group. Another problem for group studies occurs when the groups represent rather random selections of a continuous phenomenon, like 'Old' versus 'Young'. Somewhere we have to draw the line to create the categories of Old and Young, which means that we will create artificial categories that do not really exist. In these cases it is better not to use a groups-approach to the study. Still, the comparison of groups of people that share a particular characteristic is one of the most frequently occurring ways of doing research.

Another way of doing research is by closely looking at the behaviour of single individuals. These studies are commonly referred to as *case studies*. Case studies are often used for qualitative analyses, in which a detailed description can be derived from several data of a single person or from the interaction of two people. For instance, in conversation analysis or discourse analysis, a detailed analysis is done of the sequence and the quality of the interaction between two language users. In this way, we can come to an understanding of how we organize our conversations linguistically, but also how language learning takes place by putting the utterances 'under the microscope'. Detailed observations on the behaviour (including language use) of single individuals can help us to understand and illustrate theoretical principles. Case studies provide an opportunity to observe human behaviour in a real life context. Observations in case studies cannot be generalized to a larger population of similar individuals, but case studies can be used for the generalization to the theory. Theoretical principles can be falsified when not observed in the cases studied.

Although case studies are usually associated with qualitative research, quantitative case studies can be done as well. For instance, in corpus linguistics, the language profile of individual cases can be created by calculations of frequencies and distributions. Case studies can also be used to investigate an individual's language use as it develops over time. By closely keeping track of the changes in an individual's language use, we can understand how stages of development emerge and how the combination of events leads to certain types of change. Case studies in the time domain are frequently used in studies based on Complex Dynamic Systems Theory. The dynamic interaction of factors over time are best investigated by closely concentrating on single cases (see Section 1.6 on Process vs. product research below).

Some studies use multiple cases, and although in terms of numbers they may seem to be the same as a group, the approach is fundamentally different. In case studies, we typically find a holistic approach, which aims at trying to integrate as many aspects that are relevant for the individual case as possible.

1.4 Description vs. explanation

The discussion about generating hypotheses vs. hypothesis testing in the section above is closely related to the distinction between description and explanation. Before we can explain anything, we first need a good description. For instance, before we can explain why interaction in the classroom is beneficial for second language development, we need to describe what goes on in classrooms: who is actually saying what to whom, how complex is the language used, is what is said also understood, and is the language used correct or full of errors? A large part of the research we do in AL is descriptive. We describe processes of learning and teaching, giving different factors that play a role in these processes; we describe language policy programmes and their effectiveness; we describe the impact of learning environments on learning, and so on.

Many studies investigate the effect of X on Y. A randomly chosen issue of one of the leading journals in our field, *Studies in Second Language Acquisition* (2018, 40), reveals the following: there is a study on the effect of the gloss type (like a textual definition or picture) on the learning of words while reading (Warren et al., 2018), one on the effect of different types of instruction on L2 processing of causative constructions (Wong & Ito, 2018), and the effect of exposure frequency on vocabulary learning (Mohamed, 2018). All were eye tracking studies. All of these studies describe the effect of the manipulation of one variable on another one. But even if the effect studied is found (and it normally is, because journals do not usually publish null results), that is not an explanation. The only conclusion that can be drawn is that the change in Y co-occurs with a change in X. To really account for the co-occurrence observed, there must always be a rigorous and detailed theory behind the research, which provides theoretical explanations for the phenomena found.

There is another sense of the concept of explanation, which is more statistical in nature. As we will see in Chapter 3 of this book, variation within individuals and groups vs. variation between individuals and groups is the essence of statistical procedures used to compare groups. We try to explain variation in variable A by looking at the impact of the systematic and controlled variation of variable B. For instance, we look at the variation in the acquisition of new L2 words (variable A) by manipulating the methods of teaching (variable B). If the experiment works, the variation in variable A is reduced, because we have taken out the variation that is caused by variable B. Suppose we teach two different methods to two different groups. If we look at the learning results of the group that used method 1 and the one that used method 2 together, we will find some learners who improved a lot, some less, and some not at all. If we look at the groups for methods 1 and 2 separately, we may find that for one method most learners have improved a lot, while for the other method learners improved only slightly or not at all. Even though there is a great deal of variation in the two groups taken together because there will be good and bad learners, there may be less variation within the groups than between the groups. In statistical terms, this is referred to as 'variance explained', variance being a specific type of variation. In this particular example, the variation between the groups can largely be explained by the different methods they were using. The goal in experiments is to explain as much variation as possible, as that will tell us to what extent we can explain a given effect. Again, this is not an explanation in the theoretical sense, but it is a description of the effect of one variable on another.

1.5 Non-experimental vs. experimental

Applied Linguistics has positioned itself as part of the social sciences and distanced itself from the humanities by adopting research techniques and paradigms based on the science model. In this model, quantitative empirical research and controlled experiments are often considered the only way to make progress. The aim is to decompose complex processes in parts that can be studied and manipulated experimentally. Experiments and statistical manipulations provide 'hard' evidence as compared to the 'soft' evidence evolving from the more interpretative research that dominates in the humanities. If one looks at the bulk of research as reported in the most prestigious journals and books in AL, the experimental approach is still dominant, but at the same time it is obvious that it is no longer seen as the only way to practise research. The choice of an experimental or a non-experimental approach largely depends on what a researcher wants to know. For a study of the organization of the bilingual lexicon or the perception of foreign accents by native speakers, experiments may be the logical choice. How human language processing takes place is not open to introspection and we can study this effectively through controlled experiments. Other aspects, such as non-instructed L2 development, we can study better through non-experimental techniques, such as observations and analyses of spontaneous speech.

In studying Second Language Development (SLD), a wide range of experimental techniques have been used, ranging from grammaticality judgments to lexical decision tasks. More recently, different neuroimaging techniques have been used that provide insight into brain activity while processing language. A detailed discussion of various techniques is beyond the scope of this book, but a good overview of different experimental techniques that have been used for the study of SLD can be found in Mackey and Gass (2005, 2016) and thorough discussions of different brain-imaging techniques have been provided by Abutalebi and Della Rosa (2008).

ACTIVITY 1.3

One of the subdivisions we can make with regard to types of research is the one between experimental and non-experimental.

- Which of the topics from the list in Activity 1.1 can best be investigated using experimental research and which with non-experimental research?

- Mention one advantage and one disadvantage of experimental research.

Sometimes there is a choice between using an experimental technique and a non-experimental technique. The choice for one or the other is determined by the aim of the study. An interesting example is the study of L2 pragmatic competence. Hendriks (2002) studied the acquisition of requests by Dutch learners of English. Her aim was to study the impact of power relations, social distance, and conversational setting on the use of politeness strategies in requests. She could have made recordings of requests in spontaneous conversations, but she wanted to study the systematic effects of each of these variables and their interactions. She would have needed a very large corpus of utterances to find sufficient examples of requests that differed in terms of power, social distance, and setting. Therefore, she decided to use an experimental technique that tries to mimic real life interaction while allowing for systematic variation of variables. The technique used was the Discourse Completion Task. In this task, a short description of a conversational setting is presented and the participant has to construct a sentence as a reaction. Here are two examples from Hendriks (2002, pp. 110–113):

The living room

You were in your room upstairs doing your maths homework, but you were not able to do the sums. You need some help. You go down to the living room where your dad is watching a documentary on television. What do you say to your dad?

....

The supermarket

You are standing in line at the checkout with a shopping trolley full of groceries. You are late for an important meeting. There is one man in front of you. What do you say to the man in front of you?

....

The use of such tasks allows for systematic variation of the variables, but it is of course not a natural setting or real conversation. Ideally, data from such controlled experiments should be validated through a comparison with real conversational data.

1.6 Process research vs. product research

A dimension that has been introduced relatively recently is the distinction between *product*-oriented research and *process*-oriented research. Most traditional research in the field of AL works with learning outcomes and background variables at one moment in time. This can be labelled as product research, as the conclusions relate to the outcomes of a process rather than the process itself. The process dimension, on the other hand, is founded in a research perspective that is rapidly gaining ground in developmental psychology and Applied Linguistics, and is based on Complex Dynamic Systems Theory (CDST) (see, for instance, De Bot et al., 2007). This perspective emphasizes the change of development over time and focuses on the dynamic interaction of factors affecting the language system, or the overall system in general, over time. CDST is thus interested in the *process* of development rather than in the eventual learning outcomes or *products*. The focus on the process has important consequences for the research choices that are made. For instance, a CDST approach takes into account that developmental processes are complex processes in which characteristics of the individual learner interact with the environment. CDST emphasizes the iterative nature of development, that is, each next step in development is based on the state of the complex system at the previous moment. And although one step ahead can be accurately predicted, each future step is increasingly difficult to predict, as all the factors that shape the system will also change over time. The implication of the iterations is that every learner's developmental process is essentially unique. Inevitably, the complex and dynamic developmental process of an individual learner cannot be generalized to groups of individuals (populations), which means that process research is mostly done on cases. To make sense of the iterations, case studies in a CDST framework usually include a large number of observations over time, from about 30 observations in some studies to over 1000 in other studies. In this way, individual patterns of variability can tell us in detail how a language learner developed and what factors may have contributed to shaping each step in the developmental process.

Since language learning is essentially a process, it will be obvious that process-oriented case studies provide a valuable contribution to our understanding of learning. At the same time we need general tendencies, not only because of educational policy reasons, but also because we need information on the likelihood that a given factor will have an impact on the product of development, so that we can include it in the study of individual developmental patterns. This creates a research cycle in which we move from factors that seem to have an effect at the individual level to testing that effect on a larger sample to get an estimate of its strength and then back to the individual level again to study the impact in more detail. An example could be the role of motivation: its effect may be suggested when we look at the learning process of an individual learner who indicates why she was motivated to invest time and energy in learning a language at some moments in time and not at all at other moments. To know more about the potential strength of such a factor, we may then do a study on a larger sample of similar learners that we compare at one point in time (a product study). With that information, we can go back to individuals and see how it affects them. The general pattern will be less detailed and typically will not give us information about change of motivation over time in the same way that an individual case study can.

ACTIVITY 1.4

In a CDST approach, we want to take into account that developmental processes are complex processes in which characteristics of the individual learner interact with the environment. Every learner is unique, and her developmental path will be affected by the internal structure of her system and her interaction with the environment. Inevitably there will be variation between individual learners.

- Order the items in the list in 1.1 on page 3 according to the degree to which the topic could be easily investigated from a CDST perspective.

Now that we have distinguished process-based research from product-based research, we can see that we need both of these dimensions to create a full picture. This means we should be balancing two ways of looking at research: on the one hand we need attention for individual developmental patterns revealing individually unique processes, but on the other hand we need to find general tendencies for various purposes. It may be true that for some learners there is no impact of the first language when learning the second, and the variation in cross-linguistic influences between individuals may be considerable, but what remains is that *in general*, the first language does play a role in learning a second language.

1.7 Longitudinal vs. cross-sectional

Longitudinal research is research in which individuals' development over time is studied. Most studies of children growing up bilingually are examples of longitudinal research: the child is typically video/audio-recorded at regular intervals over a longer period of time, sometimes more than three years, and transcripts of the recordings are analysed with respect to relevant aspects, such as mean length of utterance and lexical richness. But also other types of development can be studied longitudinally: Hansen et al. (2010) looked at the attrition of Korean and Japanese in returned missionaries who typically acquired the foreign language up to a very high level, used it in their work as missionaries, but hardly ever used it after they returned. This study is unusual, because it is longitudinal with only two moments of measurement in 10 years. In many longitudinal studies there are more moments of measurement with smaller time intervals. Longitudinal studies often take long; even three-year data collection periods may be too short to cover a significant part of the developmental process. And funding agencies are not very keen on financing projects that take more than four or five years to generate results. Therefore, the number of longitudinal studies is small, but those projects (like the European Science Foundation study on untutored L2 development in different countries (see Klein & Perdue, 1992; Becker & Carroll, 1997)) have had a major impact on the field.

Because of the time/money problem that characterizes longitudinal studies, many researchers use *cross-sectional* designs. In cross-sectional research, individuals in different phases of development are compared at one moment in time. For the study of the development of morphology in French as an L2, a researcher may compare first, third, and fifth graders in secondary schools in Denmark. Rather than follow the same group of learners for four years as they progress from first to fifth grade, different groups in the three grades are compared at one moment in time.

Both longitudinal designs and cross-sectional designs can have their problems. In longitudinal studies, the number of participants is generally very small because a large corpus of data is gathered on that one (or very small group of) individual(s). Large numbers of participants would make both the data collection procedure and the processing and analysis of the data extremely demanding and time-consuming. Small numbers, on the other hand, mean that the findings may be highly idiosyncratic and difficult to generalize. As we discussed in 1.6, this may not be a problem in studies that use the uniqueness of the individual's development as the central issue, as is normally the case in CDST approaches to language development. Another problem of longitudinal studies is *subject mortality*, that is the dropping out of subjects in a study. With each new measurement, there is a risk of subjects dropping out, and the longer and more demanding the study, the higher the risk of drop-out. An additional problem is that in such studies drop-out is typically not random, but selective or biased: in a study on acquisition or attrition, subjects that do not perform well will be more likely to lose their motivation and drop out than more successful ones, leaving a biased sample that is even less generalizable.

Cross-sectional designs can also be problematic, because the assumption that the three groups that are compared behave like one group tested longitudinally may not be true. There may be specific characteristics of different age groups, such as changes in the school curriculum, natural disasters, changes in demographic trends, and changes in school population, that can make the three groups very different. One solution for this so-called *cohort effect* is to take more than one cohort, so rather than only testing grades one, three, and five in year x, also testing grades one, three, and five of the next year or cohort. If the findings for the two cohorts are similar, it is assumed that the groups do not behave atypically. Some studies try to get the best of two worlds by combining longitudinal and cross-sectional designs: in research on ageing such a cross-sequential design has been used frequently, and it was also used by Weltens (1989) and Grendel (1993) in their studies of the attrition of French as a foreign language in the Netherlands.

1.8 Qualitative vs. quantitative

The discussion of qualitative versus quantitative studies would take another book to discuss in sufficient detail. It has been one of the main rifts in the social sciences, including AL, in the past decades. It looks as if the fiercest controversy is over now, but the different communities still view each other with distrust. For a long time a researcher had to be in one or the other community, but now it seems acceptable to take an elective stance and use more qualitative or more quantitative methods depending on the type of research question one wants to answer. Following Mackey and Gass (2005, p. 400), the two approaches can be defined as follows:

> **Qualitative**: Research in which the focus is on naturally occurring phenomena, and data are primarily recorded in non-numerical form.

> **Quantitative**: Research in which variables are manipulated to test hypotheses, and in which there is usually quantification of data and numerical analyses.

From these definitions it follows that the two approaches differ fundamentally in epistemological terms and with respect to the research methods used. Qualitative research is holistic, trying to integrate as many aspects that are relevant into one study. It is also by definition interpretative and therefore in the eyes of its opponents 'soft'. In qualitative research a number of techniques may be used, such as diaries of learners, interviews, observations, and introspective methods such as think-aloud protocols (see Mackey & Gass, 2005, Chapter 6, and Brown & Rodgers, 2002, Chapters 2–4 for discussions of various methods). One of the main problems is the lack of objectivity in those methods: in all these methods, the researchers interpret what is going on, and some form of credibility can only be achieved through combinations of data (*triangulation*) and the use of intersubjective methods, in which the interpretations of several 'judges' are tested for consistency. All of this may not satisfy the objections raised by hard-core quantitativists. For them, only objective quantitative data are real 'hard' data. Such data are claimed to be objective; for example, there is little a researcher can change or interpret in the latencies in reaction-time experiments. The starting point of quantitative research is that the entire world is one big mechanism and by taking it apart and studying its constituent parts we will in the end understand the whole machine. Qualitative researchers criticize this approach as, as explained by Leo van Lier, 'one cannot peel away the layers of an onion to eventually get to the real onion within' (van Lier, 2004, p. 43). And that, according to qualitative researchers, is exactly what quantitative researchers tend to do. They try to explain complex phenomena by calculating the influence of a limited number of factors.

Another problem with the experimental and quantitative approach is that it is not always clear what participants in such experiments actually do. There is a substantial set of studies on the recognition of pseudo-homophones (like English 'coin', a piece of money, and French 'coin', which translates to *corner* in English). The list of words to be recognized typically consists of many regular words with some of these pseudo-homophones interspersed. The researcher's hope is that the participants will not notice these words and become aware of the fact that they are special, because that could have an effect on their strategies in processing. To what extent participants actually do notice the trick is often unclear. Participants in such experiments are typically psychology students who have to take part in many different types of experiments and who have accordingly become quite clever in detecting the trick.

 **ACTIVITY 1.5**

- **Which of the topics in the list in Section 1.1 can best be investigated using longitudinal research and which can best be investigated using cross-sectional research?**
- **Mention one advantage and one disadvantage of cross-sectional research.**
- **How can the cohort effect be avoided?**

1.9 In-situ/naturalistic research vs. laboratory research

In-situ or *naturalistic research* refers to research that studies a phenomenon in its normal, natural setting and in normal everyday tasks, while *laboratory research* refers to both isolating a phenomenon from its normal setting and to the use of data that are an artifact of the procedures used. Laboratory research aims at finding 'pure' effects that are not tainted by the messiness of everyday life. In such studies the grammaticality of sentences in isolation is tested through grammaticality judgments, or the process of lexical access is studied using reaction-time experiments. Experimental laboratory research has reached extremely high standards, mainly through a very successful experimental psychology tradition in North America and Western Europe. Therefore, that type of research stands in high regard, also in AL. The counter movement that advocates a more qualitative and naturalistic approach has long been marginalized and has created its own subculture and its own journals and societies. Their main argument is that reductionist research has no *ecological validity* in that it does not really tell us what reality looks like. Researchers in the laboratory tradition have problems countering this argument, because their research does not always lead to the kind of deeper insight it is supposed to bring. The gap between the methods used and the reality it claims to inform us about has become so wide that even researchers themselves may have problems showing the relevance of what they do. To give an example, there is a large body of research on word recognition, mostly using the lexical decision paradigm in which participants are presented with letter strings on a computer screen and asked to indicate as quickly as possible whether the letter string is a word in a given language or not. At the beginning of this field of research, it was assumed that word recognition data would inform us about the process of normal reading, but over time, researchers working on word recognition have developed their own sets of questions that have basically no link to the process of normal reading.

Researchers using naturalistic data claim that their research is more ecologically valid because it focuses on the tasks in their normal setting. Up to a point this is probably true, but with the use of different introspective methods, they may also have crossed the line and adapted methods that may create their own type of data that are as far removed from reality as the reaction times and error rates of word recognition researchers. The validity of introspection has been questioned and the core of the problem is sublimely expressed in the title of Klein's (1989) review of Kasper and Faerch on introspective methods in L2 research: 'Introspection into what?'.

 **ACTIVITY 1.6**

Here is the summary of an article from the journal *Applied Linguistics* (Webb & Kagimoto, 2011). What do you think are the main characteristics in terms of research types of the research reported on?

Learning Collocations: Do the Number of Collocates, Position of the Node Word, and Synonymy Affect Learning?

Stuart Webb & Eve Kagimoto
Victoria University of Wellington

This study investigated the effects of three factors (the number of collocates per node word, the position of the node word, synonymy) on learning collocations. Japanese students studying English as a foreign language learned five sets of 12 target collocations. Each collocation was presented in a single glossed sentence. The number of collocates (6, 3, 1) varied per node word between three of the sets, the position of the node word (+1, −1) varied between two of the sets, and the semantic relationship between collocations (synonyms, non-synonyms) varied between two sets. Productive knowledge of collocation was measured in pre- and post-tests. The results showed that more collocations were learned as the number of collocates per node word increased, the position of the node word did not affect learning, and synonymy had a negative effect on learning. The implications for teaching and learning collocations are discussed in detail.

We have presented various types of research by giving a number of more or less opposite characteristics of research types. In Table 1.1, the list is repeated again, and a reflection on the characteristics on the left-hand side and on the right-hand side will make clear that the characteristics on either side are related and co-occur: quantitative research is often experimental, based on groups, and laboratory research, while qualitative research is often based on case studies in a naturalistic setting aimed at description more than explanation. This is not to say that there is no mixing possible; many researchers nowadays are eclectic and take what suits them without caring too much about what different communities of researchers may say about this. This typology may help the interpretation of research and to structure your own research.

Table 1.1 Types of research

Hypothesis generating	Hypothesis testing
Description	Explanation
Non-experimental	Experimental
Process research	Product research
Longitudinal	Cross-sectional
Case studies	Group studies
Qualitative	Quantitative
In-situ research	Laboratory research

1.10 The approaches taken in this book

We have elaborated on the necessity of looking at individuals on the one hand, and generalizing over larger groups on the other hand. Only with these complementary research methods will we be able to advance in science and bring different theories closer together. To go into all possible ways of analysing data will be too much for an introductory book on methodology and statistics. In order to do group studies, you will need to know how to advance in structuring your research and how to analyse the data you get. We often encounter linguists who think of an interesting study to carry out, but who forget to think about how to analyse the data and then get stuck; likewise, some report on statistics but have forgotten an important step, which has rendered their results unreliable. The aim of this book is to make you aware of how to construct a quantitative study in an analysable way, and which tests you can carry out to check your hypotheses. Although we focus on group studies, we will keep stressing that there is also the possibility to look at individual data. If you want to learn more about how to analyse data from a longitudinal CDST perspective, you can consult Verspoor et al. (2011): *A dynamic approach to second language development: methods and techniques.*

2 SYSTEMATICITY IN STATISTICS: VARIABLES

2.1 Introduction

"A Pearson r revealed that there was a significant negative relationship between age of acquisition and proficiency level $r(27) = -.47$, $p = .01$."

Many students tend to skip the results sections of research reports, because they do not understand the meaning of sentences like the one exemplified above. The unfortunate consequence of this is that they will not be able to fully assess the merits and weaknesses of those studies. Moreover, they will not be able to report on their own studies in a conventional and appropriate way. This is not only unfortunate, but also unnecessary. Once the underlying principles of statistics are clear, understanding statistics is a piece of cake!

The purpose of this book is to come to an understanding of some elementary statistics, rather than providing a full-fledged statistics course. We will demonstrate why it is necessary for many studies to apply statistics and which kind of statistic is normally associated with which kind of study. After studying this chapter and the next three chapters, you will already be able to understand many of the statistical reports in articles and apply some very basic statistics to your own investigations. We will do this by encouraging you to think about problems in second language research through a set of tasks. Wherever possible, we will ask you to try and find your own solutions to these problems before we explain how they are conventionally solved. Obviously, this learning-by-doing approach will only work if you work seriously on the tasks, rather than skip to the solution right away!

In the previous chapter, we discussed the relationship between theory and empirical observations for different types of research. In the current chapter, we will move on to a more practical application of these observations: doing and interpreting research. Since an understanding of research based on traditional theories is crucial for a full appreciation of the field of Applied Linguistics, we will focus on the more traditional methodologies, and will occasionally refer to approaches that are more appropriate for the investigation of non-linear development.

One of the most important characteristics of any type of research is that it is carried out systematically and according to research conventions that are generally agreed upon. The purpose of the current chapter is to discuss the most relevant of these conventions and to outline the systematicity of empirical research.

2.2 Why do we need statistics?

Let us start by looking at a practical problem in the following activity.

A researcher wants to know whether the age at which a second language is learned (AoA) affects the learner's proficiency level. A group of 80 participants with various ages of acquisition (ranging from approximately 5 to 58) have taken an English proficiency test (maximum score is 100). A scatterplot of this hypothetical dataset might look like one of the three scatterplots below.

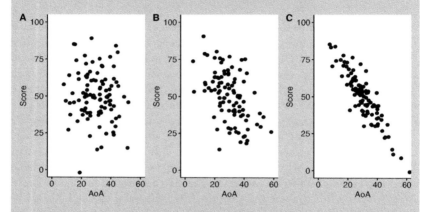

- What can you say about the potential relationship between age of acquisition (AoA) and proficiency level (Score) when looking at the different plots? Which of the plots suggest a clear relationship between the two and which one does not?
- Based on what you know, which of the plots do you think most likely visualizes the relationship between AoA and proficiency? (Explain your answer!)
- Are there any other observations you can make?
- Is there any additional information you would like to have to assess the value of this study?

The 'correct' answers to the questions in Activity 2.1 are not very relevant. The purpose of the exercise is to make you aware that it can be very difficult to make decisions based on empirical observations. In the above activity, you probably noticed that it is relatively easy to say something about the relationship between the two variables on the basis of plot C and the absence of such a relationship on the basis of plot A. The data in plot B, however, are more difficult to base conclusions on. The question is where to draw the line between a relationship or no relationship. Now, would it not be great if we could feed these numbers into a computer program and the program would tell us that we can safely decide (beyond reasonable doubt) that there is indeed a relationship as well as inform us about the strength of this relationship? That is exactly what we are doing in applying statistics to empirical data. We enter the data in, for example, JASP or R, we select or enter the right calculation for a particular problem, and the program will tell us which decision we can make (beyond reasonable doubt). The main issue in this book is the selection of the right type of calculation. The *beyond reasonable doubt* bit is, in combination with the interpretation of the strength of the effect or relationship, another issue we will have to deal with. In short, however, this is basically all you need to know about statistics.

2.3 Variables and operationalization

Many a phenomenon that we want to investigate is not measurable in an obvious way. The first step that is necessary for doing systematic research is *operationalization*. This means that the abstract phenomenon, or *construct*, we want to investigate is converted into a measurable *variable*. For instance, if we want to investigate someone's level of L2 proficiency at a certain moment in time, we need a way to express this. Level of proficiency could be operationalized as the number of vegetables that a person can mention in the L2 in two minutes (an example of the *verbal fluency test*). Alternatively, level of proficiency can be expressed in terms of a TOEFL score, one of the most widely accepted tests of English as a foreign language, or someone's final school grade in that subject. This example immediately shows how controversial operationalization may be. The translation of a construct into a variable is always the researcher's own choice; and the *validity* of the outcomes of the investigation may strongly depend on it. If the variable resulting from the operationalization does not adequately represent the underlying construct, the entire study may be questionable. In many studies, the operationalization of constructs into variables is left implicit. It is therefore one of the first questions that critical readers of an empirical study should ask themselves.

 ACTIVITY 2.2

Provide two possible operationalizations of the following constructs:

- A person's motivation (at one moment in time) to learn a particular foreign language
- A person's intelligence (at one moment in time)
- The love one person feels for another person (at one moment in time)
- A person's pronunciation of English (at one moment in time)
- A person's height (at one moment in time)

The answers to the questions asked in Activity 2.2 may vary wildly and may yield interesting discussions about the validity of empirical studies. However, the most important point appearing from this activity is that there is not one correct answer to these questions and that it is always the researcher's responsibility to carefully operationalize constructs into variables. Another important point is that all of the variables operationalized in Activity 2.2 take a synchronic perspective, which appears from the additional phrase 'at one point in time'. It will be obvious that research designs for the investigation of the development of these factors over time may be considerably more complex and require different methods and techniques from the ones needed to investigate one time slice only.

There are two more points we need to discuss in relation to variables: the type of variables and their function in an empirical study. Answering the questions in Activity 2.3 below will make you aware of the differences that can arise between different types of variables. The different functions of variables in statistics will come back in Chapter 4.

ACTIVITY 2.3

Applying statistics by definition involves doing calculations. Perform the following simple calculations:

- The height of 3 persons is 1.58m, 1.64m, and 1.70m respectively. What is the average height of these people?

- A group consists of 9 female students and 7 male students. What is the average gender of this group?

- Three students participate in a bike race. At the end of the race, Julia finishes first, Hassan second, and Nadia third. They decide to do a second race, in which Nadia finishes first, Hassan second and Julia third. In a third race, Nadia is first, Hassan second, and Julia third. Who is the overall winner?

- Four essays are graded using a grading system that has four scale points: A,B,C,D. If someone scored an A, two Bs, and a D, what is her average score?

Each of the four questions in Activity 2.3 includes a variable that represents an underlying construct. For our purpose, the underlying construct is not relevant this time, as we will concentrate on the variables themselves and the operations we are allowed to carry out with different types of variables. The calculation of the first one, a person's height as measured in metres, will not pose any problems. The average length can be calculated by the sum of the values, divided by the number of values: (1.58+1.64+1.70)/3. The answer is 1.64m. The second question is more problematic. Why is it impossible to calculate the average sex of this group? The answer must be found in the scale that we use to measure the different variables.

The scale used in the first question runs from 0 till ∞ and the scale points occur at regular intervals from each other. Such variables are often called *continuous variables* or variables with an *interval* or a *ratio* scale. Other examples of this scale are the number of vegetables a person can mention in an L2 in two minutes and the number of correct items in a test. The difference between ratio and interval data is that the ratio scale has a fixed zero point. A good example of a scale that is interval but not ratio is temperature in Celsius or Fahrenheit, because the zero point is quite random and zero does not mean 'no temperature' here. For the purpose of Applied Linguistics, the difference is not very important and we will therefore disregard the difference between the interval and ratio scale, and just refer to both as interval scale.

The implied scale for the second question is of a different nature. This scale has a limited number of scale points (or *levels*) that only serve as labels to distinguish categories. This scale type is therefore called a *categorical* or *nominal* scale. Clearly, mathematical calculations like averaging cannot be applied to nominal variables and the question cannot be answered. Another example of a nominal scale is a person's nationality. Here too, the different nationalities are no more than labels, to which mathematical operations like adding up and averaging cannot be applied.

While the categories of nominal variables typically concern labels that do not have a certain order or rank (a woman does not have more gender than a man), the third question relates to a scale that is based on ordered or ranked levels and is referred to as an *ordinal* scale. Ordinal variables may have an infinite number of scale points, but the distance between these scale points does not occur at exactly the same intervals. Therefore, calculating averages is not possible for ordinal variables. To decide who was the fastest cyclist of the three, we would need the exact distance (for instance in time) between each of the students in each of the three races. As time can be expressed as a continuous or interval variable, the results of the three races can be added up. To answer the fourth question, we would need to decide on which scale the essays were graded. As the distances between the scale points A, B, C, and D are not necessarily identical, this scale must be considered as an ordinal scale and no averages can be calculated. Users of this type of scale may be tempted to transfer A, B, C, and D to numbers (4, 3, 2, and 1), so that seemingly an average can be calculated. However, this suggests an underlying interval scale, so that an essay that is rewarded a '4' is exactly twice as good as one that is rewarded a '2'. For most types of essay grading this is not true and the transfer operation is not permitted. Similarly, essay grading on a scale of 1–10 must still be regarded as ordinal and in theory, no averages can be calculated. Examples of the different variable types are given in Table 2.1.

Table 2.1 Variable types

Variable types	Characteristics	Example
Nominal	Alphanumeric labels only	Nationality
Ordinal	Rank order	Essay grades
Interval	Numbers with fixed intervals	Temperature in centigrade
Ratio	Numbers with fixed intervals and absolute zero point	Weight in kilograms

Applied to research design, categorizing variables as nominal, ordinal, or interval is extremely relevant, as the choice of operationalizing a construct as a particular type of variable will have important consequences for the calculations that can be performed in the analysis of the results of a study.

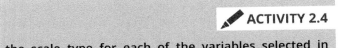 **ACTIVITY 2.4**

Determine the scale type for each of the variables selected in Activity 2.2.

Different statistics programs deal differently with how they refer to these three variable types. In JASP, variable types can be changed into nominal, ordinal, and interval through symbols at the top of the columns. In R, variables are divided slightly differently, as nominal variables are usually called 'factors', and interval or ordinal variables can either be referred to as 'numeric' or 'integer' variables. More about this will be discussed in the Practicals in Part 2.

2.4 Statistical dangers and limitations

We conduct research to find answers to questions, for example the effects of age of acquisition on second language proficiency. A hypothesis could be that the earlier L2 speakers start learning the language, the more proficient they will be when tested in adulthood. However, one experimental study finding a relationship between the two does not provide us with the definite truth. The findings only become credible if others are able to find the same or similar results. The inability to reproduce findings (e.g. Open Science Collaboration, 2015) has in recent years led to a major dispute between people ranging from those who claim published work equals the truth to those who state that all unreplicable studies are false and wrong. Although the dispute is too technical to discuss in detail, the truth is to be found somewhere in between those extremes. Just as one study cannot provide solid proof for a relationship, the failure to replicate the relationship also does not necessarily mean that the relationship does not exist. Statistically significant results, that is the results in most published studies, may be based on extreme cases that are in subsequent studies often followed by more moderate cases (a phenomenon also known as *regression towards the mean*). Thus, we can only get closer to the truth by continuing to replicate each other's work. It is therefore crucial to work systematically according to the conventions we agreed upon, keeping two major requirements in mind: *validity* and *reliability*.

Validity is closely related to operationalization, which can be seen as the link between the statistical study and the real world. Some cases of operationalization are completely obvious, like the operationalization of the construct 'height' in terms of the number of centimetres measured from top to bottom. The only point at which we may go wrong in measuring someone's height is at what is understood as the 'top' and the 'bottom'. If a person is wearing high heels, we may not want to include the heels in our measurement. The operationalization of abstract constructs like 'language proficiency' is clearly less obvious and always involves choices on the part of the researcher. In short, you could say that a valid study incorporates measures that actually measure what the study intended to measure. When, for instance, the objective is to study fluency in the second language by means of a grammaticality judgment task, you could argue that the validity is low. If the validity of a study is not warranted, this may well lead to systematic errors and the possible significant outcomes are completely meaningless. The same holds for studies in which the samples are not representative. Here, too, the validity is at stake, because it is not sure that the outcome of the study is representative for a real-world situation.

Reliability refers to the internal consistency of a study and is also closely related to the issue of replications discussed above. It is the ability of a measure to give the same results when used again under the same conditions. Contrary to validity, which is often a matter of argumentation, there are several ways to control or check the reliability of a study. We will come back to this issue in later chapters.

As will be explained in more detail in the next chapter, statistical studies can involve complex calculations that may have restrictions to their application. These calculations themselves are hidden for the user of computer programs like JASP or R, which is why it is very unwise to perform analyses on a dataset and blindly interpret their output in terms of significance. As was explained above, however, statistical studies cannot only go wrong at the level of the calculations themselves. Perhaps the biggest danger in statistics is its blind application and the assumption that statistical significance is identical to The Truth, a danger that we will discuss in more detail in Chapter 4.

In this chapter, we have introduced the first basics of statistical terminology: operationalization, variables, validity, and reliability. Before you start designing a study, one of the first steps is to think about the variables you want to use and their measurement scales. After reading this chapter, you are ready for the first practical in R or JASP. Before you start Practical 1, we recommend going through the 'Getting ready to start using' introductions to JASP or R and RStudio in Part 2 of this book.

3 DESCRIPTIVE STATISTICS

3.1 Introduction

Basically, two types of statistics can be distinguished: *descriptive* and *inductive* statistics. Inductive statistics help us in making decisions about the results of a study. They usually involve hypothesis testing, in which the results of a small *sample* are generalized to a larger *population*; something we will return to in Chapter 4. Descriptive statistics are used to describe the characteristics of a particular dataset or to describe patterns of development in longitudinal analyses. This chapter will focus on the most important notions of descriptive statistics that are commonly used in Applied Linguistics: means, ranges, standard deviations, z-scores, and frequency distributions. These descriptives are used to describe observations for two different kinds of perspectives on data: means and relationships. 'Means' are used when we want to compare different groups, like different language backgrounds or different sexes. Statistics within the 'means' perspective are used to compare the mean value of one group (e.g. males) to another (e.g. females) to see whether they differ. 'Relationships', on the other hand, are used when we are not interested in contrasting groups, but want to say something about the relationship between variables measured within a group, such as reading skills and writing skills, or age and proficiency scores.

3.2 Statistics: Means versus relationships

Let us go back to the relationship between age of acquisition and L2 proficiency that was discussed in the previous chapter (in Activity 2.1). A more elaborate visualization of this relationship is depicted in Figure 3.1.

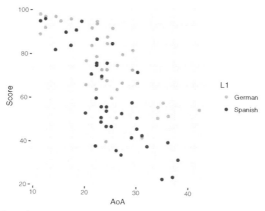

Figure 3.1 Scatterplot

Scatterplot showing the relationship between Age of Acquisition (AoA) and Score.

The scatterplot in Figure 3.1 visualizes the relationship between Age of Acquisition (AoA) and the L2 proficiency score (Score). The relationship here is negative: proficiency score decreases as age of acquisition increases. The scores of people with a German L1 background are depicted in light grey while the scores of Spanish learners of English are depicted in dark grey.

ACTIVITY 3.1

Figure 3.1 again reveals the negative relationship between Age of Acquisition (AoA on the x-axis) and the L2 proficiency score (Score on the y-axis). Negative refers to the fact that one variable decreases as the other increases, and vice versa (as will also be explained in more detail in Chapter 5). To take this one step further, we have added one more variable to the dataset. The dots, that is the people, now have different colours which indicate whether their L1 is German (light grey) or Spanish (dark grey). Try to answer the following questions before you read on.

- What are the two main variables if you are interested in the relationship between AoA and proficiency score? What are the measurement scales of these two variables?

- What are the two main variables if you are interested in the effect of L1 background on proficiency score? What are the measurement scales of these two variables?

- In your own words, try to explain how your answers to the questions above affect the way in which you should look at (and ultimately analyse) the data. Can the scatterplot provide a useful insight in both cases? Can it reveal whether there is a difference in proficiency scores between German and Spanish learners?

For the first question of Activity 3.1, you are interested in examining whether L2 proficiency score decreases as age of acquisition increases. In other words, you are interested in the relationship between two interval variables and you are mainly focusing on individual data points. Such a relationship can nicely be visually examined using a scatterplot such as the one in Figure 3.1. On the contrary, when looking at the second question, you are not necessarily interested in individual data points, but rather in comparing the data of two different groups. In this case, these groups are divided on the basis of the variable 'L1 background', a nominal variable with two levels. Although you might be able to say something about the

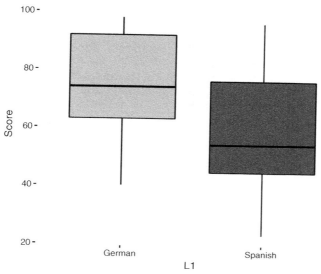

Figure 3.2 Boxplot

This boxplot visualizes the difference between proficiency scores of the people with a German L1 background (in light grey) and those with a Spanish L1 background (in dark grey).

difference in scores between the German (light grey) and Spanish (dark grey) data points on the basis of the scatterplot, a look at how the group performs in general is likely to be more useful. Consider, for example, the boxplot in Figure 3.2.

The boxplot is based on exactly the same dataset as the scatterplot in Figure 3.1, but the focus is completely different. A scatterplot shows a relationship between all available data points, while a boxplot summarizes the data points for a group of individuals taken together. As you may have realized after having completed Activity 3.1, this focus depends on the measurement scales of the variables. From Chapter 5 onwards, we will further discuss the differences between the statistical tests that are needed to answer questions that either focus on a relationship between interval variables or on group comparisons. First, we will focus on describing and visualizing data, as such summaries are a crucial first step in understanding and getting to know your data, regardless of your research questions and the focus of your research.

3.3 Describing datasets: Means and dispersion

One of the most well-known descriptive statistics is the *mean value*. Providing the mean value of a dataset (like the average exam grade of a group of students) immediately gives an insight into the characteristics of that dataset. The mean can therefore also be seen as a simple *statistical model* (Field et al., 2012, p. 36) in that it constitutes a summary or simplified approximation of the real dataset. To calculate the mean value, add the values in the dataset and divide the sum by the number of items in that dataset. This operation is summarized by the following formula:

$$\bar{X} = \frac{\sum X}{N}$$

(3.1)

where: $\bar{X}$ = mean
$\sum$ = sum (add up)
X = items in the dataset
N = number of items

ACTIVITY 3.2

Calculate the mean values of the following datasets:
3, 4, 5, 6, 7, 8, 9
6, 6, 6, 6, 6, 6, 6
4, 4, 4, 6, 7, 7, 10
1, 1, 1, 4, 9, 12, 14
A, A+, B, C−, D, D

■ **Describe in what way these datasets are similar and in what way they are different.**

■ **What can you say about these kinds of calculations with regard to variable types (refer to the last dataset in the list)?**

The last dataset in Activity 3.2 clearly shows that it is not possible to perform mean calculations for each and every possible dataset. As explained in Chapter 2, means can only be calculated for interval data and not for ordinal or nominal data. Therefore, we will exclude this dataset from our further discussion. The answer to the first question in Activity 3.2 shows that all the datasets have the same mean value. This goes to show that although a mean value may reveal one important characteristic of a dataset, it certainly does not give the full picture. Two additional descriptive statistics relating to the central tendency are the *mode* and the *median*. The mode requires no calculations, as it is simply the value that occurs most frequently. Some distributions have more than one mode (which are then called bimodal, trimodal, etc.) and some have none. The median is the point in the dataset that is in the middle: half of the data are below this value and half of the data are above.

Looking at the mean, mode, and median provides some useful information about the dataset, but it does not tell us exactly how similar (as in the second set) or different (as in the fourth set) all the items in the set are to each other. In other words, the mean as a statistical model may represent all data values perfectly (as in the second set) or it may not be such a good representation (as in the fourth set). To find out more and describe the dataset in a better way, we need details about the dispersion of the data. One of these is the *range* of a dataset, which is the difference between the highest and lowest value in the set. To calculate the range, take the highest value and subtract the lowest value.

 **ACTIVITY 3.3**

- What are the mode, the median and the range in Activity 3.2?
- Provide the mean, the mode, the median, and the range of the following dataset:

  1, 2, 2, 2, 3, 9, 9, 12

The first dataset from Activity 3.2 has no mode, as all values occur only once. In the second set the mode is 6, in the third it is 4, in the fourth it is 1, and in the final one it is D. The medians in the datasets in Activity 3.2 are 6, 6, 6, and 4 respectively. The ranges of the datasets in Activity 3.2 are 6 (9 − 3), 0 (6 − 6), 6 (10 − 4), and 13 (14 − 1) respectively.

One of the problems of the range is that it is rather strongly affected by extreme values. For instance, for the dataset 1, 2, 3, 4, 4, 5, 5, 6, 6, 8, 29 (henceforth variable *a*) the range will be 28, but that is not very telling for this dataset. What is therefore often done is to cut off the extreme values (25% of the values on either end) and then take the range (see also Figure 3.3). This is called the *interquartile range*. To calculate the interquartile range, you will have to divide the data into four equal parts. First, determine the median. The median will divide the data into two equal parts. Then take the median again, but now for each of these parts. The median of the lower half is called the *lower quartile*; the median of the upper part is called the *upper quartile*. The range between the lower quartile and the upper quartile is called the interquartile range. In the example above, the median is 5, the lower quartile is 3, the upper quartile is 6, and so the interquartile range is (6 − 3) = 3. The quartiles divide the dataset into four equal parts:

1 2 3 4 4 5 5 6 6 8 29

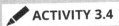

ACTIVITY 3.4

Imagine the following dataset based on variable *b*: 4, 6, 7, 8, 9, 10, 11, 12, 16, 17, 18.

- What is the median?
- What is the lower quartile and what the upper quartile?
- Compare variables *a* and *b*.
  - Which one, overall, has a higher value?
  - Which of the two variables shows a larger spread in scores?

The dispersion of a dataset based on these quartiles can be graphically represented in a boxplot. A boxplot shows the median, the extreme values, and the interquartile range of a dataset and is illustrated in Figure 3.3 for variables *a* and *b*.

What was your answer to the last question in Activity 3.4? If you took the range, your answer was probably variable *a*, which has a range of 28 (29 – 1), as compared to 14 (18 – 4) for variable *b*. When looking at the interquartile range, however, variable *b* has a larger spread in scores (16 – 7 = 9) than variable *a* (3). To overcome this problem, we prefer to use a measure relating to the 'average dispersion' of a dataset: the *standard deviation*.

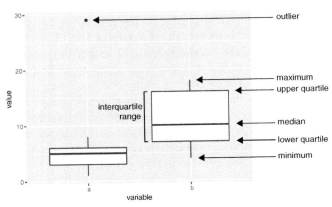

Figure 3.3 Boxplot with explanation

In this picture, you can see two so-called boxplots, one for variable a (left) and one for variable b (right). The boxplot for variable b additionally shows the different quartiles and the interquartile range. The bottom tail of the boxplot shows the first quartile. The middle two parts are the third and fourth quartile, with the median in the middle. The top tail of the plot shows the fourth quartile. You can also see that R has taken the extreme value of variable a to be an outlier, instead of including it in the boxplot itself.

ACTIVITY 3.5

When we have a large set of data, we prefer to describe a dataset by saying what the 'average dispersion' is.

- For the following data, first calculate the mean of the whole set:

  3, 4, 5, 6, 7, 8, 9

  6, 6, 6, 6, 6, 6, 6

- Then calculate how far each separate value is away from the mean.

- Then calculate the mean of those distances.

Expressing how far *on average* each value in a distribution is away from the mean reveals the dispersion characteristics for a dataset at a single glance, as it expresses the mean dispersion for that set. In calculating the mean dispersion, we could follow the standard procedure for the calculation of means. For each individual value in the list, we determine how far it deviates from the mean, which is 6 in both datasets given in Activity 3.5. For the first dataset, the mean dispersion calculation would be as is done in Table 3.1.

Table 3.1 Mean dispersion calculation

value	Distance from mean $(X - \bar{X})$	Distance from mean
3	3 – 6	–3
4	4 – 6	–2
5	5 – 6	–1
6	6 – 6	0
7	7 – 6	1
8	8 – 6	2
9	9 – 6	3
Σ		0

The next step would be to divide the sum by the number of items. However, in this case, we have a problem because the sum is zero, which is caused by the positive and negative values that are set off against each other. One way to solve this problem is to apply a common mathematical trick: we square all the values and get rid of the negative values.[1] We are allowed to

---

1   An alternative solution is to take the absolute values of the numbers. This can also be done, but the result is a different measure. We will only discuss the most commonly used way of calculating average dispersion.

do so, as long as we undo this operation by taking the square root at the very end of the calculations. The following table illustrates the squaring of each distance from the mean (Table 3.2):

Table 3.2 Calculating the standard deviation

value	Distance from mean $(X - \bar{X})$	Distance from mean	(Distance)^2 $(X - \bar{X})^2$
3	3 – 6	–3	9
4	4 – 6	–2	4
5	5 – 6	–1	1
6	6 – 6	0	0
7	7 – 6	1	1
8	8 – 6	2	4
9	9 – 6	3	9
Σ		0	28

Notes: For each and every individual value in the dataset, we subtract the mean value (X – X̄) and square the result. Then we take the sum (Σ) of the squares and take the square root of that value.

The number of items in the list (N) is 7 and, for reasons that will be explained in the next chapter, statistical formulas often use the number of items minus 1 ($N - 1$). So, to get the *variance* (s^2) of this dataset, we take the sum of all squared distances and divide it by ($N - 1$), so the result so far is 28/6 = 4.67. The final step is to take the square root of 4.67, which is 2.16. So, the average dispersion of the first dataset in Activity 3.5 is 2.16. This value is commonly referred to as the *standard deviation (SD)*. The complete formula for the standard deviation reads as follows and should now be completely transparent:

$$SD = \sqrt{\frac{\sum (X - \bar{X})^2}{(N - 1)}} \tag{3.2}$$

The standard deviation (SD) represents the amount of dispersion for a dataset. From the SD and the mean, a clear picture of that

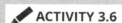

ACTIVITY 3.6

Calculate the mean and the standard deviation of the following datasets:

6, 6, 6, 6, 6, 6, 6
2, 5, 7, 8, 8, 9, 9, 15, 18

dataset will emerge. Imagine that someone told you that a group of German learners on average scored 74.7 (SD = 16.9) on a proficiency test and another group of Spanish learners overall scored 59.7 (SD = 21.1). This information should now be enough for you to visualize an overall higher score for the German learners, but an overall larger spread in scores for the Spanish. In other words, this is a very brief, but informative written summary of the visual information we saw in the boxplot in Figure 3.2.

The SD thus provides information about how similar or different the individual values in a dataset are. Moreover, it can sometimes be used to provide information about how an individual item in the dataset is related to the whole dataset: we can calculate how many standard deviations an individual score is away from the mean. The number of standard deviations for an individual item is called the *z-score:* (the score – the mean)/SD. Let us illustrate this with another example. Suppose a group of students has taken a 100-item language test. Now suppose the mean score for all the students is 60 (correct items) and the standard deviation is 8. A person who has a score of 68 can then be said to have a score that is exactly 1 standard deviation above the mean. That person's z-score is therefore +1. The z-score of someone who scored 56 on that test is half a standard deviation below the mean, which is –0.5, and a person who scored 80 has a z-score of 2.5 (80 – 60 = 20; 20/8 = 2.5). The advantage of the z-score is that it gives an immediate insight into how an individual score must be valued relative to the entire dataset.

ACTIVITY 3.7

In a 40-item language learning test, the mean score is 20. Nadia participated in this test, and her score is 30. We know that Nadia's z-score is +2.

- What is the link between the z-score and the standard deviation?

- What is the standard deviation in this test?

- If a person scored 15, what would be her z-score?

3.4 A different view on variability

This chapter has concentrated on the mean value of a group and the extent to which individual members of that group deviate from that mean. The mean and the dispersion can give us insight into general tendencies for groups. Studies that investigate language development from a CDST perspective take a rather drastically different view on variability. In traditional means analyses, deviation is generally regarded as 'noise' to be avoided. If we want to make generalizations about groups, we want the groups to be as homogeneous as possible. CDST studies regard variability as containing useful information about the developmental process. In longitudinal analyses of individual learners, we often see that an increase in variability signals a change in the process. Therefore, in CDST studies, techniques are used to evaluate the change of variability over time. One of these techniques is the *Min–Max graph*, which visualizes the degree of variability by plotting the minimum observed value and the maximum observed value of many observations of single individuals over time. Figure 3.4 is an example of such an analysis, in which the use (number of instances per session) of a particular type of negating construction ('don't V') was measured at different moments in time. Similarly, CDST studies make use of means analyses in a different way. Instead of comparing the means of groups, they tend to look at how the mean value of a variable (for instance 'average sentence length') changes over time. The longitudinal developmental perspective in CDST case studies and the group studies we focus on in this book are largely complementary. The choice of perspective will depend on the research question that is addressed in a study. For more details on these techniques, please check Verspoor et al. (2011).

Jorge

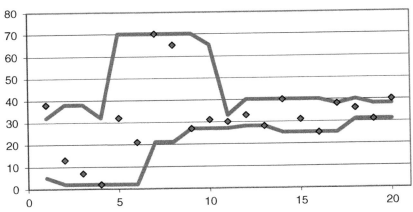

Figure 3.4 Min-Max variability analysis depicting the change over time of 'don't V' negation

Notes: the dots represent the percentage of use of this type of negation in each of the recordings: the top line is the maximum value and the bottom line the minimum value

From: Verspoor et al. (2011, p. 76), with permission

3.5 Frequency distributions

The mean and *SD* do not tell us exactly how often certain values occur and how they are distributed. For instance, a teacher may need to know how many students answered how many items correctly on an exam to be able to determine the grade. To find out, he or she can conduct a frequency tally. Tallies are recordings of the number of occurrences of a particular phenomenon. Table 3.3 exemplifies this for a 10-item test. The tallies refer to the number of correct answers on the test.

Graphically, a frequency distribution can, for instance, be displayed as a *histogram*, as in Figure 3.5(A), or it can be presented as a *line graph* (Figure 3.5(B)).

Table 3.3 Frequency distribution data for a 10-item test

Number of correct items	Number of students with that number of correct items
1	0
2	1
3	1
4	3
5	7
6	11
7	9
8	5
9	2
10	1

 **ACTIVITY 3.8**

Use the figure below to draw a graph that represents the frequency distribution exemplified in Table 3.3. The score in this distribution is the number of correct items. First put a dot for the occurrence of every score, and then use these dots to draw a line.

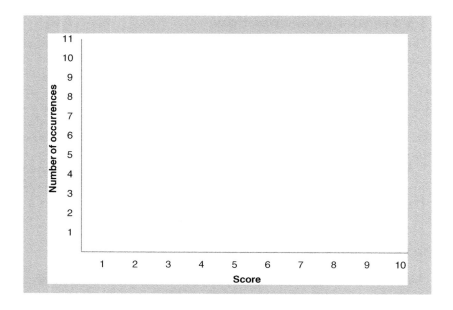

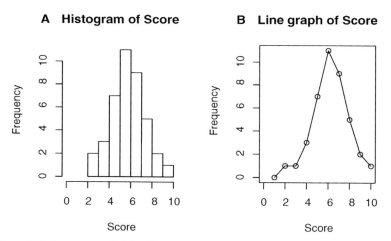

A Histogram of Score   **B Line graph of Score**

Figure 3.5 Frequency distributions

Frequencies can be presented in a histogram (A) or as a line graph (B)

The different kinds of graphs help us visualize how the data is dispersed. This brings us to an interesting phenomenon that characterizes frequency distributions that are based on natural data like human behaviour. If there are very many data points, the frequency distribution will often result in the same bell-shaped line graph that is commonly referred to as a *normal distribution*. This phenomenon will be used as a reference point for almost all of the statistics discussed in the remainder of this chapter. Figure 3.6 provides an example of the normal distribution.

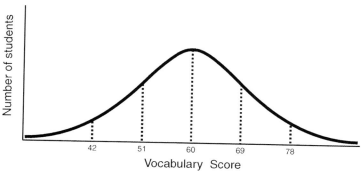

Figure 3.6 Frequency polygon representing a normal distribution

This frequency polygon (a graph type based on a histogram to visualize the overall pattern of frequency distributions) represents the scores of a very large number of scores on a vocabulary test.

Figure 3.6 is a representation of the vocabulary scores of a large number of students. The vocabulary scores in this example are distributed according to a normal distribution (also called a *Gaussian* distribution). The normal distribution has a number of typical characteristics. First of all, the mean, the mode, and the median largely coincide. In this example of a perfect normal distribution, the mean, the mode, and median are all 60. In other words, the average is 60, the most frequently occurring score is 60, and when ordering the scores from lowest to highest, half of them will be below and half will be above 60. The extreme low and high values, on the left-hand side and on the right-hand side, occur much less frequently than the scores around the mean. This makes perfect sense because extreme values are always more exceptional than the middle values. In a frequency polygon of a normal distribution, predictable regularities go even further. Let us assume that in the example in Figure 3.6, the standard deviation is 9. Now we can instantly see that the vast majority of all the students' scores in this distribution fall between –1 and +1 standard deviations from the mean (with scores between 51 and 69), while fewer students had scores in the adjacent sections (with scores between 42 and 51 or 69 and 78), and a very limited number of students' scores appear in the outlying sections that are above 2 standard deviations. In a normal distribution, the number of scores that occur in the sections related to the standard deviations is always approximately the same. This is expressed in *percentile scores*. The percentage of scores between the mean score and 1 *SD* away from that mean is always about 34.13%. Between 1 and 2 *SD*s from the mean, we always find 13.59% of all scores. Higher than 2 *SD*s above the mean is only 2.14% and lower than 2 *SD*s below the mean another 2.14% can be found. These observations are summarized in Figure 3.7 below.

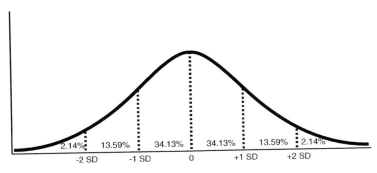

Figure 3.7 The normal distribution with *SD*s and percentile scores

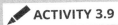ACTIVITY 3.9

100 people have taken a reading test. The test contains 11 items. The results are as follows:

Score	Frequency
11	2
10	1
9	2
8	15
7	20
6	30
5	13
4	7
3	5
2	3
1	2
0	0

- Calculate the mean and the mode.

- Draw a frequency polygon. Do you think this variable is approximately distributed according to a normal distribution?

- How many people are more than 2 standard deviations away from the mean? Is this a small or a large percentage? If someone else took the same test, which score do you think would be the most likely score for this person to get?

In a perfect world, we would always see a normal distribution in our data. However, since we test samples from the population, it could be that the distribution deviates from normality. To check this, we can look at the shape it takes and check the values of *skewness* and *kurtosis*. Skewness says something about the symmetry of the distribution being more focused to the left or to the right of the curve. Kurtosis says something about the pointedness of the curve. When the values of skewness and kurtosis are zero, they represent a perfect normal distribution. The more they deviate from zero, the more they also deviate from normality. In Figure 3.8, we give examples of distributions that suffer from negative or positive skewness or kurtosis.

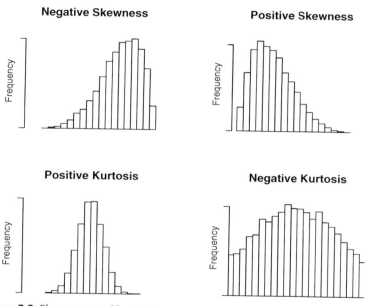

Figure 3.8 Skewness and kurtosis

This is an overview of distributions that are either negatively skewed (with a tail to the left) or positively skewed (with a tail to the right), as shown in the top left and top right graphs, respectively, or datasets suffering from positive kurtosis (a pointy distribution) or negative kurtosis (a flat distribution), as shown in the bottom left and right, respectively.

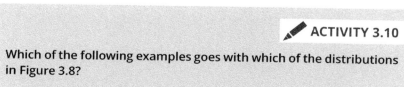

ACTIVITY 3.10

Which of the following examples goes with which of the distributions in Figure 3.8?

■ **Scores on a test that was too easy.**

■ **Scores on a test that did not discriminate well between students.**

- Giving the same test to all students in a language school (regardless of being beginners, intermediate, or advanced learners).
- Frequency of words in a language.

Now have a look at the four boxplots below. Which boxplot visualizes which of the four distributions in Figure 3.8?

In this chapter we have introduced basic descriptive statistics and the concept of a normal distribution. Looking at the descriptives and the distribution of data is an important step that many people tend to forget when they are analysing data. Before carrying out any statistical test, it is crucial to inspect data visually and look at the descriptive statistics. This will provide information that statistical tests will not be able to provide. After reading this chapter, we suggest you try Practical 2 of this book.

4 STATISTICAL LOGIC

4.1 Introduction

In the previous chapter, we discussed descriptive statistics that can be used to get a first impression of the data. The next step could be to apply inductive statistics, which will help to evaluate the outcome of the data. To illustrate this, let us go back to the data in Activity 2.1 concerning the relationship between age of acquisition and proficiency score. We could add some descriptive statistics to the data, but the descriptives, in combination with the scatterplot, will not provide us with the tools to estimate how certain we can be that the observed relationship is not based on a coincidence. Moreover, since it is generally impossible to test entire populations, researchers normally select a small representative sample. Inductive statistics will help us in generalizing the findings from a sample to a larger population. However, there are some important assumptions underlying inductive statistics, which require testing by descriptive statistics. For instance, many inductive statistical tests constitute so-called *parametric* tests that have been developed with the assumption that the data that are analysed approximately follow a normal distribution. This means that when a sample shows data that are not normally distributed, we will have to select tests that are not based on this assumption, so-called *non-parametric* tests. In this chapter, we will introduce the logic behind inductive statistics and discuss the issue of generalization from samples to populations. Before we can explain the logic behind inductive statistics, there are a few other concepts that need to be introduced, which have to do with operationalization.

4.2 Independent versus dependent variables

In Chapter 2, we discussed the scales of variables, but another consideration in the choice of variables is their function in an empirical study. This step is particularly relevant for quantitative, statistical studies with an experimental or quasi-experimental design (a design that will be explained in more detail in Section 4.4). In these types of studies, one or more *independent* variables (IVs) are systematically changed to investigate the effect of the independent variable or variables on a *dependent* variable (DV). An example would be a study that investigates the effect of instruction on vocabulary knowledge. The independent variable in such a study, that is the variable that is manipulated, would be instruction, a nominal variable with two levels: with and without instruction. In statistical programs, independent variables are sometimes also called grouping variables, factors, or predictor variables, as these variables might 'predict' the dependent variable. The dependent variable, that is the variable that is measured and that is expected to be affected by the independent variable, is vocabulary knowledge in English. This could be an interval variable that represents the outcome of a vocabulary test (for instance the number of correct items on a test). In this way, we can measure the effect of instruction (independent) on vocabulary knowledge (dependent). If the vocabulary knowledge were bigger with instruction than without instruction, we could conclude that instruction is helpful. Obviously, this example is a gross oversimplification of the reality of such a study, but only serves to illustrate the point.

 ACTIVITY 4.1

A researcher wants to know if training positively affects speed for runners. To investigate this, she has set up an experiment in which she will time two different runners who will complete a fixed distance after different training programmes. Runner A has trained twice as much as runner B. For the sake of the argument, we will assume that the two runners are otherwise identical. One of the variables in this experiment is the time (in seconds) it took the runners to complete the track. The other variable is the amount of training, represented by the two different runners.

- What is the function of each of these variables (dependent/independent) and what are the scales involved?

It can be argued that the dependent variable (like the vocabulary knowledge in our example above and running time in Activity 4.1) changes as a result of the independent variable (the presence or absence of instruction or the amount of training). What is measured is normally the dependent variable; what we want to investigate is the influence of the independent variable. In many experimental studies, more than one independent variable is included at the same time. In more complex designs, more than one dependent variable may be included. For instance, in our example of instruction and vocabulary knowledge, we could include an additional independent variable, such as the L1 of the participants. In this study, we would then have one dependent variable (vocabulary knowledge) and two independent variables (instruction, L1). The number of independent variables we can include is not limited, but the interpretation of the data may become increasingly complex. Sometimes, researchers explicitly decide not to include a variable in a study if they are not interested in the effects of this variable and want to exclude any effect such a variable may have on the dependent variable. This can be done by not changing the variable, or in other words, keeping the variable constant. Such a variable is then referred to as a *control variable*. Applied to the vocabulary study described above, the researcher may decide to include only female learners in the study. We can then say that gender is a control variable in this study. The dependency relationship between variables is not equally relevant to all types of statistical studies, such as studies examining relationships between variables; this is something we will return to in the next chapter (Section 5.2).

 **ACTIVITY 4.2**

Think of an experimental design in which:

- **Age is an independent variable**

AND

- **Language proficiency is the dependent variable**

AND

- **L1 background is a control variable**

4.3 Statistical decisions

Suppose we want to compare two groups that participated in a vocabulary test. Following our example in Section 4.2, let us assume these two groups represent two 'types of instruction': either they received instruction or they did not. Imagine the median score in the uninstructed group is 32 and the interquartile range (IQR) is 28 – 36, and the median score in the instructed group is 38 (IQR = 35 – 40.25). In Figure 4.1(A)), this hypothetical situation is illustrated in a boxplot. In the boxplot, we can compare the median score of the two groups, but we can also compare the dispersion within each group. At face value, we can see that some higher scores in the uninstructed group overlap with some lower scores of the instructed group. If we disregard all other possible differences between the groups (which is hard to imagine) and assume that the type of instruction is the only independent variable involved, how can we evaluate the difference between these groups? Is a difference of six items on this vocabulary scale large enough to say that there *is* a difference (in spite of some overlap) and that, in general, vocabulary instruction is effective in learning a second language? And what if we had a difference of only two points and a little more overlap (as in Figure 4.1(B))? Would that also be proof that instruction is better than no instruction? Or was it simply a coincidence that the instructed group in this sample scored better than the other group?

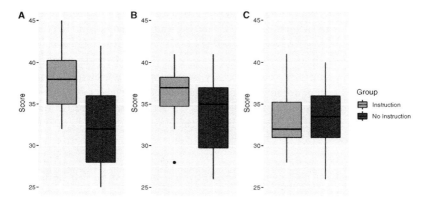

Figure 4.1 Boxplots showing the dispersion in the data of the instructed group (light grey) and the uninstructed group (dark grey) in three hypothetical situations

ACTIVITY 4.3

Figure 4.1 shows three hypothetical datasets based on the example study aimed at examining the effect of instruction (instruction vs. no instruction) on vocabulary learning.

- For which of the three datasets would you expect to find a difference between the instructed and the non-instructed group?

- For which of the three datasets would you expect to find no differences between the two groups?

- Which of the datasets is the most difficult to judge on the basis of the boxplots?

In our example of vocabulary scores, the question of whether there is a difference between the groups and how sure we are about that difference existing in reality may be very interesting, but being wrong about interpreting the results of our test would not be a matter of life or death. In many cases, the results of tests or surveys have serious consequences, and it is important that we can evaluate the differences between test scores and try to make sure that if we gave the same test to other similar groups, we would get very similar results. The purpose of this section is to show how statistics can be helpful in determining how the potential difference or relationship between scores can be evaluated. There is a lot of discussion about the best way to do this, and there are different approaches. We will present the conventional approach here, but will come back to its limitations later on.

ACTIVITY 4.4

Return to your answer to Activity 3.7, a 40-item language-learning test with a mean score of 20 and an *SD* of 5. Let us assume that the test scores are approximately normally distributed.

- Draw a frequency polygon for these test scores and draw lines at the mean and at 1 and 2 *SD*s from the mean in both directions (see Figure 3.7 for an example).

- One person who participated in this test tells you she scored 34. Someone else tells you she scored 22. One of them is not telling the truth. Who would you believe? And why?

4.3.1 The chance of making the wrong decision

Activity 4.4 should help you see the usefulness of statistics. The best guess for the last question is probably to say that the person who scored 22 was telling the truth, while the other one was not. Using the normal distribution as a starting point, we know that the person who says she scored 34 would have had a score that is between 2 and 3 *SD*s from the mean and that her score would belong to less than 2.14% of all scores. The person who said she scored 22 would have had a score that is within 1 *SD* from the mean. As about 33% of all scores fall within this range when the data are normally distributed, it is simply more likely that the person who says she scored 22 was right. It should be noted that it is certainly possible for someone to have scored 34, but if we have to make a decision based on these figures, the chance of making the wrong decision is bigger if we decide that the person who says she scored 34 was right. In other words, doing statistics is all about estimating the chance of making the wrong decision and about comparing a limited dataset (like the two persons from the example) to a larger group of people.

What are the chances of making the wrong decision? Logically, two types of errors are possible when making a decision based on observations. Imagine a teacher has rather convincing evidence that a student has cheated, but he cannot be 100 per cent certain. The immediate consequence of cheating is that the student will be excluded from further participation on a course. There are two possible correct decisions: the student did not cheat and is not excluded, or the student did cheat and is excluded. There are also two wrong decisions possible: the student did cheat but is not excluded, and the student did not cheat but is excluded. It is generally accepted that the latter is a more serious error. In statistics, the error of assuming that something is true which in reality is not true is commonly referred to as an *alpha (α) error*. The other error type (assuming something is *not* true which in reality *is* true) is known as a *beta (β) error*. The error types are summarized in Table 4.1.

Table 4.1 Error types

Decision made		Really cheated? Yes	Really cheated? No
	Excluded	OK	α-error
	Not excluded	β-error	OK

4.3.2 Hypotheses

To avoid logical errors, one of the first steps of conducting a statistical study is to formulate specific research hypotheses about the relationship between the dependent and independent variables. When we apply this reasoning to the strongly simplified example about vocabulary acquisition by instructed learners and uninstructed learners, we can formulate three possible hypotheses: instructed learners do better, uninstructed learners do better, or there is no difference between the instructed and uninstructed learners. For each of these hypotheses, a decision table can be set up like the one in Table 4.1. However, the main hypothesis that is tested is the *null hypothesis* (H_0), which states that there is no difference. The other two possible hypotheses are referred to as *alternative hypotheses* (H_1 and H_2): the instructed learners perform better, or the uninstructed learners perform better. The reason for stating the null hypothesis is that it is impossible to prove a hypothesis right, but it is possible to prove a hypothesis wrong; in other words, we can only *reject* a hypothesis. This *principle of falsification*, which was already briefly introduced in Section 1.2, is best illustrated with another example. Suppose we want to investigate whether all swans are white. If we formulate our hypothesis as 'all swans are white', we can accept this hypothesis only after making sure that all swans in the world are indeed white. However, we can easily reject this hypothesis as soon as we have seen one non-white swan. Therefore, hypotheses are always formulated in such a way that we are able to attempt to reject them, rather than accept them. In research terms, this means that we will normally test the rejectability of the null hypothesis. In our vocabulary learning example, we would thus test the hypothesis that there is no difference between instructed and uninstructed L2 learners. If we can reject this hypothesis beyond reasonable doubt, we can implicitly accept the alternative hypothesis that there *is* a difference. The mean scores of the instructed and the uninstructed learners will then reveal which group performs better.

Suppose one group does indeed score better than the other. If the groups we are testing are our only concern, we need no further analyses. But how can we be sure that this difference in scores in the sample can be generalized to an actual difference in reality? In other words, if you performed the test again and again, with new people in the instructed and uninstructed group, would you find the same difference? Or, to put it differently, how can we say beyond reasonable doubt that the findings in our sample were not found just by chance? And what do we mean by *beyond reasonable doubt*? These questions are related to the alpha error that was introduced in the previous paragraph. The alpha error concerns the possibility that we *incorrectly reject* the null hypothesis (and thereby implicitly incorrectly accept the alternative hypothesis). This is illustrated in Table 4.2.

To avoid the possibility that we reject the H_0 incorrectly, we try to calculate the degree of chance that might have been involved in obtaining these scores by chance. In other words, we want to obtain a value that signifies the exact probability of us committing an α-error, that is the chance of finding an effect in our study while it does not exist in reality. If we assume that the distribution of scores in our groups follows the normal distribution, then we can quantify which scores are the least likely to have occurred. Recall the frequency polygon of the normal distribution (see Figure 3.7). The small areas on either side of the mean beyond 2 SDs refer to a little over 2% of the scores. These scores are less likely to occur than the scores around the mean, and might have occurred by chance. Therefore, scores in this area are related to the conventionally accepted probability of an alpha-type error (abbreviated as p for probability), which is 2.5% on either side of the distribution, and 5% in total.

To elaborate on this a little further, let us go back to the data in Figure 3.6 concerning vocabulary scores. This normally distributed dataset is plotted once more in Figure 4.2 on the left. Imagine we tested a second group of students who received a new teaching method as compared to our original group and they scored 96 on average, as visualized on the right in 4.2. Our original group had a mean score of 60 ($SD = 9$) and, as we discussed on the basis of the normal distribution, a score below 42 ($-2\ SD$) or above 78 ($+2\ SD$) would be highly unlikely (around 5% in total). If a person from our

Table 4.2 Making decisions about H_0

		Reality	
		H_0 false	H_0 true
Decision made	H_0 rejected	OK	α-error
	H_0 accepted	β-error	OK

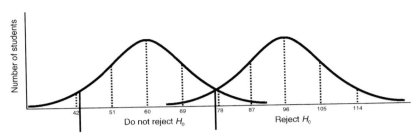

Figure 4.2 A comparison of two normal distributions

The distribution to the left belongs to the original group exposed to an old teaching method ($M = 60$; $SD = 9$) and the one to the right belongs to a group who had received a new teaching method ($M = 96$; $SD = 9$).

original group told us that they scored 96, we would highly doubt their statement as the chance of such a score occurring is extremely small. On the contrary, if a person from the group who received the new teaching method told us that they scored 96, we would probably immediately believe them.

Using that same reasoning, imagine someone cannot remember which group they were in, but really needs to know what teaching method they received. The only thing they do know is that their score was 105. In that case, you can quite safely state that they differ from the original group and hence tell them that they most likely received the new teaching method. But what if someone came up to you and said they scored 78? In that case, you cannot really say that there is a bigger chance of this score occurring in the first or the second group as the chances of obtaining such a score are approximately equal in both groups (around 2%). If you said they belonged to the original group, you might be committing a beta error, that is saying that they do not differ from the original group when they in fact do if they were in the new group. If you told them that they were in the new group, you might be committing an alpha error, that is saying that they differ from the original group when in fact they may not as they were in reality part of the original group. You can probably imagine that the degree of overlap between the curves determines the probability of making these kinds of mistakes. More specifically stated, the chance of making an alpha error decreases the further the two curves are apart. When performing inductive statistics, we want to quantify the probability of making an alpha error and this probability is reflected in the p-value.

4.3.3 Significance

In the previous paragraphs, we have explained how we can quantify 'beyond reasonable doubt' justified by general observations about the normal distribution. Yet, the interpretation of 'reasonable' varies among disciplines and is strongly based on conventions. The conventionally accepted maximum chance of incorrectly rejecting the null hypothesis is 5% or less ($\alpha = .05$), but in cases of life or death, such as clinical trials, the chance of making an alpha error is usually set to 1% or less ($\alpha = .01$). It is important to realize that it is the researcher's choice to set the alpha level and thereby define the term 'beyond reasonable doubt'. However, researchers will have to follow the conventions. For instance, it may seem attractive to set the alpha level at 50%, so that we make it easy to reject the H_0, but logically this will not be accepted. On the contrary, making it difficult to reject the H_0 will make a research conclusion more convincing. The selected chance of incorrectly rejecting the null hypothesis is closely related to the level of *significance*, that is the *p*-value. A significant result is one that is acceptable within the scope of the statistical study and a report should include both an interpretation of the significance as well as the exact probability of this interpretation being incorrect. An expression like 'a statistical analysis showed that the difference between the two groups was significant' must always be followed by, for example, '$p = .02$'. This should be interpreted as 'I accept that there is a difference between the two groups, and the chance that I have made an error in assuming this is approximately 2%'.

ACTIVITY 4.5

A researcher has investigated the relationship between reading skills and listening comprehension. She reports the following: $r_{xy} = .56$; $p < .001$.

■ What exactly is meant by '$p < .001$'? (Be as explicit as possible.)

■ What is the implied null hypothesis?

We have now seen that in statistics we can never say that a hypothesis is true; we can only express the chance of making the wrong decision. Conventionally, if that chance is smaller than 5% or 1% (depending on how serious it is to make the wrong decision), this is taken to be acceptable. In Figure 3.7 (of the normal distribution), we saw that values between $z = -2$ and $z = 2$ make up approximately 96% of the scores of the entire population (95.72%, to be precise). What z-scores do you think will belong to the 95% confidence interval? The answer should be 'slightly less than 2', which also corresponds with the two lines reflecting the values 42.36 and 77.64 in the left curve in Figure 4.2. To be precise, these lines reflect the z-scores -1.96 and 1.96, which are the *critical values* related to the top 5% of the distribution. So on either side of the 'tails' of the distribution we find 2.5% beyond these points. If a new group of people scored anywhere between 42.36 and 77.64, we would not reject H_0 and we would conclude that there is no significant difference between this new group and our original group with respect to their vocabulary scores. We would reject H_0, however, if a new group's average exceeded the critical values, that is if they scored lower than 42.36 or higher than 77.64. If the starting point is that the chance of making the wrong decision should be smaller than 1%, then the critical values (z-scores) for being 99% certain about a decision are –2.58 and 2.58 (or 36.78 and 83.22 in our vocabulary example).

4.3.4 One-tailed vs. two-tailed

Now suppose we want to calculate the relationship between height and the age of children from birth to ten years old. The null hypothesis would be: there is no relationship between age and height. One alternative hypothesis is that the older the children are, the taller they get, which sounds quite plausible. In this case, the relationship cannot really become negative: that is, it would be quite impossible to see children grow smaller as they get older. In cases like this, we would only have to consider one side of the spectrum, which is called *one-tailed testing*, and only one alternative hypothesis would be needed. In most cases, *two-tailed testing* is used, because it is uncertain in which direction the results will go. Although in some extraordinary cases one-tailed testing is allowed, it is usually better to test two-tailed. This is because it becomes easier to reject your null hypothesis in one-tailed testing, since you are disregarding one side of the normal distribution. When allowing a 5% chance of incorrectly rejecting the null hypothesis, this is usually 2.5% on either side of the distribution, while with a one-tailed distribution, the 5% occurs only on one side. Therefore, to be on the safe side, two-tailed testing is preferred unless one of the alternative hypotheses is theoretically impossible.

 **ACTIVITY 4.6**

Think of two different null hypotheses that test one aspect of second language acquisition. One of these should clearly be a 'two-tailed' problem (so there are two alternative hypotheses) and one should be a 'one-tailed' problem (so there is only one alternative hypothesis).

- **For each, formulate the null hypotheses and the alternative hypotheses as precisely as possible.**

4.4 The sample and the population

A sample needs to be representative for the population that we wish to investigate. For instance, in a study investigating the possible differences in language aptitude between men and women, it must be ensured that the participants selected represent the same population or subpopulation. If the women in this study are all university language students and the men are all professional mechanics, there is a fair chance that the outcome of this study is meaningless in spite of its possible statistical significance. There are two ways of ensuring that the sample is representative. The first is to make sure that the sample is selected purely at random from the entire population. This means that the researcher finds men and women that do not belong to any subpopulation other than that determined by sex. Theoretically, this could be achieved by randomly picking men and women from a purely random list, like a directory of all people on earth. However, this example will illustrate that, for such research questions, pure random sampling for large and general populations is very difficult to achieve.

The second way of eliminating differences between participants is to focus on a very specific subpopulation (or *stratum*) by including all possibly interfering factors as control conditions. Subsequently, a random selection can be made from this specific stratum. In the language aptitude example, this could mean that the study exclusively focuses on professional mechanics who are working at the same company, who have always lived in the same area, who went to the same school, who belong to the same socio-economic class, etc. The problem in this case may be that there are not enough female mechanics that live up to these criteria. Testing very specific populations also has the disadvantage that the results cannot be generalized beyond that specific situation. In reality, random samples are normally taken from limited populations that can be assumed to be generally representative for the variables involved. However, the critical reader must be aware of this choice. The results of a language aptitude study among university students in northern England may say nothing about the distribution of the exact same variables among mechanics in the Indian province of Punjab.

Strictly speaking, studies in which the sampling has not been done purely at random cannot be considered experimental studies. This type of study is then referred to as *quasi-experimental*. It will not be surprising that many studies in the field of Applied Linguistics belong to this group. For any study that uses representative sampling, it is crucial that the sample size is sufficiently large. But how can it be determined whether a sample size is sufficient? The required sample size is related to the strength of the effect. The stronger the effect (that is the bigger the difference between groups or the stronger the relationship between variables), the smaller the sample needed to demonstrate that effect in a statistical study. The strength of the effect in relation to the sample size is referred to as the *power* of a study. Although the experimenter has little control over the size of the effect, it may be possible to estimate this and to take a sample that is more than sufficient to demonstrate the effect. In language studies, the sample size is often confined by practical limitations. In these situations, a very small sample size of, say, 20 cases for each level, might be the maximum number a researcher can practically use. This will often mean that small effects cannot be demonstrated in these studies (see Section 4.7 for more details about this).

To preclude confusion in whether we are talking about a sample or a population, the conventions are that Greek symbols are used for the population (σ for standard deviation, μ for mean, and α for the chance of making the wrong decision), while Latin letters are used for the sample (SD for the standard deviation of the sample, M or $\bar{X}$ for the mean, and p for the chance of making the wrong decision).

As we have described above, inductive statistics can help us in generalizing the findings from a sample to a larger population. Logically, we can never select a sample that is fully representative of the population. Fortunately, we can calculate the representativeness of our sample by expressing how much it deviates from the population. This standard way to express the error of our sample is called the *Standard Error* (*SE*), and it can be seen as a standard deviation for the sample when compared to the population. The *SE* can be calculated using the equation below:

$$SE = \frac{\sigma}{\sqrt{N}} \qquad (4.1)$$

For statistical calculations, the difference between the sample and the population has some important consequences. The generalizability of the results found in the sample to the entire population will 'automatically' be taken into account in the calculations done by, for instance, JASP or R. We have already seen one example of this: in Equation 3.2 of the *SD*, we used $N - 1$ for the number of participants in the group, rather than simply N, and the reason for this is explained in the following section.

4.5 Degrees of freedom

In reporting our statistical outcomes, we also report the *degrees of freedom* (*df*). *Df* is a necessary correction that is needed for the calculation of the probability of the sample and is related to the number of 'free choices' that can be made. The principle can best be explained by a simple example. Suppose we have five numbers and a total that is given. Say the total is 100. We can then randomly choose four numbers, though the last number will always be fixed. If we choose 11, 41, 8, and 19, the fifth number must be 21. In a calculation of probability, we then say that there are four (5 − 1) *df*. For our purpose, it will suffice to understand that *df* is related to the total size of the sample. The bigger the sample size, the larger the *df*, the more lenient we can be in rejecting the H_0 and the more relevant is the value. When different groups are compared, the *df* is determined by taking the total number of participants in the groups and subtracting the number of levels of the independent variable (which is the number of groups). When there are two groups and 20 participants in each group, the *df* value would be (20 + 20) − 2 = 38.

 **ACTIVITY 4.9**

How many participants does each group have, where the numbers in each group are the same, for the following *df*s and number of groups:

- *df* = 28, 2 groups?
- *df* = 57, 3 groups?

4.6 Checking assumptions

As we have mentioned in Section 4.1, inductive statistics can be divided into parametric and non-parametric tests. The choice between these types of statistics depends on the type of data that are analysed, the perspective the researcher wants to take, and on the question as to whether all assumptions of the tests have been fulfilled. For instance, when interval data are used and when the assumption of normality of the distribution is met, parametric statistics can be used, like a 'Pearson *r*' or a 'Student *t*-test' (which will be explained in detail in Chapter 5). However, if we want to analyse ordinal or nominal data, or if the interval data in the sample do not prove to follow the assumptions, we will have to use non-parametric alternatives to these tests. These non-parametric tests are in general a bit stricter and take into account that the data are, for example, not normally distributed or of an ordinal nature. Parametric tests are only allowed when the data:

- Consist of an interval dependent variable and, very often but not always, independent observations;
- Approximate the normal distribution (especially for small sample sizes);
- Comply with homoscedasticity/homogeneity of variance (to be explained in more detail below);

When assessing relationships, it is additionally important to assess:

- Linearity.

The question of whether your dependent variable is measured on an interval scale is important for the design of your study and should be considered before you proceed. For instance, if we want to assess essay questions, the ratings must be considered as subjective grades, so the data are not interval and regular parametric tests should not be used. The assumption of independent observations is, just as the interval dependent variable, an assumption that can only be checked using common sense knowledge and this independence assumption is two-fold. On the one hand, the observations between groups should be independent. That is to say, the different groups should be made up of different people. On the other hand, the assumption of independence also means that the observations within each group should be independent. In other words, two or more data points in one group should not be connected to, or dependent on, one another. It should be noted that there are some commonly used parametric tests that can account for such dependency relationships and one of them will be introduced and discussed in Chapter 5 (Section 5.3.2).

An additional important assumption of parametric statistics is a normal distribution of the data. We have seen that we can draw a frequency plot to assess whether the curve approaches the bell-shape. We have also shown how the values of skewness and kurtosis can give a rough idea of the normality of the distribution. However, if you want to make a more objective decision on the normality of the data, you can run a separate statistical test to see if the normality hypothesis can be reliably assumed (for instance with 95% confidence). An example of such a test is the *Shapiro-Wilk* test.

Another important assumption of parametric statistics is *homoscedasticity* or *homogeneity of variance*. Homoscedasticity is the term most often used when assessing relationships and homogeneity is generally used in the context of group comparisons. Both terms, however, refer to the similarity of variation in the data. For relationships, the assumption holds that the spread in scores is comparable across the relationship line (more details on this follow in Section 6.4). For group comparisons, this assumption refers to the similarity in distribution within the groups: the variance within each sample should be approximately the same. The variance is very similar to the *SD*, because it is the total sum of the deviation from the mean. Since the deviations from the mean are based on squared values (to neutralize the negative values), the notation for variance is s^2 or σ^2. For the application of parametric statistics, the variance across the dataset and, if applicable, in the different groups must be approximately the same. A rule of thumb to check whether different groups show similar variance is to compare the *SD*s. If one *SD* is more than twice as big as that for another group, then you know that the variance is not homogeneous. Different from the violation of the normality of the distribution, this violation can usually be corrected for, so that in most cases, parametric statistics can still be used.

Finally, an important assumption for virtually all parametric statistics used to assess relationships is that the relationship between variables is linear. For non-parametric correlations, the relationship does not necessarily have to follow a perfectly straight line as long as it is *monotonic*. The latter term refers to the fact that the line should go up or go down, but should not include both an increase and a decrease in (one of) the variables. This assumption can best be assessed by creating a scatterplot: a relationship is linear when the dots approximately follow a straight line (see Figure 3.1 for an example).

When data do not match one or more of the points mentioned above, we will need to apply non-parametric tests. These tests do not necessarily require the dependent variable to be interval or the distribution to be bell-shaped as they, for example, do not involve the calculation of means (in case of group comparisons). These non-parametric versions are generally also less powerful and often more difficult to interpret.

Note that the assumptions we mention here are needed for the basic statistical tests, but that for some tests, other assumptions play a role. Whenever this is the case, this will be pointed out in the discussions of these specific tests.

4.7 Alpha, beta, and effect sizes

In Sections 4.2 and 4.3, we talked about setting our alpha to, for example, 5% or 1%, and about the risk of getting an alpha error (or Type I error) or a beta error (or Type II error). The alpha error is important, because we would not want to incorrectly reject our null hypothesis. This means that the stricter we are, the less chance we have of getting an alpha error. The beta error is the chance that we incorrectly accept the null hypothesis. Although this error may seem to be less serious, it is also an error we will want to avoid. Similar to why we have a convention for the alpha error (of a maximally 5% chance of making the wrong decision), the conventionally accepted beta error (β) is 20%. This means that if there really is an effect (such as the difference between the groups), we want to be 80% certain that we really find that effect in our sample. This number, 80%, is the desired *power* of an experiment: the power is $1 - \beta$, since β is .20. Let us briefly return to the two groups we compared in Figure 4.2. Imagine that the two groups are indeed different, but their scores overlap a lot more. The area of overlap would also constitute an increased chance of making a beta error (β) and incorrectly concluding that the groups do not differ. In the current situation, a person scoring 75 would most likely belong to the old teaching method group as the chance of obtaining such a score with the new method is very small (or at least smaller than 5%). If, however, the mean of the second group was 87, then the likeliness of obtaining a score of 75 in the old teaching method group is the same, but the chance of obtaining such a score in the new teaching method group has become less unlikely. There is thus a bigger chance that we will not be able to reject H_0. Not only has this increase in overlap led to an increase in β, but the power has also decreased. If, on the other hand, there was no overlap whatsoever between the two curves, then β would be 0 as we would always correctly reject H_0. Consequently, the power of the experiment, the chance of finding the difference between the two groups, would be 100%.

The power of an experiment is logically related to the number of participants in a sample. Theoretically, if the entire population were tested, we would also be 100% certain that we find an effect that really exists. The smaller the samples are, the weaker the power and the more difficult it is to demonstrate an existing effect.

The chance that we find an existing effect is not only dependent on the sample size, but also on the size of the effect. A big effect can be found with a limited sample size, but to demonstrate a small effect, we will need really large samples. The following numbers are suggested for this by Field et al. (2012, p. 59) based on work by Cohen (1992). Using an alpha level of .05 and a beta level of .2, we would need 783 participants (per group in a means analysis) to detect a small effect size, 85 participants to detect a medium effect size, and 28 participants to detect a large effect size. This means that to assess meaningfulness based on the power of an experiment, we will have to calculate the *effect size* of the experiment and we will have to be able to interpret the effect size. But what is a 'small' and what is a 'large' effect size? There are several statistical calculations that can be used for this purpose. We will discuss this when we dig more deeply into inductive statistics in Chapters 5, 6, and 7.

For now, it is important to realize that the smaller the effect, the larger the sample needs to be in order to actually find the effect. In other words, trying to find a small effect with a limited number of participants may be a waste of time, as it is like finding a needle in a haystack. At the same time, if we are looking for a large effect, it is a waste of time to try and find a large sample. Therefore, it is important for the evaluation of the meaningfulness of a result that the effect size be calculated. In the past years, it has become more and more common to report effect sizes in addition to the chance that the found difference or relationship was based on chance. In fact, the American Psychological Association (APA) recommends to always report effect sizes (Vanden-Bos, 2010). In the following chapters, you will thus also learn how effect sizes can be calculated for the different statistical tests we will discuss.

4.8 Significance revisited

In Section 4.3 we promised to return to the discussion about the best way to quantify 'beyond reasonable doubt'. We have presented the conventional approach of *Null Hypothesis Significance Testing* (NHST), simply because it is still widely used and it is important to be familiar with the method. However, there has been much criticism on the approach and we would like to point to the most important issues to put it in a present-day perspective.

The most important problem with NHST is the all-or-nothing approach of significance. Within a set alpha level, a result is significant or not significant. For instance, if the alpha level has been set to 5% and the outcome of a statistical calculation is that $p = .049$, we would safely reject the H_0 (p is smaller than 5%), while we cannot reject H_0 when $p = .051$. It will be obvious that this is a dubious interpretation of the results of a study. A more realistic method that has been suggested is to report the confidence interval (CI) in addition to the p-value. In our explanations we have concentrated on the continuity of the difference between the distributions of H_0 and H_a, so this is a rather small step. As we illustrated in Figure 4.2, the CI associated with an alpha level of 5% (the chance of incorrectly rejecting H_0 is 5%) is the 95% CI, which ranges between $z = -1.96$ and $z = 1.96$ for each hypothesis. Similarly, we can report on the 90% CI or the 99% CI. The essence of the calculation is the same as that of the p-value, but it leads to a less binary interpretation of the results. We would recommend avoiding the all-or-nothing interpretation of significance and using the p-value in research reports with caution or in combination with the relevant CI.

A second problem is the interpretation of alpha itself. Cohen (1994) claims that the implications of H_0 rejection are based on a logical fallacy due to the inverse probability: 'If H_0 is true, then this result (statistical significance) would probably not occur – This result has occurred – Then H_0 is probably not true and therefore formally invalid' (Cohen, 1994, p. 998). Cohen explains that while we would like to test if H_0 is true, what we are actually testing with NHST is the probability of finding the data in the sample if the H_0 is true. This is explained by the fact that our calculation of probability is based on the data we have gathered, which is not the same as the probability that H_0 is true prior to the experiment. Ioannidis (2005) has shown that when the probability prior to the experiment is included in the calculations, the probability of the H_0 can easily change from 5% to 60%. There are two solutions to this problem. The first is to include the chance of finding H_0 prior to the experiment in our calculations. This is done by applying so-called *Bayesian* statistics (after the statistician Thomas Bayes) instead of conventional statistics as discussed in this book (also called *frequentist* statistics). Bayesian statistics are also based on probabilities, but Bayesian methods allow for continuously updating the probabilities of an effect really existing as soon as new information is added. The trend in modern statistics is gradually shifting towards these Bayesian methods: JASP actually offers both the Bayesian and the traditional versions of the statistical tests in the program, and for R there are packages available to run Bayesian statistical tests. However, the underlying argumentation requires a deeper understanding of statistics that goes beyond the scope of this book. In spite of this, conventional statistics can still be used, as long as we are aware of the pitfalls. Yet, for high-stakes research projects we would definitely recommend considering the use of Bayesian statistics. A second solution to this problem is to replicate studies with different samples and in different contexts. The awareness of these observations has led to what has been called the 'replication crisis', as many effects reported in the social sciences could not be replicated (also see Section 2.4). This is not surprising in the light of this fallacy; finding an effect is simply not the same as finding truth, and we must be aware of the fact that we may just have been lucky in finding our data. Only by repeated replication can we avoid spurious research findings. It will be clear that this adds a rather inconvenient limitation to statistical studies that we have to live with.

So what do we conclude from these complications of statistical logic? Some people have said that there are 'lies, damned lies, and statistics'. Does this mean that we should avoid doing statistics at all? Certainly not! But what we can learn from these complications is that we must be careful in interpreting the results of our studies. When something is 'significant', it is not necessarily true, and a higher level of significance does not mean that it is more true. Some journals consider no longer accepting papers that report on *p*-values, to avoid the all-or-nothing fallacy. We would not want to go that far, but there are some practical implications. The most important one is that we always report on descriptives combined with visualizations of the data and use our common sense in interpreting these. Second is that we always report on the effect size of a study, which should be leading in the interpretation of the results. The *p*-value and the confidence interval can give us additional insight and can safely be used as a tool in addition to the other observations, but should not be used in isolation. As long as we are aware of the limitations of our method, the use of statistics can be an invaluable tool to help us quantify the probability of our observations.

4.9 Steps in statistical studies

In this section, we will summarize the most important steps we have to go through in making statistical decisions. To quantify the probability of the outcome of a study, we have to consider the following steps:

4.9.1 Operationalization and forming hypotheses

The first step is to operationalize the constructs under investigation into variables and determine the scale for each variable (see Section 2.3). At this stage, it should also become clear which is the independent and which the dependent variable, and whether there is a control variable in the research design. It is important to realize that a particular variable may serve as a dependent variable in one design, but as an independent variable in another. If a pharmaceutical researcher wants to investigate the effectiveness of a new anti-ageing medicine, he or she may regard the variable age to be a dependent variable and taking or not taking the medicine as the independent variable. However, if an applied linguist wants to investigate the effect of age on second language development, he or she may regard age as the independent variable and some proficiency measure as the dependent variable.

The second step is to formulate the hypotheses that will be tested. Even though the null hypothesis remains implicit in many reports on statistical studies, it is crucial to understand that this is in fact the hypothesis that is tested. Apart from the null hypothesis, the alternative hypothesis or hypotheses also have to be made explicit at this stage.

4.9.2 Selecting a sample and collecting data

The third step is to select a representative sample and subsequently collect data. As was discussed in Section 4.4, it is difficult to select a purely random sample.

ACTIVITY 4.10

In many language studies, samples are taken from naturally occurring groups, like a specific class at a specific school.

■ How can you make sure your samples of German and Spanish learners of English are comparable?

When gathering data, different kinds of dangers are lurking. Some of the dangers relate to the selection of the participants of the study, others relate to the method of elicitation that is used. We will briefly mention some of these dangers, but the list is far from exhaustive.

Since it can be difficult to find participants for a study, it is tempting to work with volunteers only. The danger in this is that volunteers may well be the ones who tend to be very good at a particular skill. For instance, in testing pronunciation skills in a second language, it is not likely that very poor pronouncers will voluntarily participate. In more general terms, this danger is often labelled as *self-selection*. Volunteering is one example of this. Another example would be a study in which participants can choose which group they want to join. Although self-selection should be avoided, for some studies it may be the only way of carrying out the investigation.

It is the researcher's responsibility to take this into account when drawing conclusions about the study. The best studies from a methodological point of view are those in which neither the participants nor the people who conduct the study are familiar with the research hypotheses. Researchers may (subconsciously) influence the procedure due to the expectations they have (*researcher expectancy*) and participants may want to please the researcher and respond in a desirable way rather than objectively (*subject expectancy*). In gathering data, researchers have to take into account what has been referred to as the *observer's paradox*. A researcher who wants to investigate the pronunciation of, say, /r/ in certain words could simply ask people to pronounce those words. However, these people may notice that the task is about the pronunciation of /r/ and (possibly subconsciously) adjust their pronunciation to a more desirable variety. In such a case, the presence of the observer will affect the observation. To avoid this, an elicitation method must be used that does not reveal the purpose of the study.

ACTIVITY 4.11

One way to investigate if the pronunciation of /r/ is related to socio-economic status would be to ask people from different social classes to read out some words containing /r/. However, asking people to pronounce words may affect people's pronunciation. Think of a strategy of eliciting these data while avoiding this observer's paradox.

4.9.3 Conducting and interpreting statistics

The fourth step is where the statistics come in. Of course, the researcher will always first consider the descriptive statistics of the data (e.g. mean, range, *SD*) and create some visualizations to get a clear first impression of the data gathered. Subsequently, we will use statistics to estimate the probability of finding the effect if the H_0 is true. This will be explained in the coming chapters.

As discussed in Sections 4.7 and 4.8, the interpretation of the statistical outcomes should be combined with a critical evaluation of the study and the statistical analyses. Statistical studies can involve complex calculations that may have restrictions to their application or for which underlying assumptions have to be met. As both the calculations themselves and the assumptions are hidden for the user of computer programs like JASP or R, it is unwise to perform analyses on a dataset and blindly interpret its output in terms of significance. The meaningfulness of a study is definitely not only established by the statistical significance of the outcome. All steps have to be considered carefully, from operationalization to sampling (and the extent to which a sample is representative!) and from checking the assumptions to considering effect sizes.

Before continuing, you can do the assignments of Practical 3 that go with this chapter. In this Practical, we will give you a first introduction to one of the statistical tests that will be discussed in the following chapters.

5 ASSESSING RELATIONSHIPS AND COMPARING GROUPS

5.1 Introduction

In Chapter 3, we already introduced two different kinds of perspectives on data: comparing groups and looking at relationships. In the coming three chapters, we will elaborate on specific types of statistical tests within, and to a certain degree slightly beyond, these two categories. The steps that need to be taken when conducting inferential statistics, as summarized in Section 4.9, apply to all these tests. Moreover, more or less the same principles hold for these tests. The only differences between the various statistical tests concern the researcher's perspective and, consequently, the scale and number of the variables involved in the study.

It should be noted that our broad division in the present chapter, comparing groups versus investigating relationships, is one possible way of presenting these statistics and some of the types may overlap. For each of the parametric options, we will also give you the non-parametric alternatives. Remember that for parametric tests, you will always need to make sure that your data are normally distributed, show homogeneity of variance, and are measured on an interval scale. If one or more of these assumptions are violated, you should opt for a(n) (non-parametric) alternative. In addition, as we argued in Chapter 4, virtually all parametric statistics are based on the assumption of linear relationships between variables.

5.2 Assessing relationships

If we want to investigate the relationship between two interval variables, we cannot use a group analysis, for the simple reason that there are no groups. The relationship between interval variables is commonly tested with a set of statistical techniques that is referred to as *correlations*.

5.2.1 Relationships between interval and/or ordinal variables

An example of a correlation study is a research design in which the question is whether the number of hours of language instruction in English as a second language is related to English language proficiency measured on an interval scale. It could be expected that someone's proficiency in English increases with increasing duration of language instruction. The relationship between two interval variables is commonly plotted in a scatterplot, as exemplified in Figure 5.1.

Looking at this scatterplot, we can see that after a limited number of hours of instruction, the proficiency scores are rather low, but they increase quite rapidly after about 50 hours and continue to increase after that. Although there is some variation, we can generally say that the proficiency scores seem to increase as hours of instruction increase. Although this is a fictitious example, it will be clear that an XY-graph like the one presented here can give an important insight into the relationship of the two variables under examination. However, this cannot be the end of our statistical analysis, as we also want to test if these two variables are significantly related, and how strong this relationship is. The null hypothesis that is tested in a correlation study, that is, the hypothesis that we want to reject, is that there is no relationship between the two variables. The statistic we can use to test this is the *correlation coefficient*. If both variables are measured on an interval scale, the most appropriate correlation coefficient is *Pearson r*, also referred to as the Pearson product-moment correlation, or simply r_{xy}. The value of r_{xy} runs from –1 to 1. If r_{xy} = 0, there is no relation.

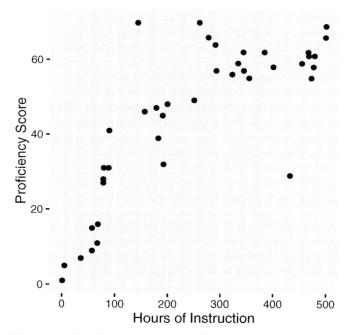

Figure 5.1 Scatterplot showing the relationship between hours of instruction (x-axis) and proficiency score (y-axis)

The more closely r_{xy} approaches 1 or –1, the stronger the relationship is. Evans (1996) suggests the following interpretation:

- .00–.19: very weak;

- .20–.39: weak;

- .40–.59: moderate;

- .60–.79: strong;

- .80–1.0: very strong.

A positive correlation, as in Figure 5.1, means that if one variable goes up, the other also goes up. A negative relationship, however, means that if the values of one variable go up, the other one goes down. In SLD research, negative correlations are sometimes reported for the starting age of L2 learning and the level of L2 proficiency in adulthood. The older a person is when he or she starts learning the language, the lower the L2 proficiency later in life tends to be (also see Figure 3.1). Besides the strength of a correlation, the output of a Pearson r analysis also reports on the significance of the correlation, that is, the estimated chance of incorrectly rejecting the H_0 that there is no relationship, and the 95% Confidence Interval (CI). The CI provides two values showing that, if we were to repeat the correlation analysis using different samples, the correlation coefficient would lie somewhere between the estimated upper and lower bound CI values approximately 95% of the time. In the example mentioned above, on the relationship between the hours of instruction and L2 English proficiency, the analysis yields the output in Tables 5.1 for R and 5.2 for JASP.

Table 5.1 R output correlation analysis

```
> cor.test(dat$proficiency, dat$hours_instruction, method="pearson")

        Pearson's product-moment correlation

data:  dat$proficiency and dat$hours_instruction
t = 7.8086, df = 38, p-value = 2.036e-09
alternative hypothesis: true correlation is not equal to 0
95 percent confidence interval:
 0.6265909 0.8809996
sample estimates:
      cor
0.7848971
```

Table 5.2 JASP output correlation analysis

Pearson Correlations			Pearson's r	p	Lower 95% CI	Upper 95% CI
proficiency	–	hours_instruction	0.785***	< .001	0.627	0.881
* p < .05, ** p < .01, *** p < .001						

From the output in Tables 5.1 and 5.2, it follows that the two variables in our example show a rather strong correlation of .78 (bottom lines of the R output and the first figure in the JASP output). The H_0 can be rejected, as the level of significance, that is, the p-value, is smaller than .001 (the chance of incorrectly rejecting H_0 is thus less than 1%) and the 95% confidence interval [0.63, 0.88] shows that the relationship is highly likely to be a strong positive one.

A common pitfall of correlation studies is that a correlation is interpreted as a causal relation. Although it is tempting to say that the increasing proficiency scores are caused by the hours of instruction, this is certainly not testified in a simple correlation study. The correlated variables are not in a dependency relation. Therefore, the distinction between dependent and independent variables is not relevant for correlation studies. To determine causality, advanced statistical methods are required, referred to as *causal modelling*, but this type of statistics goes beyond the scope of the current book.

ACTIVITY 5.1

Eight students have participated in a reading test and a listening comprehension test. Reading ability and listening comprehension are operationalized by the variables *R* and *L* respectively. Both variables are measured on an interval scale. The results have been summarized in the table below.

Student	R	L
1	20	65
2	40	69
3	60	73
4	80	77
5	100	80
6	120	84
7	140	89
8	160	95

- **What would be H_0 if we want to test the relationship between reading and listening comprehension?**

- **Draw a plot of the results.**

- **A computer has calculated for these data that r_{xy} = .996. What would be your first impression?**

- **The critical values (also see Section 4.3.3) for this to be significant at α = .05 and *df* = 6 are −.707 and .707. Can we conclude that reading skill and listening comprehension are significantly related?**

So far, we have only discussed correlations for interval data that show a linear, homoscedastic relationship between two normally distributed variables. In case one or more of these assumptions are violated, correlations can still be calculated by using a type of correlation that is based on mean rank orders. The most commonly reported statistic in this case is the *Spearman's Rho* (ρ). The interpretation of Spearman's Rho is largely identical to that of Pearson *r*. When you have small sample sizes and many identical scores, it may be better to report *Kendall's Tau* (τ).

Correlations can also come in handy when you want to assess the reliability of an experiment or exam, that is, whether the experiment or exam you created is in fact a good one and does what it claims to do. An exam is reliable when students would perform the same if they had to take the exam again (*test-retest reliability*), but it is also reliable when students who are equal receive the same score. These two ideas of reliability are difficult to test, because you cannot really test students again and again on the same test and you can also never be sure how equal students are. There is another type of reliability, however, that we can test. When we create a test or an exam we expect the better participants to outperform the less good ones on every question. If the less strong participants do better on one of the questions than the better participants, what does that tell us about that question? Clearly, it indicates that this might not be a reliable question for the test. In other words, there should be a strong (positive) correlation between the items in order to have a reliable exam.

The easiest way to check this is to use a measure of *split-half correlations*. With this method we can divide the scores in two (e.g. the average scores on the odd and even questions or the scores on part one and part two of an exam) and check the correlation between them. The problem is that a difference is produced depending on how you make this division. Every time you make a new division, you will probably get a different correlation coefficient. A way to escape this is to use *Cronbach's Alpha*. This method takes all the items separately and relates all scores on each item to the scores on the other items. If you get a high outcome for this test (higher than .7 or .8) this means that your items are highly correlated. You can also see which items are not representative for your exam or experiment. If one item is negatively correlated with the other items, then this means that the item is not a very reliable one.

5.2.2 Correlations and effect sizes

Before we explain effect sizes in relation to correlation research, have a look at Activity 5.2.

ACTIVITY 5.2

Below you see two scatterplots, one with a small sample (left) and one with a larger sample (right).

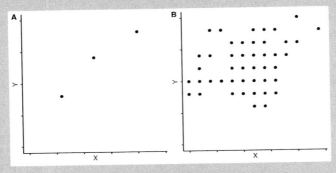

- Which of the two scatterplots shows the clearest relationship between variables x and y?

- If we told you the statistical test only revealed a relationship beyond reasonable doubt in one of the plots, which one would that be?

- And if we told you that the effect size in one of the two plots is a lot larger than in the other, which one would we probably be referring to?

The two scatterplots in Activity 5.2 are an illustration of the difference between effects or relationships themselves, whether they are found, and the actual size or strength of the effect or relationship. In scatterplot A on the left, the correlation is positive and very strong, almost perfect ($r = .98$), but the relationship is not significant ($p = .13$). The data seem to be more spread out in scatterplot B, resulting in a weak relationship ($r = .32$), but the chance of incorrectly rejecting H_0 is only about 3% here ($p = .03$). In other words, the relationship in the left plot (A) is very strong (the points almost follow a perfectly straight line), but there is a fair chance that we are mistaken, simply because we only have three data points. On the other hand, while the relationship is less strong and there is more variation in the data points in the plot on the right (the dots clearly do not all follow a straight line), we can be more sure that the somewhat weaker relationship we found is a 'real' one. This is simply because the decision is based on more data and adds to what we already discussed in Chapter 4: big effects can be detected with relatively small sample sizes (about 28 participants per group if the β-error is set to 20%), but to detect smaller effects, larger samples are required.

The above example also illustrates that a genuine interpretation of statistical results involves both information on the chance of making the wrong decision as well as information on the size of the effect. Therefore, the APA citation format now also explicitly requires researchers to include effects sizes in their scientific papers (VandenBos, 2010).

Every test has its own effect size measure and the effect size for a correlation is the easiest, as the r-value itself is already an expression of the strength of the relationship. This value is sometimes squared to obtain an effect size that is related to the amount of variance that can be explained by the variables in our experiment. The explained variance is thus calculated by taking r^2. This means that if $r = .50$, $r^2 = .50^2 = .25$. So then 25% of the variance is explained by the variables in our experiment. This is considered a large effect. Conventionally, the interpretation of effect sizes is as follows:

- $r = .1$ ($r^2 = 1\%$) is considered a *small* effect
- $r = .30$ ($r^2 = 9\%$) is considered a *medium* size effect
- $r = .50$ ($r^2 = 25\%$) or higher is considered a *large* effect

In the example datasets in Activity 5.2, the effect size r^2 of plot A is thus $.98^2 = 96\%$. The effect size r^2 of plot B, on the other hand, is $.32^2 = 10\%$. So, as the dots in plot A almost follow a perfectly straight line, without a lot of variance, the amount of variance in this dataset that can be explained by the relationship between x and y is 96%. It should be clear that the relationship between variables x and y in plot B cannot explain all the data points as there is more spread in the data.

For every statistical test, we will introduce the most commonly used effect size measure. The interpretation of these, however, largely resembles the one given here.

5.2.3 Associations between nominal variables

The last type of analysis that we will discuss here in Section 5.2 concerns another non-parametric test: the analysis for designs that have no interval variables at all. If a study wants to investigate a relationship between two variables that are measured on an ordinal scale and/or that do not follow the normal distribution and/or a relationship that does not follow a straight line, a Spearman or Kendall correlation can be carried out. In all other cases (for instance, one nominal and one ordinal variable, or nominal variables only), however, no statistics can be used that require regular calculations. As no calculations can be done with nominal variables, the only thing we can do is count the number of occurrences. Therefore, this type of non-parametric analysis is also commonly referred to as *frequency analysis* and it is used to measure the strength of the potential association between nominal variables.

The example we will use here is a sociolinguistic study in which a researcher wants to investigate the association between socio-economic status and the use of two alternative grammatical constructions for negation, 'haven't got' and 'don't have'. The nominal variable 'construction used' has been operationalized as the number of times the participants used one of these constructions in an elicitation task. Socio-economic status has been operationalized as the answer to a series of questions about income and education and is represented by two levels: 'higher' and 'lower'. The null hypothesis is that there is no association between the use of the grammatical construction for the two levels of socio-economic status (SES). Frequency data of two nominal variables are most clearly presented in a *cross-tabulation*. The cross-tabulation of the data from this particular study looks as follows in Table 5.3:

Table 5.3 Contingency table (from JASP)

	reply		
class	haven't got	don't have	Total
lower	58	30	88
higher	68	62	130
Total	126	92	218

Contingency Tables

Table 5.3 shows that the participants with a lower SES used 'haven't got' 58 times and 'don't have' 30 times. The participants with a higher SES used 'haven't got' 68 times and 'don't have' 62 times. At face value, it looks as if there is a difference in the use of this construction for the participants in the lower SES, but that the constructions are approximately levelled for the higher SES group. The question we want to answer, however, is if this difference is significant. What is the chance of incorrectly rejecting H_0?

The statistic that is most appropriate for this type of data is the *chi-square* (or χ^2) analysis. The chi-square calculates the number of occurrences in a particular cell relative to the margins of that cell, that is, the total number of instances of each construction and the total number of participants in each group. The value of the statistic, χ^2, runs from 0 to infinity; the most common values reported are between 0 and 10. The (simplified) R output of this chi-square analysis can be found in Table 5.4, with the same JASP output in Table 5.5.

Table 5.4 R output chi-square test

```
Pearson's Chi-squared test
--------------------------------------------------------------
Chi^2 =  3.980075     d.f. = 1     p =  0.04604151
```

Table 5.5 JASP output chi-square test

Chi–Squared Tests ▼			
	Value	df	p
X^2	3.980	1	0.046
N	218		

This outcome shows that, if we chose an alpha level of .05, we would be inclined to reject H_0. As H_0 states that there is no difference in the use of 'haven't got' and 'don't have' between the two social classes, we can infer the reverse.

The analysis in our example yields a result that can be interpreted without any problems. However, if we want to analyse the association between nominal variables that have more than two levels, the interpretation may be less obvious. If the χ^2 analysis of a four-by-four crosstable yields a significant result, the only conclusion we can draw is that the values in the cells are not equivalent. For frequency analyses, the effect of the different levels cannot be determined by post-hoc analyses, so inspection of the association by plotting the data is crucial for the interpretation. An example of a useful plot in this case would be Figure 5.2, which was created in R. (Note that two separate plots would have to be created in order to visualize this in JASP, which is also explained in Practical 4.)

The barplot in Figure 5.2 reveals that the association can be explained by the fact that people with a lower SES tend to use 'haven't got' more often than 'don't have'. No preference for one of the two constructions can be found in the people with a higher SES.

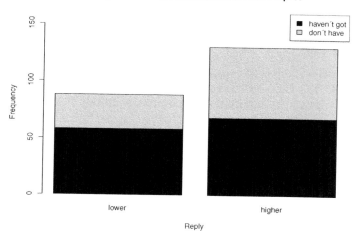

Figure 5.2 Barplot of the use of 'haven't got' and 'don't have' by people with a lower and higher socio-economic status

 **ACTIVITY 5.3**

At the university theatre, a movie is playing about Spanish culture. Before the movie starts, 70 randomly selected people who enter the theatre are asked whether they are planning on visiting Spain in the next two years. Of the 70 people, 55 answer NO and 15 answer YES. The movie shows all the wonderful characteristics of the Spanish language and culture. After the film, 80 people are asked the same question, again randomly selected. This time 5 people answer NO and 75 people answer YES. The question the producers of the film are interested in is if the film affects the number of prospective visitors to Spain.

a) Draw a crosstable similar to the one in Table 5.3 for this study and fill in the observed value (F_O) of each cell.

b) Label the cells in the crosstable A and B for the top row and C and D for the bottom row.

c) Calculate the 'marginal frequencies' by adding up the totals of A and B; C and D; A and C; B and D; and the Total Frequency: A, B, C, D.

d) What is your H_0?

e) The first step to calculate the appropriate statistic for this situation is to determine the 'expected frequency' for each cell. The expected frequency (F_E) of a cell is expressed as the product of its margins (row x column), divided by the Total Frequency. So for cell A, the expected value is:

$$\frac{(A+B)(A+C)}{TotalFreq}$$

f) Now calculate the expected value for each cell. Are any of these expected values below 5?

g) The next step is to calculate ($F_E - F_O$) for each cell. For some cells, this is bound to result in negative values. To neutralize the negatives, square the outcome of each cell: $(F_E - F_O)^2$.

h) Finally, divide this value by the F_E, so

$$\frac{(F_E - F_o)^2}{F_E}$$

i) Then add up this value for each cell (A, B, C and D), so

$$\sum \frac{(F_E - F_o)^2}{F_E}$$

As no square root is taken for the resulting value, this remains a 'squared' value. The name of this statistic is therefore 'chi-square' (χ^2).

j) Now calculate the degrees of freedom (df). For the χ^2, this is defined as the (number of rows − 1) x (number of columns − 1).

While chi-square is a non-parametric test, there are still three assumptions that need to be checked. First of all, you must have nominal variables only. Secondly, chi-square does require the assumption of independence of observations to be met in that each case must occur in only one cell of the cross-table. Finally, the *expected* frequencies in should not be too low. This latter assumption can be checked relatively easily in R and JASP, as will be explained in Practical 4 in Part 2.

For chi-square, most researchers report either *Phi* or *Cramer's V* as a measure of the effect size. Phi (φ) is used for variables with 2 levels and Cramer's V for variables with more than 2 levels. Phi and Cramer's V are, like *r*, numbers between 0 and 1 and the closer it is to 1 the stronger the association between the two nominal variables. This measure is relatively easy to obtain both in JASP and R (as will be explained in Practical 4).

5.3 Comparing two groups

The second perspective that we already introduced in Chapters 3 and 4 requires a research paradigm in which the mean scores of different groups are compared. The *independent samples t-test*, also known as the Student or two sample *t*-test, can be used only to evaluate interval data of two groups (levels) representing one nominal independent variable. An example would be an IQ test that is given to two different groups (such as men and women) to find out which group has a higher score. In all other cases (more than two groups, no nominal independent, no interval dependent, etc.) a different statistic will have to be used and those alternatives will be discussed in Chapter 7. Here, we will focus on the *t*-test to compare two groups.

5.3.1 Comparing two groups: The *t*-test

The *t*-test makes use of the following descriptives: the number of participants in each group, the mean scores of each group, and the standard deviations of each group. Although in our computer age it is very unlikely that anyone will ever have to calculate the value of t manually, we will give the calculation in order to provide more insight:

$$t = \frac{\overline{X}_{Group1} - \overline{X}_{Group2}}{\sqrt{\frac{SD_{Group1}^2}{N_{Group1}} + \sqrt{\frac{SD_{Group2}^2}{N_{Group2}}}}} \tag{5.1}$$

The outcome of this calculation expresses the magnitude of the difference between the groups, taking into account the variation within the group (the SDs) and the group sizes (the Ns). The bigger the difference between the groups (the part of the equation above the line), the larger the value of t becomes, but the bigger the variance within the groups (the part below the line), the smaller the value of t becomes. Values of t range from minus infinity to infinity, but values between 0 and 5 (or – 5 and 0) are most commonly reported. If there is no difference between the groups, $\overline{X}_{Group1} - \overline{X}_{Group2}$ will be zero, so the closer the value of t approaches 0, the weaker the difference between the groups will be. Whether the value of t is positive or negative is not very meaningful as it is simply the result of the order of the groups (1 and 2) in the equation.

 **ACTIVITY 5.4**

Explain in your own words what the formula for the t-test does. In your description, do not use technical terms (like 'standard deviation' or 'variance') but language that people without a background in statistics would also understand.

When the value of the statistic has been calculated, the next step is to interpret that value by determining the probability (the chance of incorrectly rejecting H_0) associated with that value. The simplest way is to feed the data into a computer program like JASP or R and to read the probability from the output. To illustrate the t-test, let us return to our example of the Spanish and German learners of English that we also contrasted in the boxplots in Chapter 3 (Figure 3.2). When we compare the two groups using an independent samples t-test, R provides us with the output in Table 5.6, which is slightly simplified here (the output from JASP will follow in Table 5.8).

Before dealing with the more general output of a t-test for both JASP and R users, we will first briefly look at the R output in Table 5.6. R users will see that the table first reveals our code for the

Table 5.6 Example code and simplified output for an independent samples *t*-test in R

```
> t.test(data$score ~ data$group, var.equal=TRUE)

        Two Sample t-test

data:  data$score by data$group
t = -4.8532, df = 63, p-value = 8.348e-06
alternative hypothesis: true difference in means is not equal to 0


sample estimates:
mean in group 1 mean in group 2
      55.18750        71.24242
```

t-test, followed by the output that starts with the test that we have conducted: a two sample *t*-test, which is the same as an independent samples or Student *t*-test. It then shows that we have looked at Score by Group (first line) and that, at face value, the scores in Group 2 are higher than the scores in Group 1 (bottom lines of the output). However, we will need to apply inductive statistics to estimate the probability of the difference between the groups. In other words, can the H_0 (that there is no difference between the groups) be rejected beyond reasonable doubt? The answer to this question can be found in the first few lines in Table 5.6 or, for JASP users, in Table 5.8, which contain the most important information in the output for the *t*-test: the value for *t*, for *df*, and for *p*, where you can see that the calculated value of *t* is – 4.853. For this value, the chance of incorrectly rejecting the H_0 that is related to these specific conditions is .000008348 (R output), which is smaller than .001 (JASP output). As this value is extremely small, the H_0 that there is no difference between the means of the two groups can be rejected. Given the relatively large difference between the groups (55 vs. 71), this outcome is not surprising. Of course, the chance of us making a mistake can never be exactly .00 and we therefore report that the chance of incorrectly rejecting the H_0 is smaller than .001 (i.e. $p < .001$).

You may also come across another parametric version of the *t*-test: the one sample *t*-test. Although it is used when the researcher has collected data from one sample, the goal is still to compare two groups. It can be used, for example, to compare the mean score of a sample (e.g. the IQ score of Linguistics students) to a known value (e.g., the average IQ of the population).

5.3.2 Alternatives to the *t*-test when assumptions are violated

Now, we have also conducted a *t*-test on the same data using a slightly different code in R that yielded the output in Table 5.7. For JASP users, the output for both of the *t*-tests can be found in Table 5.8.

Table 5.7 Example code and output for a Welch's independent samples *t*-test in R

```
> t.test(data$score ~ data$group, var.equal=FALSE)

        Welch Two Sample t-test

data:  data$score by data$group
t = -4.8686, df = 61.176, p-value = 8.267e-06
alternative hypothesis: true difference in means is not equal to 0
95 percent confidence interval:
 -22.648555  -9.461293
sample estimates:
mean in group 1 mean in group 2
       55.18750        71.24242
```

Table 5.8 JASP output for the independent samples *t*-test showing the outcomes of both the Student (parametric) *t*-test and the Welch

Independent Samples T-Test

	Test	Statistic	df	p	Mean Difference	SE Difference	95% CI for Mean Difference Lower	Upper
score	Student	−4.853	63.00	< .001	−16.05	3.308	−22.67	−9.444
	Welch	−4.869	61.18	< .001	−16.05	3.298	−22.65	−9.461

For R users, it is important to note that the output of Table 5.6 and 5.7 is not identical. When you compare the output here to the simplified version provided in Table 5.6, you will notice that we previously not only left out the 95% confidence interval for the difference in means, but also that almost all the values are slightly different. For JASP users, the same holds when comparing the first line (the Student *t*-test) to the second line (Welch's *t*-test) in the output. In Table 5.6, we used `var.equal=TRUE` in R when performing the *t*-test and we have changed this to FALSE in the code in Table 5.7 (also see the first line that repeats the code to perform this *t*-test). This code refers to the assumption of homogeneity, the equality of variances (also see Section 4.6). In R, TRUE is used in case your variances are equal and FALSE in case they are not comparable. When equal variances are not assumed and the Welch's adjustment is used, the degrees of freedom (*df*) are adapted slightly.[1]

Since the *t*-test is especially very sensitive to violations of homogeneity of variance, and especially in cases with unequal sample sizes, researchers often first run a *Levene*'s test to assess whether the variances in the groups are

---

[1] The actual formula for this adaptation is extremely difficult to understand, even to statisticians (e.g. Field et al., 2012), but relates to power. The more people we test, the more power our study has. If we cannot benefit from the assumption of homogeneity of variance and especially if our sample sizes are very different, we have to adjust the degrees of freedom to be somewhere between the larger and the smaller sample we are testing. That is what the Welch-Satterthwaite correction to the degrees of freedom does for us.

approximately similar. If this test is significant, this means that the assumption is violated. Although it is good practice to test homogeneity of variance using Levene's test, Welch's adjustment can easily be used in both JASP and R to correct for unequal variances. Because of this, some statisticians recommend using this Welch's *t*-test in all situations (also see Field et al., 2012, p. 373).

When comparing the interval scores of two groups of subjects, such as the Spanish and the German learners of English, we are dealing with one interval dependent variable that might be influenced by one nominal variable ('L1 background') with two levels ('Spanish' and 'German'). We therefore have to conduct an independent samples *t*-test that is based on a calculation of the *t*-statistic (also see the formula in 5.1). As can be seen in Table 5.9, however, there is also a *dependent* or *paired* version of the *t*-test in which the scores of the two groups are related to one another. Imagine we are not comparing Spanish and English learners, but instead we focus on the Spanish learners by comparing their scores on an English proficiency test before and after they followed an English course. In this particular example, every learner has been tested twice and the data of the groups we are comparing are thus related, dependent, or 'paired'. As the two groups mostly consist of the same people, the assumption of homogeneity of variance does not have to be met for the paired *t*-test. Additionally, the paired version does not assume that the data within the two different groups are normally distributed. Instead, the difference in scores should approximate normality.

Before being able to conduct an independent or paired samples *t*-test, we need to look at our data using descriptive statistics and test the assumptions. If one or more of these assumptions have been violated, we have to use (non-parametric) alternatives. As we have seen above, Welch is used when variances are not equal or homogeneous in an independent samples *t*-test. When the data are not normally distributed, the *Mann-Whitney U* test is used to compare groups. The most commonly used non-parametric alternative for the dependent *t*-test is the *Wilcoxon signed-rank* test (also see Table 5.9).[2] The Mann-Whitney and the Wilcoxon are generally interpreted as comparing medians as opposed to means.

Table 5.9 (Non-parametric) alternatives for the *t*-test

Parametric test	(Non-parametric) alternatives most commonly used (assumption violated)
Student Independent Samples *t*-test	Welch (homogeneity of variance) or Mann-Whitney *U* (normality)
Student Paired Samples *t*-test	Wilcoxon signed-rank (normality)

---

2 Do note that the Mann-Whitney is sometimes also referred to as the Wilcoxon rank-sum test (or even as the Mann-Whitney-Wilcoxon or Wilcoxon-Mann-Whitney test).

5.3.3 Comparing groups and interpreting effect sizes

To make well informed judgments about the outcome of a statistical test, effect sizes are indispensable. For the t-test, one of two different effect sizes are commonly reported: r^2 and Cohen's d. The first one, the r^2 value, should be familiar to you now and we can calculate this r^2-value relatively easily once the calculations of t have been carried out:

$$r^2 = \frac{t^2}{t^2 + df} \tag{5.2}$$

So if $t = 2$ and $df = 36$, then $r^2 = .096$ (a medium effect), which means that 9.6% of the variance in the data can be explained by the impact of the independent variable. The effect size of the same t-value will be smaller if the sample gets bigger. For example, if $t = 2$ and $df = 136$, then $r^2 = .029$ (a small effect), which suggests that only 2.9% of the variance can be explained. At the same time, larger t-values will result in larger effect sizes if sample sizes remain the same. The interpretation of this effect size is identical to the one for correlations explained in 5.2.1.

Cohen's d is very similar, but reflects the difference in means of the two groups divided by the average of their standard deviations. So, a value of 1 simply means that the means of the groups differ by one SD and a d of .5 reveals a mean difference of half an SD. The interpretation difference is thus related to either a difference in terms of standard deviations (Cohen's d) or the amount of variance explained (r^2). Although they are both often used, the values for different effect sizes differ slightly as exemplified in Table 5.10.

Table 5.10 Comparison of effect size value for Cohen's d and r^2

	Cohen's d value	r^2 value
Small effect	0.2	.01
Medium effect	0.5	.09
Large effect	0.8	.25

It should also be noted here that the interpretation of Cohen's d in terms of effect size is less straightforward and often also depends on the field of study. Both measures explained above, d and r^2, are easily calculated in both JASP and R, so we will provide the means for both during the practicals in Part 2. Some journals will ask for specific measures of effect sizes, but both d and r^2 are generally accepted and you are often free to choose the one you like best.

The present chapter has introduced you to the most common statistics for examining relationships and for comparing the means of two groups. When interested in the relationship between two interval variables, we can use a Pearson *r*. When interested in a relationship that is not perfectly linear, or a relationship between ordinal or non-normally distributed variables, we can use Spearman's Rho or Kendall's Tau. When we are interested in the association between nominal variables, we can use a chi-square frequency analysis. When we are interested in examining whether the means of two groups differ significantly, the type we have to choose depends on whether we compare two groups or whether we want to compare one group to a population mean. In the latter case, we should opt for a one sample *t*-test. For the comparison of two groups, we should use an independent *t*-test in case of two separate groups and a dependent *t*-test in case the two groups are related (and are in fact not two separate groups). For reasons that will be explained later, a special version of means analysis should be used in case the independent variable contains more than two levels, such as when we are comparing three groups, or when multiple independent nominal variables are involved. In that case, we should opt for ANOVAs, a group of tests that will be explained in detail in Chapter 7. When our design is somewhat more complicated, for example because it contains multiple independent variables that are nominal and/or interval, we can opt for a multiple regression analysis, a technique that will be explained in the next chapter.

Before continuing, we advise you to work through Practical 4 in which you will practise performing correlations and group comparisons.

6 SIMPLE AND MULTIPLE LINEAR REGRESSION ANALYSES

6.1 Introduction

When we are doing research, we are usually interested in testing the difference between groups or determining the relationships between two variables. However, especially in Applied Linguistics, it is often worthwhile to predict the outcome based on one or various independent variables. We might additionally want to know what the exact influence is of the independent variable and, in case of multiple predictor variables, which of these contributes most to the outcome. For example, a language teacher may want to estimate what the influence is of motivation and time spent doing homework on learning a second language. To find the answer to this question, we can do a *regression* analysis.

You will see that regression is very similar to correlations as it can establish the strength of a relationship between two numeric variables. Interestingly, regression can also be compared to means analyses, as it is also a technique that allows us to compare the means of two (or more) groups. In a sense, regression, and then we are talking about multiple regression (as discussed in Section 6.3), allows us to combine what we can do with correlations (Pearson r) and mean comparisons (t-tests or ANOVAs) and can be seen as a technique used to predict the value of a certain dependent variable as a function of one or more nominal and/or continuous independent variables. Interestingly, multiple regression additionally allows us to examine which of these variables contributes most to the outcome by controlling for the effect of the other variables.

As experimental researchers, who traditionally mostly used to choose ANOVAs (an extension of the t-test that will be discussed in detail in Chapter 7) to compare various groups, are increasingly using more flexible and advanced regression techniques to analyse their data, we will spend an entire chapter on regression. It should be noted, however, that regression is a very broad field and we will only introduce you to the basics here.

6.2 Assessing relationships and simple regression

Before considering a real dataset, have a look at the two lines in Figure 6.1 below to examine the characteristics of straight lines. The solid line visualizes a positive relationship between variable X and variable Y and the dashed line

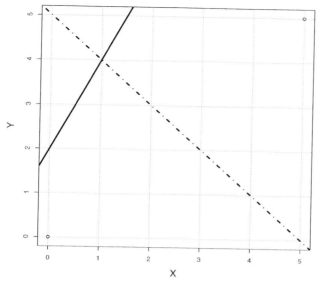

Figure 6.1 Two straight lines depicting a hypothetical relationship between X and Y

a negative relationship. We could summarize the direction (positive versus negative) and the strength of the relationship between X and Y by reporting a correlation coefficient r. In these cases, however, the strength and hence the effect size would be the same: $r = 1$ for the solid line and $r = -1$ for the dashed line. As there are no data points outside of the lines, all the variance is explained by the perfectly straight line. We can see, however, that the steepness of the lines is not the same. How can we define the difference?

 **ACTIVITY 6.1**

Have a look at Figure 6.1 and answer the following questions.

- **For the solid line, with every increase of X, how much does the line go up?**

- **And for the dashed line, what is the decrease in Y for every single increase in X?**

Figure 6.1 shows two perfectly straight lines: one reflecting a positive correlation and one reflecting a negative one. For every increase in X for the solid line, the Y value goes up by 2 points. For the dashed line, however, the Y value goes down by 1 point for every increase in X. The value of Y thus increases more rapidly in response to a change in X in case of the solid line as compared to the dashed line. This exact steepness of a line is often referred to as the *slope* and finding this number is exactly what is aimed for when performing a regression analysis, as it tells us exactly how much a change in a predictor variable (X) affects the value of the outcome variable (Y). When performing a regression analysis, the null hypothesis that is being tested is that the slope equals 0 (there is no relationship or effect of the IV) and the alternative hypothesis is that the slope is not 0 (there is a relationship or an effect of the IV).

There is, however, another important difference between the lines, which concerns their starting point. The solid line crosses the y-axis at a lower value, 2 to be precise, than the dashed line, which starts at 5. In addition to the slope, this *intercept*, that is the point at which the line crosses the y-axis, helps us characterize and summarize a straight line. Before explaining these terms in more detail, let us go back to the relationship between hours of instruction and proficiency.

ACTIVITY 6.2

Have a look at Figure 5.1 in Chapter 5. When we draw a straight line through the data in the scatterplot, the line represents a model of what happens when the number of hours of instruction increases. With every hour of instruction, this model assumes that the proficiency is also increasing.

- Try to draw a straight line through the plot (you can also make a similar-looking scatterplot on a piece of paper).

- With every hour of instruction, how much does the line approximately go up?

- What is the estimated proficiency of someone with 200 hours of instruction according to your line?

When adding a straight line to a scatterplot, as you have done in Activity 6.2, the difficulty is to draw a straight line that most closely resembles all data points in the sample. Very much like a mean value that summarizes a dataset, this straight line is used to summarize the effect of a predictor variable (X) on an outcome (Y). In other words, the line represents a model of what happens to the proficiency score when the number of hours of instruction increases. We have added a straight line to the scatterplot visualizing and modelling the relationship between hours of instruction and proficiency in Figure 6.2.

The idea of a regression analysis is that it can be used to predict the outcome as a function of one variable (simple regression) or multiple variables (multiple regression). So all we do in a simple regression analysis like this one, in which we have only one predictor variable, is find out how much this predictor variable contributes to the variance in our dependent, or outcome, variable.

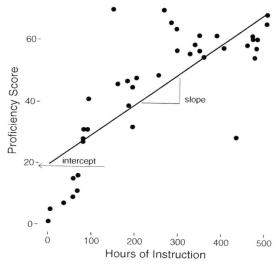

Figure 6.2 Scatterplot with regression line through the data

In Activity 6.2, we took the scatterplot and drew a so-called regression line through the data points. This regression line will be the closest-fitting linear line that can summarize, model, and therefore predict the data. In Figure 6.2, the regression line starts around the proficiency score of 19. If we want to create a formula for a regression line, we need several elements. First, we need the starting point, that is the intercept, also called the constant, which is referred to as *b0* in the formula. Secondly, we need to know the exact steepness of the line, that is the slope, *b1* in our formula. So if we want to create a model that can predict a specific value (i) of our outcome variable (Y), we take the slope (*b1*) multiplied by the number of hours of instruction (X) and we add this to the intercept (*b0*). The slope and intercept are often referred to as the *regression coefficients*. Of course, the actual students in this study deviate from the line (the *model*). As you can see, for example, there is one person in the sample who had exactly 200 hours of instruction. How far is this person approximately away from our model? This deviation of a particular person from the model is referred to as the *error* (ε). So to express the difference between the real data and the model, we need to add the error of a particular person to the equation to get the real data points. With this equation (see 6.1) we can then calculate the outcome on the y-axis for each specific participant (if we know the error). The equation for the model then becomes:

$$\text{Outcome } Y_i = b0 + b1X_i + \varepsilon_i \qquad (6.1)$$

We can run a simple regression analysis to calculate the exact numbers for the intercept and the slope. Tables 6.1 and 6.2 show the output from R and JASP, revealing that the constant or the intercept is 19.572, and the slope is (almost) 0.100.

Table 6.1 R output table for the linear model (lm) and its regression coefficients

```
> lm(proficiency ~ hours_instruction)

Call:
lm(formula = proficiency ~ hours_instruction)

Coefficients:
        (Intercept)   hours_instruction
           19.57208             0.09976
```

Table 6.2 First half of the JASP Output table for the linear model and its regression coefficients

Coefficients		
Model		Unstandardized
1	(Intercept)	19.572
	hours_instruction	0.100

So, to illustrate the use of such a model using the equation we introduced before, let us fill in the details for the person who had 200 hours of instruction:

$$\text{Outcome } Y_i = b0 + b1X_i + \varepsilon_i$$

$$\text{Proficiency score}_i = 19.572 + 0.100*200 + \varepsilon_i$$

The above calculation reveals that, after 200 hours of instruction, the model predicts a proficiency score of 39.57. Of course, a model is a simplification and you can see in Figure 6.2 that the person who received exactly 200 hours of instruction scored higher than the model would predict (around 47 or 48).

An important concept in regression concerns these *residuals*, that is, the error-term (ε) in the equation above, which are simply the deviations of each data point from the model and very similar to the deviations away from the mean that we used to calculate the *SD* in Chapter 3. In other, more statistical, words, the residuals refer to the difference between the observed values (the actual data) and the fitted values (as predicted by the model). The person who received 200 hours of instruction, for example, had a fitted value of about 39, but an observed value of about 48.

 **ACTIVITY 6.3**

Using the formula above, calculate what score the model would predict for the following people. Take into account that you do not know the error and you cannot add that to the formula:

- John had 300 hours of instruction: what is his proficiency score according to the model?

- Elena had 17 hours of instruction: what is her proficiency score according to the model?

- Belinda has a proficiency score of 50: how many hours of instruction should she have had according to the model?

Can you think of a problem with these kind of data? What would have happened to the regression line if you had only measured up to 200 instruction hours? What do you think would happen if we had more data from people with more hours of instruction? Would the slope go up or down?

Figure 6.3 clarifies the concept of residuals by showing two regression models in which the dependent variable Y was predicted by the independent variable X. The left picture (A) shows a regression line that fits the data quite well: the actual data points are very close to the line. The picture to the right (B) reveals relatively large residuals with some of the data points being relatively far away from the regression line. This interpretation is the same as in a correlation analysis.

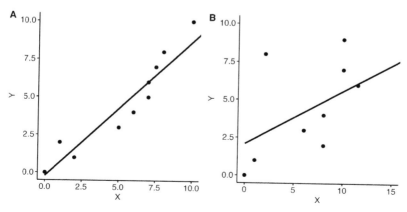

Figure 6.3 Scatterplots with regression lines through the data with relatively small (A) and larger residuals (B)

ACTIVITY 6.4

When comparing the two regression models or lines in Figure 6.3, which of these would you say best predicts the actual data? Knowing what you know about effect sizes, which of the two models do you expect to have a larger effect size? (Explain your answer!)

The straight lines plotted through the data points represent the best fitted lines and are also referred to as the *regression model*. As negative and positive deviations even each other out, the *sum of squared differences* is often used to assess how well the linear line fits the data. The smaller the squared differences, the better and more representative a model is, and it is exactly this line with the lowest sum of squared differences that is aimed for when performing a regression analysis (the so-called *least squares approach*).

Let us go back to our model that predicted proficiency on the basis of hours of instruction. We can obtain a full picture of the model in R or in JASP. The regression formula in R (Table 6.3, box A) and the output of the models in both R and JASP are shown in Tables 6.3 and 6.4, respectively.

Table 6.3 R summary table for the linear model and its regression coefficients with (A) a repetition of the code and the regression formula; (B) the residuals of the model; (C) the coefficients table and; (D) a summary of the model

```
> summary(lm(proficiency ~ hours_instruction))          A

Call:
lm(formula = proficiency ~ hours_instruction)
```

```
Residuals:
     Min       1Q   Median       3Q      Max           B
 -33.669   -7.310    0.379    6.907   36.162
```

```
Coefficients:
                  Estimate Std. Error t value Pr(>|t|)
(Intercept)        19.57208    3.79896   5.152 8.25e-06 ***    C
hours_instruction   0.09976    0.01278   7.809 2.04e-09 ***
---
Signif. codes:  0 '***' 0.001 '**' 0.01 '*' 0.05 '.' 0.1 ' ' 1
```

```
Residual standard error: 12.9 on 38 degrees of freedom
Multiple R-squared:  0.6161,    Adjusted R-squared:  0.606     D
F-statistic: 60.97 on 1 and 38 DF,  p-value: 2.036e-09
```

Table 6.4 JASP tables for the linear model and its regression coefficients

Model Summary

Model	R	R^2	Adjusted R^2	RMSE
1	0.785	0.616	0.606	12.90

ANOVA

Model		Sum of Squares	df	Mean Square	F	p
1	Regression	10144	1	10143.9	60.97	< .001
	Residual	6322	38	166.4		
	Total	16466	39			

Coefficients

Model		Unstandardized	Standard Error	Standardized	t	p
1	(Intercept)	19.572	3.799		5.152	< .001
	hours_instruction	0.100	0.013	0.785	7.809	< .001

Important information about the potential effect of your predictor variable can be found in the coefficients table, which can be found in box C in Table 6.3 and is presented in the third table in 6.4. These coefficients tables provide an estimate of the intercept (19.57) and the slope (0.100) and the accompanying standard error values. You will also find a t-value and the corresponding p-value for both the intercept and our predictor variable hours of instruction. For the intercept, the t-test simply tests whether the intercept is significantly different from 0, which in this case is not so important. For hours of instruction, which we are more interested in, the t-test evaluates whether the effect (i.e. the slope) of hours of instruction differs significantly from 0. In this particular example, as we could have expected, both are significant ($ps < .001$). But how do we assess this model's so-called *goodness of fit*?

The residuals are important in regression models, as they tell us something about how well the model fits the actual data. A residual value is negative when the actual data point is below the regression line and a positive residual means that the real value is higher than the one predicted by the model. As can be seen in box B of Table 6.3, R provides information about the spread in residuals in the output. It tells us that the most negative residual is –33.67 (the minimum), which means that we have one extreme data point that is 33.67 below the regression line. There is also one data point that is about 36 points above the line (the maximum), which we can also locate in Figure 6.2. Luckily, when all residuals are ordered from lowest to highest, the middle value (median) is very close to 0, which again means that it is a good fit. Apparently, when our model misses, it makes mistakes in both directions equally often. Such an equal spread in residuals is an important assumption for regression and we will come back to this in Section 6.4.

The most important thing about residuals to remember at this point is that if the data points are all very close to the line, and the residuals are low, the model fits the data well (as in Figure 6.3(A)). If, however, the observed data are quite far from the line, we can say that the model fits the data less well (as in Figure 6.3(B)). Looking back at Figure 6.3, we can state that the strength of the relationship between X and Y appears to be stronger when the data points are closer to the regression line and, in a simple regression model, the strength of the relationship between the independent and dependent variables is also measured with the correlation coefficient r. Normally, people tend to refer to r^2, the squared Pearson r value, for regression models to assess the goodness of fit. The r^2 value gives us a measure of how much of the variation in the dependent variable can be explained by variation in the independent variables and it is provided in the output (also see Section 5.2.2). In both Table 6.3 (box D) and Table 6.4 (first table in the output), you will see that 61.61% (the multiple r-squared value) of the variance in our data can be explained by our regression model. In other words, the impact of hours of instruction explains 61.61% of the variance in the proficiency scores, which is a relatively good model.

Related to the explained variance, we can also have a look at the bottom line of the output in box D in Table 6.3 or the second table in Table 6.4. This contains an F-value, which we will discuss in detail when we introduce the ANOVA test in the next chapter. The F in the ANOVA, like the t in the t-test, tests whether there is a difference between groups by comparing the difference between groups to the difference within groups. As will be explained in Section 7.2, the ANOVA's F-value is calculated by dividing the explained variance by the unexplained variance, and its computation is very similar here. The F-value of a regression model, and its associated p-value, is calculated by dividing the variance explained by the model divided by the residual (or unexplained) variance. The F-value that we then get shows us the overall strength of the complete model (instead of the effects of a single variable), together with a p-value giving us the significance of this effect. In our example, the model is significant, which confirms the effect of hours of instruction on proficiency.

6.3 Multiple linear regression

What we did in the simple regression analysis can also be done with more variables in a multiple regression analysis, with which we can rule out the importance of certain variables and investigate potential interactions (a term that will be explained in more detail in Chapter 7). So all we do in a multiple regression analysis is find out what the most important predictor variables are in our study and how much they contribute to the variance of our data. The nice thing about regression is that we can add multiple independent variables that are interval (as in the example above), but we can also add categorical independent variables to predict the value of our dependent variable. The latter is not (yet) possible in JASP, so when working in JASP, we can only analyse categorical independent variables with an ANOVA (or a so-called ANCOVA when we also have continuous independent variables). For the sake of clarity, we will now stick with an example containing continuous predictors only, but an example of a multiple regression model in R with both continuous and categorical predictors can be found in the How To unit (for R) on multiple regression on the companion website.

Imagine that the students in the previously mentioned example not only had different amounts of instruction, but that they also had varying levels of foreign language anxiety. The output of a multiple regression model with this additional explanatory variable can be found in Table 6.5 (R output) and Table 6.6 (JASP output).

Table 6.5 R output table for the linear multiple regression model and its coefficients

```
> summary(lm(proficiency ~ hours_instruction + anxiety))

Call:
lm(formula = proficiency ~ hours_instruction + anxiety)

Residuals:
    Min      1Q  Median      3Q     Max
-33.885  -6.189   0.193   6.620  37.523

Coefficients:
                  Estimate Std. Error t value Pr(>|t|)
(Intercept)       29.23170    5.77635   5.061 1.17e-05 ***
hours_instruction  0.08982    0.01305   6.880 4.10e-08 ***
anxiety           -0.13911    0.06471  -2.150   0.0382 *
---
Signif. codes:  0 '***' 0.001 '**' 0.01 '*' 0.05 '.' 0.1 ' ' 1

Residual standard error: 12.32 on 37 degrees of freedom
Multiple R-squared:  0.6587,    Adjusted R-squared:  0.6402
F-statistic:  35.7 on 2 and 37 DF,  p-value: 2.308e-09
```

The R output in Table 6.5 again starts with a repetition of the model and its code and information on the residuals. After that, we find the coefficients table, which is the third table in Table 6.6, that can tell us whether the explanatory variables have an effect on proficiency and how big this effect is. We find an estimate of the intercept (that slightly changed with the added variable) and the estimates of the slopes for the two different independent variables with their accompanying standard error values. As explained in

Table 6.6 JASP output table for the linear multiple regression model and its coefficients

Model Summary

Model	R	R²	Adjusted R²	RMSE
1	0.812	0.659	0.640	12.32

ANOVA

Model		Sum of Squares	df	Mean Square	F	p
1	Regression	10846	2	5422.9	35.70	< .001
	Residual	5620	37	151.9		
	Total	16466	39			

Coefficients

Model		Unstandardized	Standard Error	Standardized	t	p
1	(Intercept)	29.232	5.776		5.061	< .001
	hours_instruction	0.090	0.013	0.707	6.880	< .001
	anxiety	−0.139	0.065	−0.221	−2.150	0.038

Section 6.2, the table also provides *t*-values and the corresponding *p*-values for each independent variable, denoting whether the effect is significantly different from 0.

ACTIVITY 6.5

Can you tell by looking at Table 6.5 or Table 6.6 whether there is a significant effect of foreign language anxiety?

Remember that the slope (the estimate) tells us how much the dependent variable goes up or down for every added value to the predictor. So, from Table 6.5 and Table 6.6, we can deduct that the proficiency score goes up by about 0.09 for every added hour of instruction. What is the effect of anxiety? Is this what you would have expected?

In this particular example, we could say that the base proficiency score is 29.23 (the *intercept*). Now, the slope for hours of instruction is 0.09. This means that for every additional hour of instruction, the proficiency score goes up with 0.09. So, after 300 hours of instruction, this model predicts that the proficiency score will be around 56 (29.23+(300*0.09)), which is slightly different from the prediction based on the simple model. The model additionally shows that the effect of anxiety is significant (*p* = .038) and the direction of the effect is a negative one: with every added value on the used anxiety scale, proficiency is expected to decrease with a value of –0.14. This value of the slope can be used to make specific predictions with respect to proficiency for different levels of anxiety. If someone scored 86 on the anxiety scale (the maximum was 120), this person's estimated proficiency would be about 17 (29.23+(86*–0.14)). A person who scored very low on anxiety with a score of, for example, 12 would be expected to obtain a higher level of proficiency around 28 (29.23+(12*–0.14)). We can now combine information about the influence of hours of instruction and the level of anxiety on proficiency by extending the regression equation that was introduced in Section 6.2:

$$\text{Outcome } Y = b0 + b1X_1 + b2X_2 + \varepsilon \tag{6.2}$$

ACTIVITY 6.6

Using the equation above and the output presented in Table 6.5 or Table 6.6, what would be the expected proficiency score for someone who had 100 hours of instruction and an anxiety score of 30? And what about their classmate who also had 100 hours of instruction, but a maximum anxiety score of 120?

Our previous calculations on this research question already showed that the more hours a person received instruction, the higher their proficiency score will be. The above calculations additionally reveal that, after 100 hours of instruction, the person with a very low anxiety score is predicted to do relatively well in terms of proficiency level when compared to the classmate with a very high anxiety score. While the former would be expected to have a proficiency level around 34, the anxious student would only obtain a score of about 21. Our new model revealed that both our predictor variables have a significant effect on proficiency level. Interestingly, regression also allows to examine the relative impact of each predictor, but then we cannot look at the unstandardized coefficients as these are based on measurements of different units. Luckily, we can compare the size of the effects directly by looking at standardized coefficients. These standardized, or beta, coefficients reveal how many *SD*s the outcome changes if the predictor variable changes with one *SD* as well. Because they are based on standardized values of the variables involved and measured in the same unit, that is, *SD*s, they can be directly compared; the higher the standardized beta coefficient, the stronger the effect of that specific variable. The output provided by JASP automatically contains standardized coefficients and, when looking at Table 6.6, it can be seen that the variable hours of instruction has a relatively higher impact on proficiency than anxiety (which is also reflected in the *t*-value). While R by default only provides the unstandardized coefficients (i.e. the estimate), the standardized beta coefficients can be easily retrieved (as will be briefly explained in Practical 5).

It might often be informative to also say something about the variance that our new model explains and to compare it to the simple linear regression model. For our simple regression model we looked at the multiple R-squared value. For multiple regression models, it is better to look at the adjusted R-squared value instead. This R-squared version has been adjusted for the number of predictors that we added.[1] When comparing Tables 6.3 and 6.4, our simple regression model, to Tables 6.5 and 6.6, our multiple regression model, it becomes clear that the multiple R-squared value has increased from 61.61% to 65.87%. The adjusted R-squared value, however, has only increased from 60.6% to 64.02%. While the multiple R-squared value will increase with every added predictor, regardless of whether they have a significant impact or not, the adjusted R-squared only increases if the addition of the predictor improves the model more than would be expected by chance. For our multiple regression model, we can thus say that 64% of the variance in proficiency scores can be explained by the effects of hours of instruction and foreign language anxiety.

6.4 Assumptions for regression and (non-parametric) alternatives

Regression as outlined above constitutes a parametric test that assumes the different observations to be independent, the dependent variable to be measured at interval scale, and the relationship between the IV and DV to be linear. The assumption of linearity can easily be checked by creating a scatterplot. If the data points all roughly follow a straight line, it can be assumed that the relationship is linear. In addition to this assumption, two other assumptions in regression are *homoscedasticity of variance* and, for multiple regression, *multicollinearity*.

To understand homoscedasticity, let us go back to the data of our simple regression model predicting proficiency as a function of hours of instruction, as plotted in Figure 6.2. As can be seen, our dataset contains both negative residuals, that is, the dots below the regression line, and positive residuals, that is, the dots above the line. As explained in Section 6.2, the closer the dots are to the regression line, and hence the lower the residual values, the better the model fits the data. A perfect model would make no mistakes and would perfectly predict every data point, which would lead to a residual value of 0. Real data will never follow a perfectly straight line, but on average we would still want the residuals to be close to 0. Moreover, the points that deviate from the model should not all deviate in the same direction and to the same amount. Consider the two datasets in Figure 6.4.

---

1 Traditionally, the *r*-squared value is often written in a lower case (r^2) when reporting the results of simple and linear regression and a capital letter is often used (R^2) for multiple and non-linear regression. These two values are, however, identical.

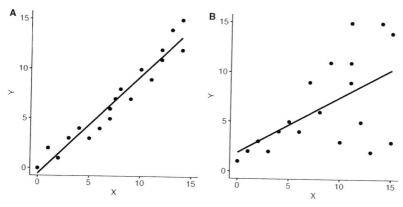

Figure 6.4 Scatterplots with regression lines through the data with a homoscedastic (A) and and a heteroscedastic pattern (B)

The regression line in the left plot (A) in Figure 6.4 obviously presents a better-fitting model with overall lower residuals than plot B on the right. Homoscedasticity is, however, not related to the closeness of the actual data points to the regression line. Instead, it refers to the equality of the closeness across the entire regression line. In the left plot (A), the residuals form a band around the regression line: some points are above the line and some are below, but their deviation from the line is approximately the same for lower and higher values. In the right plot (B), on the other hand, the actual data points are close to the line for lower values, but deviate increasingly the higher the values get. To put it differently, you could say that the model in B is good at predicting lower values, but it is not good at predicting values in higher ranges. The deviations from the model are thus not equal across the regression line in plot B. Homoscedasticity is thus similar to the homogeneity of variance assumption and assumes that the residuals or errors, that is the differences between the observed values and the ones fitted by the model, vary constantly.

Multicollinearity is very specific to multiple regression and refers to a situation in which multiple variables relate to the same underlying variable. Imagine you are testing the effects of proficiency on the motivation level of students and you have included both listening proficiency and reading proficiency. The two proficiency measures are likely to correlate and when you enter both of them as independent explanatory variables, you will likely find that they both impact motivation level. But how much does each of these variables contribute? Is reading proficiency a more important predictor for motivation than listening proficiency, or is it the other way round? The problem with predictor variables that correlate is that you cannot answer these questions. Reading correlates with listening and so they are, together, influencing motivation. In this particular situation, you will not be able to assess the individual contribution of each of these variables. This is referred to as multicollinearity and should be avoided.

Finally, the errors in a regression, that is, the residuals, should be normally distributed (see Levshina, 2015 for a more detailed explanation of each of these assumptions). Luckily, R and JASP have functions to check each of these assumptions and they will be explained in detail in Practical 5 and the How To units on Regression on the companion website.

Regression can also be done to predict the outcome of ordinal or categorical data, in which case you cannot use the regular parametric version. Imagine, for example, that a group of participants was asked to perform a lexical decision task in which they saw both actual as well as non-words pop up on a computer screen. For every word, they had to decide whether it was a real word or not and they had to do this as fast as possible. When the question is whether it is possible to predict the response times for the words, we can use the regression analysis outlined above, but when the question is about predicting the accuracy for each word, we would need to opt for *logistic regression*, as we would be predicting a binary outcome (correct vs. incorrect).

As you have probably realized, a dataset can influence the model greatly, depending on what was measured. In addition to a linear regression line to fit the data, it is also possible to choose to use different regression lines, for example a logarithmic model. Just make sure that you are aware of the choices you make. For more information about regression and the more advanced versions (such as logistic regression and mixed-effects regression, which we will briefly touch upon in Chapter 8), we recommend Baayen (2008).

The present chapter has given an introduction to regression analyses. When we are interested in the relationship between two interval variables, we can use a Pearson *r* correlation. When, however, we want to predict one variable on the basis of a continuous predictor variable, we should use simple regression instead. When the design is somewhat more complicated, for example because it contains multiple independent variables that are nominal and/or interval, we can opt for a multiple regression analysis. In addition to revealing which variables significantly impact the values of the dependent variable, it can also determine how much each variable impacts the dependent variable. Please remember that when you are dealing with multiple independent nominal variables and an interval dependent variable, you can choose either regression or more complicated versions of ANOVA. This latter group of tests will be discussed in more detail in the upcoming chapter. For now, we suggest you work through Practical 5 to get some hands-on experience performing a regression analysis and to practise some of the other tests that you have learned thus far.

7 ADDITIONAL STATISTICS FOR GROUP COMPARISONS

7.1 Introduction

When you start to get the hang of research, you will probably start to add more groups or more variables to your research designs. For example, you might want to examine the influence of L1 background on proficiency level in English as a second language, but you want to compare three or more language backgrounds. Or you might want to look at the differences between two groups that receive a different type of instruction while learning French as a second language, but you additionally want to look at the effect of their L1. Or maybe you want to investigate the effect of instruction, but you want to do so comparing vocabulary scores to listening and reading skills. Or you may want to investigate the differences between these instruction groups at different points in time on a vocabulary test. In these situations, you would not only have two levels of your independent variable instruction, but you would have either an additional independent variable (L1) or more than one dependent variable.

In the very first example, when comparing three or more groups, you cannot use the *t*-test that we used to compare two groups, but you will have to use *Analysis of Variance* (ANOVA, also see Table 7.1). Various versions of the ANOVA exist that can deal with almost all possible combinations of designs consisting of more than two groups. The second situation, in which the effects of both instruction and L1 are examined, allows for a multiple regression with independent categorical predictors, but traditionally most experimental linguists would choose to perform a two-way ANOVA on these data (also see Table 7.1). In the third example, vocabulary scores, listening skills, and reading skills are independent measures of each other, although they might correlate (the more vocabulary knowledge, the better the listening and reading skills). This can be tested using a Multivariate ANOVA (see Table 7.1). In the final example, the different measures of vocabulary knowledge at different times cannot be called independent from each other, as they are repeatedly measuring the same thing. The latter should therefore be tested with a so-called Repeated Measures design, which treats the related dependent variables as different levels of one dependent variable.

We will not give detailed examples for all means analyses here; the principles and interpretations of these are largely the same as those for the *t*-test and the one-way ANOVA that will be discussed in detail in Section 7.2 below. After introducing the basic one-way ANOVA, we will look into factorial (*n*-way) ANOVAs and alternatives in case of violations of one or more of the assumptions.

7.2 Comparing more than two groups: The ANOVA

You have been introduced to the *t*-test that is used when comparing two independent or related groups. We cannot simply use multiple *t*-tests to compare more than two groups or more than one dependent variable, because we cannot run multiple comparisons with the same dataset within the same alpha level. For different comparisons, different statistics can be used to avoid this problem. The number of groups related to the same independent variable is referred to as the *levels* of that variable. The analyses we will discuss go up to three levels for each variable (see Table 7.1).

An example of a study that uses a nominal independent variable with more than two levels would be a study in which an interval proficiency score is compared for learners with different L1 backgrounds. The different

Table 7.1 Choice of parametric statistics for group means analyses

Number of nominal independent variables	Number of levels (groups) for the nominal independent variable	Number of interval dependent variables ('scores')	Statistic to be used	Statistical expression
1	2	1	Independent samples *t*-test	*t*
1	1	2	Paired-samples *t*-test	*t*
1	More than 2	1	one-way ANOVA	*F*
2	Any	1	two-way factorial ANOVA	*F*
N	Any	1	*n*-way factorial ANOVA	*F*
N	Any	Any	MANOVA	*F*

Table 7.2 Descriptives comparing the proficiency of 3 groups

	n	Mean	St. Dev
Chinese	12	54.08	14.49
Spanish	12	39.62	10.84
Sutu	9	50.75	9.91

first languages, say Spanish, Chinese, and Sutu, would each form a different level of the variable L1 background. The null hypothesis of this study would be that there is no difference between any of these groups. The descriptive statistics of this fictitious study are shown in Table 7.2 and a boxplot of the data can be found in Figure 7.1.

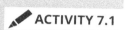 **ACTIVITY 7.1**

■ What are your first impressions about the group results summarized in Table 7.2 and when comparing the boxplots in Figure 7.1?

■ Referring to the data in Table 7.2, what are the dependent and the independent variable(s)?

■ Which statistic should be used to test the significance of the difference between these groups (consult Table 7.1)?

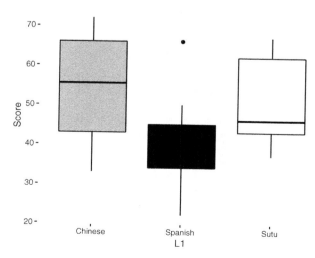

Figure 7.1 Boxplot showing the spread in scores for the Chinese, Spanish, and Sutu learners of English

At face value, the mean proficiency scores for the Chinese learners are the highest; the scores for the Spanish learners are the lowest. The Sutu are the most homogeneous (smallest *SD*), and the Chinese learners show the largest differences within their group. The question we want to answer is whether the H_0 can be rejected. The appropriate test, as illustrated in Table 7.1, is the one-way Analysis of Variance (ANOVA). This is a test that calculates *F*, which represents the proportion of the variance between the groups to the variance within the groups, which is very similar to *t*. To reject the H_0, we would obviously prefer a large difference between the groups, while the variance within the groups (as expressed by the *SD*) should be as small as possible:

$$F = \frac{Variance\ between\ groups}{Variance\ within\ groups} \tag{7.1}$$

This equation shows just this. Like the value of *t*, the value of *F* increases with increasing between-group differences, but decreases with increasing *SD*s within groups. So the greater the value of *F* is, the more likely it is that we can reject H_0. Whether or not we can actually reject H_0 not only depends on the value of *F*, but also on the sample size (as expressed by *df*) and on the significance value. Running a one-way ANOVA in R on the data of the Chinese, Spanish, and Sutu learners using aov()[1] yields the result in Table 7.3. The outcome of the same test in JASP is shown in Table 7.4.

In this case you will see that there is a *df* referring to the number of groups minus one (3 – 1 = 2) and one referring to the number of participants

Table 7.3 R code and output for a one-way ANOVA

```
> Model1 <-aov(Score ~L1, data = dat)
> summary(Model1)
            Df Sum Sq Mean Sq F value Pr(>F)
L1           2   1449   724.3    5.13 0.0113 *
Residuals   34   4800   141.2
---
Signif. codes:  0 '***' 0.001 '**' 0.01 '*' 0.05 '.' 0.1 ' ' 1
```

Table 7.4 JASP output for a one-way ANOVA

ANOVA – Score ▼						
Cases	Sum of Squares	df	Mean Square	F	p	η²
L1	1449	2	724.3	5.130	0.011	0.232
Residual	4800	34	141.2			

Note. Type III Sum of Squares

---

1   Some might prefer to use lm(), but here we provide an example using aov() to show the more 'traditional' ANOVA output and to be able to do planned contrasts later on.

minus the number of groups (37 – 3 = 34). Tables 7.3 and 7.4 additionally show that, for an .05 level of significance, the H_0 can be rejected. This signals a difference in English proficiency scores between the groups. But this is not the end of our analysis, because the output does not reveal whether all groups differ from one another or whether only one group differs from the other two. We would thus want to know if the scores for each of the groups differ significantly from both of the other groups. To test this, it would be tempting to do three t-tests, one for each L1 pair. However, we cannot use multiple comparisons on the same dataset, because every time we run the test we are again allowing the 5% chance of making the wrong decision. If we ran several t-tests on the same sample, we would therefore 'capitalize on chance' and the eventual level of significance would be more than 5%. Therefore, any program that can calculate the F for a one-way ANOVA also provides the opportunity to run a *post-hoc* test. A post-hoc test does the same as a t-test, but includes a correction for the multiple comparisons. A post-hoc test makes two-by-two comparisons between all the levels of the independent variable. Table 7.5 is the output of a post-hoc analysis for the current example where we used the *Tukey Honest Significant Differences* (HSD) test, which provides 'honest' or corrected p-values:

Table 7.5 shows the differences in means for every L1 pair (diff) and also the lower (lwr) and upper (upr) boundaries revealing that, if we were to repeat the test on different samples, R estimates that the mean difference would lie somewhere between those two values in approximately 95% of the cases (95% CI). The last column contains the adjusted p-values for every L1 pair comparison and shows us that the mean proficiency of the Spanish and Chinese learners differs significantly at p = .012, but that no difference is found between the Sutu and the Chinese (p = .77). Judging by the p-values, the difference between the Spanish and Sutu learners is not very convincing with p = .064 and might at the most be reported as a trend towards a significant difference.

The output for the Tukey HSD in JASP can be seen in Table 7.6 and shows approximately the same outcomes, but with additional information on the t-value, which can be compared to the t-value in a t-test, and the

Table 7.5 R output of a Tukey post-hoc analysis

```
> TukeyHSD(Model1)
  Tukey multiple comparisons of means
    95% family-wise confidence level

Fit: aov(formula = Score ~ L1, data = dat)

$`L1`
                      diff         lwr        upr      p adj
Spanish-Chinese -14.467949 -26.1237780 -2.812119 0.0122250
Sutu-Chinese     -3.333333 -15.2199936  8.553327 0.7725194
Sutu-Spanish     11.134615  -0.5212139 22.790445 0.0635628
```

Table 7.6 JASP output of a Tukey post-hoc analysis

Post Hoc Comparisons – L1

			95% CI for Mean Difference				
		Mean Difference	Lower	Upper	SE	t	P_tukey
Chinese	Spanish	14.468	2.812	26.124	4.757	3.042	0.012
	Sutu	3.333	−8.553	15.220	4.851	0.687	0.773
Spanish	Sutu	−11.135	−22.790	0.521	4.757	−2.341	0.064

Note. Confidence intervals based on Tukey's HSD.

Standard Error. Note that the differences between the groups are positive here, when they were negative in R, and the other way around. This just depends on which group is subtracted from which group, but makes no difference for the interpretations of the difference.

 **ACTIVITY 7.2**

■ The lower (lwr) and upper (upr) bound values in Table 7.5 and Table 7.6 reveal that, if we repeatedly test other participants in each language group, the mean difference is estimated to fall between those two values in approximately 95% of the cases. If the table had not provided any *p*-values, would you be able to use these lower and upper values to assess whether there is a significant difference in means between the groups? To put it differently, what is the difference between the lower and upper values for the case in which the *p*-value is .012 and the case with a *p*-value of .77? And can you explain why the *p*-value of the last comparison would be lower if the lower and upper values were both negative or both positive instead of containing the 0 value?

■ Suppose we added an additional independent variable to the research design discussed in this section, for example gender. In that case, would you still be able to analyse the data using a one-way ANOVA? If not, which statistic should you choose? Use Table 7.1 to help you make a decision.

Looking closely at the output in Tables 7.5. and 7.6 will help you to interpret how R and JASP calculated the *p*-values. For the Chinese and the Spanish, the mean difference is estimated to fall on one side, that is either positive (JASP) or negative (R), in approximately 95% of the cases. If all estimated differences fall on the same side, the adjusted *p*-value will be below .05. If, however, the upper and lower values include a 0, this means that the mean difference might also be 0. Hence, the difference is unlikely to be significant.

If our independent variable contains more than two levels, such as when we are comparing three groups, we should opt for a one-way ANOVA. When our design is somewhat more complicated, for example because it contains multiple independent variables that are nominal, we should opt for a factorial ANOVA, which will be explained in the next section.

7.3 Factorial ANOVA

In Chapter 5, we discussed a test to compare two groups (the *t*-test) and in the previous section, we discussed a test to compare more than two groups (the one-way ANOVA). As can be seen in Table 7.1, these tests are used when there is only one independent variable involved. Let us go back to the example where we compared the Spanish, the Chinese, and the Sutu groups. Imagine that we are additionally interested in potential effects of two teaching methods, for example explicit and implicit teaching of grammar, and that this nominal variable is added to the design and analysis. In this particular example, we would have two independent variables, one with three levels (language background) and one with two levels (teaching method), and we would have to conduct a two-way *factorial ANOVA* instead.

ACTIVITY 7.3

Let us assume you are adding yet another variable to the analyses in the design described above: gender. What are the dependent and the independent variables and which statistic should be used to test the significance of the difference between these groups (consult Table 7.1)?

When performing *n*-way factorial ANOVAs, we can find differences between the levels of each of the independent variables, such as an effect of language background and/or an effect of teaching method. Consider, for example, the effects of both teaching method and L1 background in the hypothetical situation depicted in Figure 7.2.

Figure 7.2 depicts a hypothetical situation with both an effect of language, with the Chinese and Sutu learners performing better than the Spanish, as well as an effect of teaching method, with those following explicit instructions scoring higher than those receiving implicit instructions. What should be noticed in the graph is that the effect of teaching method seems to be very comparable in each group tested: the difference between the scores of the implicit and explicit groups is almost identical regardless of whether we are looking at the Spanish, Sutu, or Chinese learners. Similarly, when

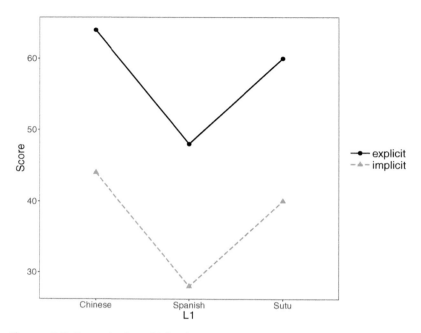

Figure 7.2 Example in which there is both a main effect of language background, with the Chinese and Sutu scoring higher than the Spanish, and a main effect of teaching method, with higher scores for the explicit teaching method

looking at the effect of L1 background, this is almost identical in both the group receiving implicit as well as those receiving explicit instructions. The effect that one independent variable has on the dependent variable without looking at the differences caused by any of the other independent variables is referred to as a *main effect*. Figure 7.2 shows both a main effect of L1 background and a main effect of teaching method.

When incorporating several independent variables, however, we are especially interested in so-called *interaction effects*. Maybe the implicit method works better for Chinese learners, while explicit teaching is more beneficial for Sutu learners, or the other way around. The different effects of one independent variable on different levels of another independent variable are referred to as interaction effects and they can often only be interpreted on the basis of graphs, such as the other hypothetical example in Figure 7.3.

Considering the hypothetical data plotted in Figure 7.3, if you took the average of the students in the explicit instruction group and the average of the students in the implicit instruction group, you would probably find a very minimal difference. In the explicit group, the Chinese score around 36, the Spanish around 48, and the Sutu a little over 60. When ignoring L1, this explicit group overall thus scored around 48 ((36+48+60)/3). We could also calculate the average for the implicit group in this way, which would result

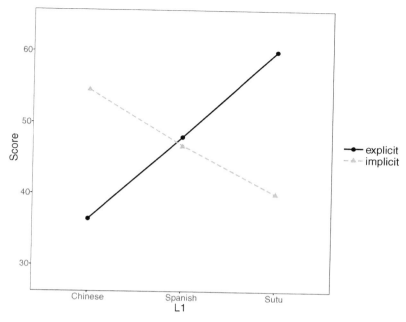

Figure 7.3 Example in which there are no main effects, but there is an interaction between language background and teaching method

in a score around 46.7 ((54+46+40)/3). Looking at main effects means ignoring any differences related to other variables and hence, if you want to examine the main effect of teaching method, you should ignore and hence average over L1 background. If you do that, you will be comparing a score of 48 to a score of 46.7, which can hardly be called a difference.

Similarly, when taking the average score for the Chinese, and hence averaging over teaching method, and comparing that score of approximately 45 ((36+54)/2)) to the average obtained by the Spanish ((48+46)/2) and Sutu ((60+40)/2), you will also find only a very minimal difference. In other words, we would not expect to find any main effects of teaching method or L1 background on the basis of the data depicted in Figure 7.3. But can we conclude that there is no effect?

No, as we can clearly see from the data, there is an effect. The effect, however, differs for the different groups involved. While the Spanish show no effect of teaching method, the Chinese score a lot better when implicitly instructed and a lot worse when explicitly instructed. On the other hand, those Sutu learners who received explicit instruction perform a lot better than those who received implicit instruction. The effect of one of the independent variables, that is teaching method, is thus different for the different levels of the other independent variable, that is L1 background. Such a combined effect is referred to as an interaction effect.

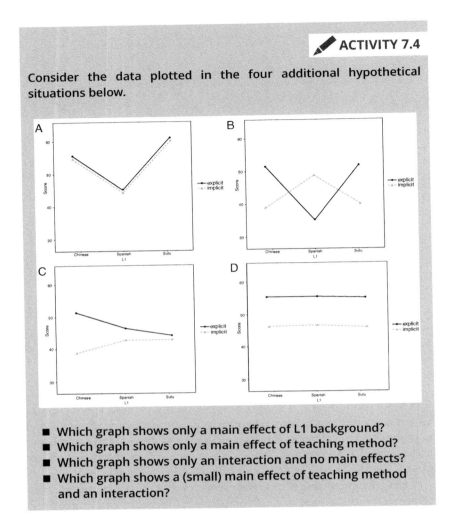

✏ **ACTIVITY 7.4**

Consider the data plotted in the four additional hypothetical situations below.

- Which graph shows only a main effect of L1 background?
- Which graph shows only a main effect of teaching method?
- Which graph shows only an interaction and no main effects?
- Which graph shows a (small) main effect of teaching method and an interaction?

The upper left plot (A) clearly shows no difference between the two teaching methods, but there is a difference between L1 backgrounds with Spanish learners scoring lower as compared to the other two groups. Such a main effect of L1 is absent in plot B in the upper right corner: if you compare the average score of all Chinese, Spanish, and Sutu learners, there is hardly a difference. Similarly, the overall average scores of implicit versus explicit learners are very comparable. This upper right plot, however, does show an interaction effect, that is a differential effect of teaching method for the different L1 groups, with Chinese and Sutu learners benefiting more from explicit teaching methods while the Spanish seem to gain more from implicit teaching.

The lower right plot (D) shows a main effect of teaching method: when we average across the L1 groups, there will be an overall higher score for

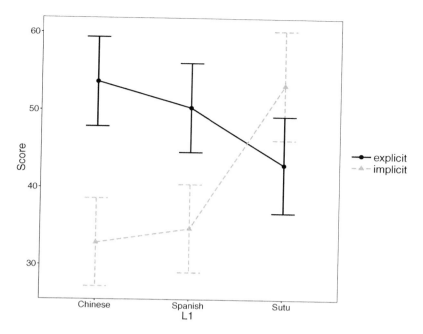

Figure 7.4 Example in which there is a main effect of teaching method and an interaction between L1 background and teaching method

the explicit as compared to the implicit group. There is no effect of L1 and the effect of teaching method is the same for all groups and hence there is no interaction effect. This is slightly different for the plot on the lower left (C). If we were to compare the average score for Chinese, Spanish, and Sutu learners, and hence average over teaching method, we would not find any differences. If we were to average over L1, however, we might find a slightly higher average for the explicit than the implicit condition. That is, however, not the entire story of this dataset. The effect of teaching method is very pronounced in the Chinese group, with higher scores in the explicit group, but smaller in the Spanish group and absent in the Sutu group. The effect of teaching method is thus different for the different L1 backgrounds: there is an interaction effect.

Figure 7.4 shows yet another possible combination of effects in the data and also shows the variation in each group as visualized by the whiskers known as so-called *error bars*.

If we were to perform a two-way ANOVA using the particular dataset plotted in Figure 7.4, we would get the output in Tables 7.7 (R) and 7.8 (JASP). The tables reveal that performing and interpreting the results of a two-way ANOVA are not that different from the one-way ANOVA. Instead of adding one independent variable, we added two, and you can imagine, it is just as easy to add a third one. In the two-way ANOVAs in

Table 7.7 R output for a two-way ANOVA with the variables L1 and teaching method added both as main effects and as an interaction

```
> model =  aov(Score ~ L1*Teaching, data=data)
> Anova(model, type="III")
Anova Table (Type III tests)

Response: Score
            Sum Sq Df    F value    Pr(>F)
(Intercept) 128400  1 1301.5357 < 2.2e-16 ***
L1             364  2    1.8465 0.1666484
Teaching      1234  1   12.5100 0.0007877 ***
L1:Teaching   2714  2   13.7574 1.208e-05 ***
Residuals     5919 60

---
Signif. codes:  0 '***' 0.001 '**' 0.01 '*' 0.05 '.' 0.1 ' ' 1
```

Table 7.8 JASP output for a two-way ANOVA with an interaction between the variables L1 and teaching method

ANOVA – Score

Cases	Sum of Squares	df	Mean Square	F	p	η²
L1	364.3	2	182.16	1.846	0.167	0.036
Teaching	1234.1	1	1234.14	12.510	< .001	0.121
L1 * Teaching	2714.4	2	1357.20	13.757	< .001	0.265
Residual	5919.2	60	98.65			

Note. Type III Sum of Squares

Tables 7.7 and 7.8, score is modelled on the basis of both L1 and teaching method and the asterisk (*) and/or colon (:) signify an interaction between these two variables. The results reveal that there is no main effect of L1 ($p = .167$), but there is an effect of teaching method ($p < .001$). As can be seen in Figure 7.4, the students receiving explicit instruction did better overall. This is, however, not the case for the Sutu learners, who performed slightly better in the implicit group. This differential effect of teaching method for the different L1 groups is confirmed in the output by the presence of a significant interaction between L1 and teaching ($p < .001$). We can thus conclude, based on the statistical output and the visualization of the data in Figure 7.4, that the effect of teaching method is not the same for the different L1 backgrounds: while both the Chinese and the Spanish seem to perform a lot better when the instruction is explicit, the Sutu learners show a slightly higher score in the implicit teaching condition instead.

7.4 Alternatives for comparing means in case of assumption violations

In Chapter 5, we already mentioned some of the non-parametric alternatives for mean comparisons for comparing two groups, such as the Mann-Whitney U test (also see Table 5.9). Now, let us suppose the proficiency scores of the Chinese, Spanish, and Sutu groups were essay grades. In this case, we have ordinal data and we should not do a parametric one-way ANOVA. If the data violate the assumption of normality or if the data are of an ordinal nature, a so-called *Kruskal-Wallis H* test can be done.

Instead of using means, these non-parametric alternatives often base their p-values on the ranked data instead. The Mann-Whitney U test and the Kruskal-Wallis H test, for example, rank all data points from low to high. Now, if the null hypothesis were true and we ranked all individuals within the Spanish, Sutu, and Chinese group (without taking L1 background into account), we would expect each group to contain a similar number of low and high ranks. Using the ranking system, we could also number all ranks from lowest to highest and then calculate the sum of ranks. If there is no difference, the summed rank should be similar across groups. If there is a difference, one or two of the groups should have a higher sum of ranks than the other(s). Many non-parametric tests use this ranking system instead of raw numbers.

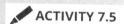

ACTIVITY 7.5

Imagine your dataset suffers from skewness and/or kurtosis. Try to explain in your own words why a statistical test based on a ranking system would be preferred over a test based on mean scores.

The assumptions for a one-way and a factorial ANOVA are identical to the ones previously mentioned for other parametric tests: the observations are independent from one another, the data of the different groups need to be normally distributed, the data show homogeneity of variance, and the dependent measure should be interval. If one or more of these assumptions are violated, you should opt for an alternative version.

Table 7.9 provides an overview of the most commonly used tests for comparing means and their alternative versions when one or more of the assumptions are violated. Although you will find that the values for the different tests may differ (W-value for Wilcoxon and H-value for Kruskal-Wallis), the interpretation of the output is very similar to the interpretation of the equivalent regular versions of these tests that we have discussed so far.

Table 7.9 Mean comparison tests and equivalents in case of violations of one or more of the assumptions[2]

Regular test	Assumption violated	Equivalent most commonly used
Independent Samples *t*-test	*homogeneity of variance*	Welch's *t*-test
	interval data/ normal distribution	Mann-Whitney *U*
	independent observations	Paired Samples *t*-test
	interval data/ normal distribution/ independent observations	Wilcoxon signed-rank
One-way ANOVA	*homogeneity of variance*	Welch's ANOVA
	interval data/ normal distribution	Kruskal-Wallis *H*
	independent observations	Repeated Measures/ Mixed ANOVA

As with a parametric one-way ANOVA, a significant Kruskal-Wallis result should be followed by post-hoc procedures, and the most commonly used one is the Dunn test. The interpretation of the output is similar to the interpretation of the Tukey HSD discussed in Section 7.2. If the data are normally distributed and interval, but the assumption of homogeneity of variance is not met, we can opt for the Welch's ANOVA for unequal variances. This test corrects for heterogeneity in variance, but is otherwise identical to the regular one-way ANOVA (also see Levshina, 2015: Chapter 8). Note that we could also opt for linear regression in most of these cases!

In the examples in this chapter thus far, we have compared effects of groups using a so-called *between-subjects* design: a person can either be Spanish, Sutu, or Chinese, and a person received either implicit or explicit instruction. In many experimental designs, however, we also include

---

2   The attentive reader will have noticed that Table 7.9 contains no row for the factorial ANOVA. The simple reason is that there is no suitable (non-parametric) equivalent for this test. Luckily, ANOVAs are generally used by researchers who carefully set up their design. In these cases, ANOVA is known to be able to deal with non-normal data pretty well.

so-called *within-subjects* effects. Imagine, for example, that we are conducting a lexical decision experiment in which we compare people's responses to both high frequency and low frequency words and maybe even their responses to pseudo-words. Individuals are then not tested in one condition only, but their responses for all possible conditions are recorded and compared. In such a within-subjects design, the independent variable is often referred to as a *within-subjects factor* as we are testing that variable within each individual. As we are testing each individual multiple times, we are violating the assumption of independence of the observations. Luckily, there is a specific type of ANOVA, the *repeated measures ANOVA* or the *mixed design*, that can account for dependence among measurements and this ANOVA can be seen as an extension of the paired or dependent samples *t*-test (also see Table 7.9).

As you have probably guessed by now, you can make a design as complex as possible and you can include both multiple independent as well as multiple dependent variables. A detailed explanation of all these ANOVAs goes beyond the scope of an introductory textbook, but we would like to stress that the output and interpretation of these various ANOVAs largely follow the steps of statistical logic of the *t*-test and the one-way and two-way ANOVA that we have discussed. For more detailed discussions and example analyses of factorial and repeated measures ANOVAs, we would like to refer to Field et al. (2012), Chapters 12 (Factorial ANOVA) and 13 (Repeated Measures Designs).

7.5 Effect sizes

As for any analysis the interpretation of the results is informed by effect sizes, we will elaborate on effect sizes for ANOVAs here. In Chapter 5, we calculated the effect size r^2 for a *t*-test and this measure can also be calculated for the one-way ANOVA using the values of the Sum of Squares of the Model (SSM) and the Sum of Squares of the Total (SST). These values were already provided in Tables 7.3 and 7.4 under the column 'Sum Sq' or 'Sum of Squares' where the first value is the Sum of Squares of the Model (between-subjects) and the sum of the first and second row would be the value for Total Sum of Squares (within-subjects).

To calculate the effect size of a one-way ANOVA, we can use the following equation.

$$r^2 = \frac{SSM}{SST} \tag{7.2}$$

Based on the output in Table 7.3/4, our r^2-value would be 1449/(1449+4800), which equals .23. In articles, they often refer to this value not as *r*-squared but as *eta-squared* (η^2), but it is the same value obtained using the same equation. The interpretation of these effect sizes is the same as what we explained for correlations in Section 5.2.1.

Some statisticians, however, prefer to use a slightly different effect size measure, *omega-squared* (ω^2), for both one-way and factorial ANOVAs. This preference has to do with the fact that the eta-squared is only based on numbers from the sample, but we want to say something about the population. An adjustment of the eta-squared for predicting the effect size in the population is reflected in the value of omega-squared. If you compare the two measures, you will see that omega-squared is always a bit lower and hence more conservative than eta-squared.

Of course, it is also possible to calculate effect sizes for non-parametric statistics. One possible calculation of the effect size r for a Mann-Whitney as well as a Wilcoxon rank-sum is using the following formula (where N refers to the total number of cases and Z to the value of the test statistic):

$$r = \frac{Z}{\sqrt{N}} \tag{7.3}$$

In Chapter 7, you have learned about the ANOVA and the more complicated versions of ANOVAs in studies in which you are using several independent variables (factorial ANOVAs). We have also given an overview of the various (non-parametric) alternatives for mean comparisons. We suggest you now try Practical 6 before reading the final chapter of this book.

8 SUMMARY AND CONCLUDING REMARKS

8.1 Introduction

In this book, we focused on the most basic and most common statistical tests used within the field of Linguistics and Applied Linguistics. Based on these chapters, you should be able to understand and judge the statistics done in most studies conducted in the field. In this final chapter, we will summarize the different statistical tests we have discussed, their most important aspects, assumptions, and how to report the results of each particular test. Where appropriate, we will also briefly mention more advanced statistical tests and provide references to explore such tests for future use.

8.2 Overview and summary of tests

Although most chapters focused on inferential statistics, it is important always to describe and plot the data before conducting any statistical test. Not only should we check assumptions before running parametric tests, but it is also crucial to know the characteristics of the data. Descriptive statistics and visualization of data are crucial to this end!

Table 8.1 gives an overview of the tests that we have discussed.

8.2.1 Investigating relationships

We started our overview of inferential statistics in Chapter 5 with statistical tests to investigate *relationships* and in Chapter 6, we added *simple and multiple regression* with (a) continuous predictor(s) to this group. As can be seen in Table 8.1, a design with one interval 'independent' and one interval 'dependent' variable provides you with a choice between Pearson r and simple regression. Remember that correlations such as the Pearson r are only used to assess a potential relationship between two variables, while simple regression can be used to predict an outcome. Other than that, simple regression with an interval independent variable and an interval dependent variable is very similar to a Pearson r in which the relationship between two interval variables is examined. The only real difference between the two is the perspective and hence the question of the researcher.

In case you want to examine a relationship between two ordinal variables, or if one of the two variables in your design is ordinal, you should opt for a Spearman's ρ or a Kendall's τ. These non-parametric alternatives should also

Table 8.1 Overview of the tests discussed in this book

		"Independent" Variable					
		interval		ordinal	nominal		
	nr of IV's	1	more than 1		1		more than 1
	nr of IV levels				2 levels	> 2 levels	
"Dependent" Variable — interval		Pearson r or simple regression (to test causal relationship) / Paired Samples t-test (to test the difference)	Multiple linear regression	Treat the interval as ordinal	Independent Samples t-test (Student/Welch) / Paired Samples t-test	One-Way ANOVA	Factorial ANOVA or Multiple linear regression
"Dependent" Variable — ordinal		Treat the interval as ordinal	Multiple logistic regression	Kendall's tau or Spearman's rho (to test relationship) / Wilcoxon (to test the difference)	Mann-Whitney U	Kruskal-Wallis	Multiple logistic regression
"Dependent" Variable — nominal		Chi-Square					

be used in case of violations of normality or non-linearity. Although Spearman's ρ is generally more popular in use, it is better to use the more conservative Kendall in cases of small samples that additionally contain little variance or many identical values (also called ties). Tables 8.2 and 8.3 summarize the specific tests we have discussed for correlations and regression respectively.

As with any of the other tests, always report the value of the test statistic, the degrees of freedom, the exact significance value (or $p < .001$), and the effect size. Furthermore, it is customary in research papers to plot the findings appropriately and refer to the plot by explicitly reporting the direction of the effect. Reporting a correlation could be done as follows (in this case for Kendall's *tau*):

> 'There was a significant positive relationship between the minutes of conversation practice and the oral exam grade, $\tau(21) = .650, p < .001$ (two-tailed). The longer a student practises conversation, the higher their oral exam grade. This relationship can also be seen in the scatterplot below and the effect size is large.'

In case we only have nominal variables (see Table 8.1), the only choice would be to conduct a chi-square analysis. Table 8.3 summarizes the chi-square, a test to assess *frequencies* and, more specifically, whether two categorical variables are associated.

Since it is a non-parametric test, we do not have to check normality or homogeneity of variance. We should, however, check the expected frequencies. The results can be reported as follows:

> 'A chi-square analysis revealed that the association between social class and the use of 'haven't got' and 'don't have' is significant $\chi 2 (1, N = 224) = 3.91, p = .048$. People from lower social classes tend to use 'don't have' less than people from higher social classes. There appears to be no large difference between lower and higher social class and their use of 'haven't got'. The association was small ($\varphi: .132$).'

While Tables 8.2 and 8.3 address relationships or associations between variables, we can also predict the value of the dependent variable (the outcome) on the basis of a continuous predictor. Table 8.4 summarizes simple linear regression analyses.

Note that, as with mean comparisons that will be discussed below, there are more assumptions (such as independence) that should be considered for (multiple) regression. These have not been added to the table as they can mostly only be assessed by common sense (also see Chapter 6 and the How To units on the companion website that deal with regression for details). As most assumptions that need to be tested for regression involve

Table 8.2 Correlations (Pearson, Spearman, and Kendall) and information to check and report

Assumptions	Linearity	Before conducting the test, we can make a scatterplot to assess whether the relationship is indeed a linear one. **This assumption is especially important for Pearson r. For Spearman and Kendall, the line does not have to be perfectly straight, as long as it goes into one direction (i.e. as long as it is monotonic).**
	Homoscedasticity	Also always use the scatterplot to ensure that the distance between the points and the imaginary straight line is equal throughout the plot. **This assumption is especially important for Pearson r.**
	Normal distribution	Best is to plot a histogram with a normal curve, check skewness and kurtosis (2SE in R and the z-score in JASP; also see 'How To Check Assumptions' on the companion website), and/or perform a Shapiro-Wilk per variable. **❗ not for Spearman's rho and Kendall's tau, because these are non-parametric tests.**
Strength of relationship	The values of r, ρ and τ are, in essence, already measures of an effect size: they reflect the strength of the relationship. For r:	
	.00–.19 = very weak;	
	.20–.39 = weak;	
	.40–.59 = moderate;	
	.60–.79 = strong;	
	.80–1.0 = very strong.	
Effect size	You can also square the value of r and report r^2, in which case:	
	.01 = small;	
	.09 = medium;	
	.25 = large.	
Tables	Tables are generally not necessary for correlation analyses	
Graphs	Scatterplot	

Table 8.3 The chi-square and information to check and report

Assumptions	Homogeneity of variance	-
	Normal distribution	-
	Expected values	Check whether all expected values in each cell are above 5.
Effect size	Report phi – φ for variables with 2 levels or Cramer's V for variables with more than 2 levels. These values are mostly very similar. For both: .1 = small; .3 = medium; .5 = large.	
Tables	Cross-tabulation or contingency table (observed values)	
Graphs	Bar chart	

Table 8.4 Simple and multiple linear regression and information to check and report

Assumptions	Linearity	Plot the relationship between x and y (or the residuals).
	Normal distribution	For regression, this assumption applies to the residuals and it is best is to plot them in a Q-Q plot or perform a Shapiro-Wilk on the residuals of the model.
	Homoscedasticity	Plot the fitted values against the observed values and make sure that the residuals are equally spread around the regression line.
	Multicollinearity	Check for correlations between the different predictor variables. ***This assumption only holds for multiple regression!***
Effect size	r^2 (provided in output)	
Tables	Coefficients, standard errors, t-values, and p-values	
Graphs	Depends on the nature of the variables and their effects	

Table 8.5 Regression coefficients for the linear model of reaction times as a function of age

	Estimate	SE	t-value	p-value
Intercept	383.129	57.686	6.642	3.43e-09 ***
Age	9.649	1.089	8.864	1.62e-13 ***

the residuals of the model, these assumptions are generally only tested after fitting the regression model.

The results of a regression are often displayed in a table with additional information concerning the model and the variance it explained, as in Table 8.5. Consequently, the table is referred to in the report, as in the following example:

'We constructed a linear model of reaction time as a function of age. This model was significant ($F(1,80) = 78.57$, $p < .001$) and explained 50% of the variance in the data (multiple R-squared). Regression coefficients are shown in Table 8.5. The positive coefficient for age reveals that, as age increases, the reaction times also increase significantly. To be very specific, for every added year in age, the RT increases with 9.65 milliseconds.'

8.2.2 Comparing means

With respect to group comparisons, we looked both at the *t*-test to compare two groups and at the ANOVA to compare three or more groups. Additionally, we discussed factorial ANOVAs that allow for the inclusion of multiple independent variables and potential interactions between these variables. Tables 8.6 and 8.7 summarize the *t*-test and the ANOVA, the assumptions to check, and information on what kinds of descriptives and graphs would be useful. Note that the tables only contain assumptions that need to be tested: there are also other assumptions that can only be assessed by common sense, such as whether the dependent variable is measured at an interval scale!

As mentioned before, we can also predict the value of an interval outcome variable on the basis of multiple categorical variables using multiple regression. ANOVA and regression are thus very comparable. One important advantage of multiple regression is that it can deal with a combination of both continuous and categorical predictor variables.

For all mean comparisons it is important to report the means and standard deviations of the groups compared (or medians in case of non-parametric testing!). Additionally, as with any of the other tests, the report should always contain the values of the test statistic, the degrees of freedom, the significance value, and the effect size. Note that statistical variables should

Table 8.6 The *t*-test and information to check and report

Assumptions	Homogeneity of variance	Levene's test **Not necessary for the paired-samples t-test!**
	Normal distribution	Best is to plot a histogram with a normal curve, check skewness and kurtosis (2SE in R and *z*-scores in JASP, also see 'How To Check Assumptions'), and perform a Shapiro-Wilk per group **! For the paired-samples t-test, the difference in scores should approximate normality.**
Effect size	r^2 or Cohen's *d* For r^2: .01 = small; .09 = medium; .25 = large For Cohen's *d*: 0.2 = small; 0.5 = medium; 0.8 = large	
Tables	Descriptives (means, *SD*s)	
Graphs	Boxplot	

Table 8.7 The ANOVA and information to check and report

Assumptions	Homogeneity of variance	Levene's test
	Normal distribution	Best is to plot a histogram with a normal curve, check skewness and kurtosis (2SE in R and *z*-scores in JASP, also see 'How To Check Assumptions'), and perform a Shapiro-Wilk per group.
Effect size	r^2, which is generally referred to as eta-squared (η^2) when reporting ANOVA results and is interpreted in the same way. Omega-squared (ω^2) is preferred for two-way ANOVAs and some would prefer to use it for both one-way and two-way ANOVAs. The partial version of ω^2 partials out other effects, which is what you need when you have multiple independent variables. Interpretation of (partial) η^2 is identical to the interpretation of r^2: .01 = small; .09 = medium; .25 = large For (partial) ω^2: .01 = small; .06 = medium; .14 = large (Kirk, 1996; Field et al., 2012)	
Tables	Descriptives (means, *SD*s)	
Graphs	Boxplot	

be italicized (VandenBos, 2010). The careful reader of the report below will notice that homogeneity of variance has also been implicitly dealt with in the report by mentioning Welch's t-test:

> 'On average, group 2 performed better on the vocabulary test ($M = 64.0$, $SD = 12.3$) than group 1 ($M = 50.4$, $SD = 14.6$). A Welch's t-test revealed that this difference was significant, t (16) = -2.13, $p = .024$, and shows that instruction positively affects the score on the vocabulary test. The effect size is large, $r^2 = .40$.'

For some journals, it is also common practice to add information about the assumptions in the report. For example:

> 'The vocabulary scores on the pre-test and post-test approximated the normal distribution because neither the result of the Shapiro-Wilk test for the pre-test scores nor the Shapiro-Wilk test for the post-test scores was significant ($W(42) = 0.98$; $p = .57$ and $W(42) = 0.99$, $p = .90$, respectively).'

Remember to always include information on the direction of the effect! People often make the mistake of only reporting the finding of a significant effect, but always also explicitly report the actual relation, difference, or association found!

8.3 Additional statistics

As mentioned throughout, this book is meant to introduce the basics of statistics. A lot of research within the field of Linguistics and AL requires the use of more advanced statistical methods. In this section the most common of these more advanced methods will be mentioned, together with references that allow a little more digging into these methods.

8.3.1 More advanced relationships

Many studies in Linguistics use surveys or questionnaires to answer questions about particular (groups of) people. *Factor analysis* is a rather common statistical method used to (1) assess the reliability of such questionnaires and/or (2) reduce the amount of data they provide to allow for more simple analyses such as the ones discussed in this book. Imagine that a researcher wants to examine the role of out-of-class exposure to English on English L2 proficiency. She might add a fill-in statement to her questionnaire, for example 'On average, the percentage of English spoken films I watch is about …%'. Another question might be about the amount of music with English lyrics and yet another one might focus on the amount of English-spoken radio shows and/or podcasts. Such questionnaires mostly contain several questions that examine the same construct, which in this case might be referred to as the 'amount of media-driven English input'. One might expect that someone who prefers to watch English spoken films would also choose to listen to English podcasts relatively more often than someone who prefers watching films and listening to podcasts in his or her native language. In other words, answers to questions that supposedly address the same underlying construct would be expected to highly correlate with each other. If such correlations are not found, this might suggest that those questions do not tap into the same underlying construct after all.

A factor analysis can be used to assess whether the answers to different questions in a survey correlate and hence measure the same overarching construct. If this is indeed the case, the researcher may combine the answers to these questions into one construct or variable. For example, if the researcher's aim is to predict someone's L2 proficiency, the researcher cannot simply add all questions as predictor variables as some of these will highly correlate. As mentioned in Chapter 6, such situations of multicollinearity should be avoided as they will never allow the researcher to examine which of the different questions really influences L2 proficiency. When combining the correlating questions in one or more factors, however, the researcher can create a regression model without multicollinearity issues or, if there is only one factor left, choose to perform a correlation, a t-test, or an ANOVA instead.

For R users who need more information on factor analysis, we recommend Field et al., (2012, Chapter 17) or Levshina (2015, Chapter 18). For JASP, there is a link on the JASP website to a video on Exploratory Factor Analysis.

8.3.2 More advanced group comparisons

This book provides a basic introduction to group comparisons, but as mentioned in Chapter 7, there are many more versions of ANOVA that are regularly used in the field of Linguistics and AL. Many research designs are, for example, based on reaction time data or accuracy data in which participants are tested on the same factor repeatedly. A simple lexical decision task may contain a category of high and a category of low frequency words and additionally it may contain a category of pseudo-words. Such within-subjects designs allow the researcher to compare response times to different categories (high frequency, low frequency, and pseudo-words) within the same individual, but they also have the consequence that he or she is testing each individual multiple times. This thus leads to a datafile with multiple non-independent observations for each level of the dependent variable. In this case, a Repeated Measures ANOVA would be a good solution. In case additional between-group factors exist, a mixed design would be a better option as this is an advanced ANOVA that allows to combine the analysis of within-subjects variables with between-subjects variables. In case of several different dependent variables, a multivariate ANOVA could be chosen (also see Chapter 7).

We discussed that, at least for R users, there is an option to predict an interval dependent variable on the basis of both continuous and categorical variables using multiple linear regression models (also see Section 8.3.3), but there is also a version of ANOVA that allows the researcher to assess the effect of a nominal variable on an interval DV while controlling for the influence of other, to the researcher less important, interval variables. These other variables are called covariates and hence the test to assess this is called *Analysis of Covariance* (ANCOVA). Whereas JASP does not (yet) allow multiple regression with categorical variables, it does provide the option to run ANCOVAs with categorical and continuous predictor variables.

We have not discussed these additional ANOVA versions in detail here, but it should be noted that the underlying principles and the interpretation largely match those for the one-way and factorial ANOVA discussed here. For more details, please consult Field et al. (2012) for R, or Field (2009) for SPSS, which in these cases is similar to JASP: Chapter 11 (ANCOVA), Chapter 13 (repeated measures ANOVA), and/or Chapter 14 and 16 (Mixed designs and MANOVA).

8.3.3 Regression with both continuous and categorical predictors

The discussion of regression models in this book only covers the very basics. We did not really touch upon the difficulty of adding predictors to a multiple regression model. How to decide which predictor to add is a difficult question to answer and there are various methods that differ in many ways, with the two most well-known ones contrasting on whether we add all possible predictors and step by step remove those that have no effect (the backward method), or whether we start with one variable and add predictors step by step to arrive at the best fitting model (the forward method). Whatever method is used, the best model is usually one with the least possible predictors. Moreover, we would advise the researcher to only include predictors that can be expected to have an effect and whose effect can be explained based on theory or previous research. Also, we would recommend that the researcher start the analysis with the most important predictor. For R users, we added an example method using ANOVAs in Practical 5C and in the How To unit ('How To: Multiple Regression Analysis') on the companion website that can be used to assess whether an additional predictor makes your model better (based on Baayen, 2008, Chapter 6).

JASP currently only allows users to create multiple regression models with continuous predictors, but R users can create regression models with multiple continuous and/or categorical predictors. We did not discuss models with both continuous and categorical predictors in Part 1, but as the combination is rather common in research designs, the example of a regression model in 'How To: Multiple Regression Analysis' on the companion website contains both a continuous and a categorical predictor with two levels. One assumption in regression is, however, that categorical predictors have only two levels. There is a way to deal with categorical predictors that have more than two levels, but this is rather complicated. In the case of a categorical predictor with multiple levels, a similar problem arises as with the output of an ANOVA: we know there is a difference, but the regression model has not compared all three (or more) groups. In order to overcome this problem, we will have to use contrasts very similar to those introduced in Practical 6 for factorial ANOVAs. For a more detailed explanation of contrasts and how to create them in R, consult Field et al. (2012, Chapter 7) or Levshina (2015, Chapter 7).

8.3.4 Even more advanced regression models with mixed-effects

In Chapter 6, we introduced regression models that allow the researcher to predict the outcome of an interval dependent variable. Suppose, for example, that in a dataset we find that the effect of word frequency on reaction times is about 30 ms. To put it differently, participants are overall 30 ms slower to respond to low frequency compared to high frequency words. Even though such an analysis would constitute a useful summary of the dataset, it does not take into account potential differences between individuals or differences between words used in the experiment. Some people may overall be slower to press a button than others and some words in the experiment may generally evoke faster response times than other words. Similarly, we might expect different effects of our predictor variables per participant or per word. The effect of word frequency, for example, is likely to be larger for L2 learners than for native speakers and it is likely to be larger for those with relatively lower levels of L2 proficiency. A simple or multiple linear regression model cannot take this variation into account, but *mixed-effects regression* models can by, for example, allowing different intercepts for different participants and, if necessary, even allowing the slopes of an effect to vary across participants.

A very easy-to-read tutorial on mixed-effects analysis in R was written by Winter (2013). It would be advisable, however, to also consult more elaborate discussions and explanations of regression and mixed-effects regression analysis written by Baayen (2008). The field of statistics is still emerging and, even more recently, researchers have started using *generalized additive mixed models* (GAMMs) to also model non-linear relationships between predictors and a dependent variable. For a practical introduction to this advanced technique, the reader is referred to Wieling's tutorial (2018) or Winter and Wieling (2016).

8.3.5 A final remark on assumptions and distributions

Another important assumption for all parametric statistics is that the relationship between variables is linear, that is, the relationship follows a straight line (see Figure 3.1. for an example). For instance, in investigating the effect of motivation on language attrition, the assumption is that levels of motivation will have a linear effect: equal amounts of motivation will have equal effects on attrition. Advocates of CDST approaches to language development have argued that relationships between variables are non-linear and change over time. Applied to the example, this implies that at different moments in time, the same amount of motivation may have a different effect on language attrition. This also means that the more variables are involved in non-linear relationships, the less predictable development will be. Therefore, these researchers have argued that parametric statistics are of limited use for the evaluation of language development. Consequently, those who take a purely CDST approach to language development mostly make use of descriptive statistics and non-parametric statistics, in addition to non-linear statistics and longitudinal time-series analyses such as GAMMs. These analyses go well beyond the scope of this book, but it is important to realize that the choice of statistics is strongly related to the theoretical framework that is taken.

All common parametric statistics we have addressed in this book are based on the normal distribution (see Chapter 4). The essential underlying assumption is that any distribution in large populations will always follow the normal distribution (also called a Gaussian distribution). However, for many populations and for many variables this assumption is not correct. Think for instance of exam grades on a 10-point scale. In practice, the mean, mode, and median will not be around 5, which in most systems will mean a fail. For this variable, the data can always be expected to be skewed, so the hypothetical distribution deviates from the Gaussian distribution. Another frequent deviation of the normal distribution occurs in cases where we expect more than one peak (Binomial distribution). Several more advanced statistics therefore use distributions other than the Gaussian distributions, such as Poisson, Binomial, or Geometric distributions, leading to different calculations for inductive statistics, but also for descriptives (like SD). These statistics go well beyond the scope of this book, but it is good to know that the Gaussian distribution is definitely not the only standard.

8.4 Concluding remarks

After reading everything up to now, we hope that you will have reached a sufficient amount of understanding of statistics to read research reports and to critically approach what other researchers have done in terms of statistics. You will also have a rough idea about how to apply statistics to your own empirical work. It may still be wise, however, to consult a statistician when you are analysing (or even conducting) your own empirical studies.

Also remember that research goes beyond being able to analyse data: an important issue concerns the interpretation of your results in light of the bigger picture. In the activities, when a result was statistically significant, we have regularly asked whether you would consider the result *meaningful* as well. In most cases where we illustrated research with very few cases, your answer would correctly have been 'no'. If we want to say something sensible about the difference between two groups, it will be obvious that we need more than about ten participants per group! The number of participants needed to make an experiment meaningful depends on the β-error, the effect size, and the power of an experiment, as we explained in Chapter 4. There we saw that to demonstrate the existence of a small effect, the group size should be at least about 780 participants. In Applied Linguistics this is rather exceptional. We can only hope that the effects we are looking for are large effects, so that we can make do with about 30 participants per group to make it meaningful.

When the decision is made to conduct a certain study in such a way that the data can be analysed according to a certain statistical tradition, then there should be an awareness of the written and unwritten rules that this tradition brings. It is important to remember that if there is a significant effect, then this does not directly 'prove' your hypothesis; it only 'supports' it within the context of the study. As we explained in Section 4.8, we should interpret the concept of significance with great care for several reasons. Conversely, if there is no significant effect, then it should be clear that it is not acceptable to say that there is a difference, but it is also rather preliminary to claim that this 'proves' that there is no difference at all. The absence of a significant effect could be due to many factors, like limited power and/ or sample size, or a flaw in the study. The only time when we could even possibly begin to think about claiming to 'prove' something is after replicating the same outcome (once or maybe even more than once) and finding a significant effect in each replication.

Nevertheless, even when all conditions of a statistical study have been met, the validity is ensured, and the study is sufficiently reliable, the application of statistics is no more than one way of evaluating research data. Although it may be valuable, a statistical study is not the final answer to just any research problem. There are many ways to analyse data, which makes the choice of which statistics to use a subjective one. A researcher needs to give good arguments for why he or she has decided to use a specific statistical measure. And most importantly, careful interpretation of the research findings is required, which should be reflected in our reports. We should avoid the all-or-nothing interpretation of significance, always report the descriptive statistics as well as effect sizes and sample sizes (and preferably the power), and always be sufficiently tentative in our conclusion.

Finally, all the statistics discussed in this book are limited to the description of a synchronic situation, a measurement at one point in time. For the investigation of development over time, more advanced techniques and statistics are required that all have their own limitations and drawbacks. One severe limitation of quantitative studies in general is that they are strongly geared toward generalization of human behaviour. This becomes obvious when we realize that the very basis of statistical argumentation is created by the normal distribution. When the emphasis on generalization becomes too strong, it may obscure the variation of individuals in a sample. In CDST-based research it is precisely this variation that may reveal the true nature of language development. We cannot do without statistical methods if we want to make generalizations about human behavior, but parametric statistics do not possess the magical power to provide a solution to all research questions.

With this book we have tried to give a very basic introduction into the world of statistics. We hope you now feel confident enough to continue doing statistics by yourself.

We recommend you now perform Practical 7, which contains 8 problems and the corresponding datasets to answer these problems. You should be able to conduct all steps necessary to conduct the correct analyses and answer these research questions in a report that follows the conventions. The problems are also listed in Activity 8.1 below, so you can already answer some of the questions needed to determine the correct statistical test to use for each dataset.

ACTIVITY 8.1

For the following problems, provide the independent and dependent variable(s) and the scale of each variable. Then indicate which statistic would be most suitable to assess the results (first determine the nature of the problem and pick an appropriate perspective: assessing relationships, comparing means, predicting an outcome, or perhaps a combination of these; then choose the most appropriate statistic).

a. A researcher wants to investigate if motivation affects the pronunciation of English by Dutch learners. To investigate the possible effect of motivation on pronunciation, she makes recordings of 40 Dutch learners of English pronouncing English sentences. She then measures the difference in vowel length before voiced and voiceless obstruents (e.g. tap vs. tab). A questionnaire has determined that 20 of these students are highly motivated and 20 students are not very motivated to pronounce English correctly. Tip: the dependent is the DIFFERENCE in vowel length between the two phonological contexts.

b. A researcher wants to find out whether the age at which one starts to learn a foreign language is related to language proficiency. To investigate this, she finds 20 Polish learners of French who had all been learning French for 10 years. The starting age of these learners ranges from 1 to 20, in such a way that each starting age is included precisely once. All learners take a 50-item French proficiency test; the proficiency score is based on the number of correct items.

c. To investigate the effect of input on second language learning, 120 randomly selected Japanese learners of Hebrew are divided into two groups: one experimental group of 60 is isolated in a dark room and exposed to Hebrew television 24 hours a day (thereby achieving maximum exposure to Hebrew); one control group of 60 is not exposed to Hebrew. After two months, both groups are submitted to a 100-item Hebrew proficiency test; the proficiency score is based on the number of correct items.

d. Another experimenter is also interested in Japanese learners of Hebrew, but for ethical reasons, chooses to focus on the effect of age and not on the effects of exposure. He also tests 60 Japanese learners of Hebrew and equally subdivides them into three age groups: 11–30, 31–50 and 51–70. Does age influence proficiency?

e. A researcher is interested in the effects of social reinforcement on toddlers' motor skills. In an experiment, 56 three-year-old children have to take marbles from a vase and put them through a tiny hole into a box. The number of marbles is counted that have been put into the box after four minutes. The children are randomly attributed to two groups. In a 10-minute learning period preceding the experiment, the children in the first group are encouraged by smiles and words of praise. The children in the second group are not encouraged.

f. In what way would the experiment in e) change if, in addition, the researcher wanted to find out if social reinforcement equally affects the boys and girls in the experiment? Reconsider the number and type of variables accordingly, and decide on the type of analysis that would be required for this new situation.

g. To investigate the relation between active sports performance and stress a questionnaire is set up. The questionnaire determines if the participants are active sportswomen and sportsmen (Yes or No) and the degree of stress they experience in their daily lives (on a 3-point scale).

h. Imagine that a researcher partly replicates the study in b) and adds another variable to his design: whether the participants have ever visited France ('yes' or 'no'). He wonders whether he can predict proficiency score based on a visit and/or starting age.

PART
2 -R

PRACTICALS IN R/RSTUDIO

GETTING READY TO START USING R AND RSTUDIO

This section briefly explains why a student or researcher would want to use R (R Core Team, 2018) and/or RStudio (RStudio Team, 2016) as opposed to, for example SPSS, and how to download and open the program. The most important components are also briefly discussed and after this short introduction to R and RStudio, you can start doing your first calculations in the program by following the instructions in Practical 1.

R and RStudio are continuously being updated, so some features might be slightly different from what we present here. The versions used for this book are R version 3.5.1 and RStudio 1.1.456.

Why use R?

R (R Core Team, 2018) is becoming more and more popular, and is used for processing and analysing data as well as for creating graphics. A lot of analyses that can be done in R can also be done in SPSS, but R is more capable of working with larger datasets and performing more advanced statistical analyses. One of the most important benefits of R is that it is free software that runs on Windows, Mac, and a variety of UNIX platforms (e.g. Linux). R is free in that (1) you do not have to pay for it and (2) anyone can download and modify the code. Moreover, R is actively maintained and continuously improved and can be extended by add-on packages for specific purposes that are continuously created and made freely available by excellent programmers around the world.

When compared to a program such as SPSS or JASP, where the user primarily has to learn where to find the menu options for the specific calculations and analyses he or she wants to perform, R has one major disadvantage in that R users normally have to give R assignments in the form of codes or syntax. This might initially cause frustration, especially for students who are unfamiliar with programming and programming languages. R therefore has a steep learning curve, but is invaluable for most (graduate) students in

Linguistics, and especially those who would like to conduct quantitative research using large datasets. To make the learning curve slightly less steep and the focus on programming slightly less pronounced, we will make use of RStudio (RStudio Team, 2016), which is an interface that allows you to use R in a more user-friendly environment that is less focused on solely codes and syntax.

Download and start using R and RStudio

Go to the following website to download R: https://cran.r-project.org/. You will have to select a so-called CRAN mirror (i.e. distribution sites across the world that contain copies of the software) that is close to your location to minimize network load. The R website also provides links to online manuals, mailing lists, conferences, and publications.

The R installation also includes a standard graphical user interface (GUI), but we will be using RStudio. Go to the following website to download RStudio (the free version suffices): https://www.rstudio.com/products/rstudio/download/. RStudio provides you with an interface that, especially if you are just starting to learn R, gives you more overview of the program and its options. Once you have installed R and RStudio, start RStudio. You should be presented with something like this:

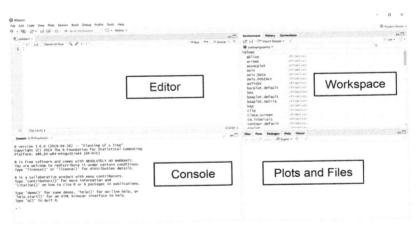

Figure R.1 Overview of RStudio and its different windows

Do not panic if you do not immediately see four windows as in Figure R.1, but select 'Show All Panes' by clicking on the ⊞ icon or select 'Panes' from the 'View' tab as depicted in Figure R.2 (or combine Ctrl+Shift+alt+0 or for MAC ^⇧0).

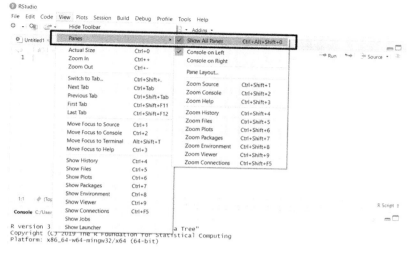

Figure R.2 Select *Show All Panes* in order to see the four windows (in case they do not show automatically)

When using RStudio, there are four windows that you will use (also see Figure R.1): in the **Console**, you can type commands and see output; in the **Editor** window, you can write collections of commands and store them as a file (script and/or output file) so you can use them later and neatly present your work to others; in the **Workspace** window, you can see all the active objects (environment tab), and the history tab shows you a list of commands used so far; finally, the **Plots and files** window shows all the files and folders in your default workspace (files tab) and any graphs you make (plots tab). The plots and files window additionally contains tabs with information about packages, a topic that will be discussed in more detail in Practical 1, as well as tabs linking to online help, manuals and tutorials (help tab), and local web content (viewer).

In the next section, Practical 1, we will use R as a simple calculator to get familiar with the program.

R PRACTICAL 1 EXPLORING R AND RSTUDIO AND ENTERING VARIABLES (CHAPTER 2)

In this practical, you will become familiar with the statistical program R and the RStudio interface. You will perform simple calculations, practise defining variables, enter data in R, and open and save a dataset. You will also learn to work with a package called 'R Markdown' (Allaire et al., 2018) that allows you to turn your calculations, analyses, and interpretations into an easy-to-read document. All this will prepare you for the statistical analyses we will be carrying out in the following practicals.

For this practical, we assume that you know how to open RStudio. It is thus important that you have read, carried out, and understood 'Getting ready to start using R and RStudio' before starting this practical.

Open RStudio, read the instructions, and enter the codes below (typed in grey in this font) to perform some simple calculations. The grey font will be used for all code and text that is either typed in or provided by RStudio.

Part A: Simple calculations, vectors, and scripts

We will eventually use R for more complex calculations, but we can also use it as a very simple calculator. If you, for example, want R to provide the sum of 11 and 11, you simply type the following code (11+11) in the (bottom-left) Console window of RStudio (also see Figure R.1 in 'Getting ready to start using R and RStudio') and it will immediately give you the answer (22).

```
> 11+11

[1] 22
```

The answer is preceded by [1] which simply indicates that this is the first (and, in this case also the only) element in your answer.

It is important to note that the commands can be entered into R by directly copying the examples from the book. The '>' character in the window is a prompt produced by R and is not part of the command, so you should not copy that character!

Let us say you want to work with the sum of this equation, in this case the number 22. You might just type 11 + 11 and that would definitely be doable for this single example, but you can also store your equation in a variable. In R this is done using the following operator: <- (or by using the equals sign (=)). In our example this would look as follows:

```
> x <- 11+11
```

When you ask R now to show x by simply typing x and pressing enter it will show the outcome:

```
> x
[1]  22
```

Our object x is now stored in memory, linked to the answer of our calculation, and can be used as such in all sorts of analyses and calculations. Try the following:

```
> 2*x
[1]  44
```

These variables can in turn also be stored in other variables:

```
> y <- 2*x
```

You will see that R keeps track of the variables you created and lists them as well in the workspace view in the top-right window.

Using objects in this way may seem a bit redundant when you only have one number and/or one object, but it is very useful when you are working with large datasets. Programming basically means that you get the computer to do the work for you, something we already did in the above examples, and this is even more important when you are working with large datasets. A regular dataset, in which you for example need to look at the sum of a person's scores, normally contains at least 20 and maybe even a million rows of data. It would be very cumbersome if we had to calculate the sum of scores for each individual person and this is exactly where a program like R can help.

Before looking at a real dataset, let us look at a sequence of elements of the same type, often referred to as a *vector* in R.

We will create our first vector, a simple list of numbers, using the c command (where c comes from concatenate or combine). Type in the following code (without the '>' character):

```
> List <- c(2,4,8,10,12)
```

What R has done now, is create an object called List containing 5 numbers. If you ask R to show the list, it will provide all numbers you entered previously:

```
> List
[1]  2  4  8  10  12
```

Now, R does not do anything else unless you ask R to do something. We could, for example, create a new list in which we add another number (say 14) without having to type all numbers in again. (Note that your vectors and their characteristics are again added in the workspace window.)

```
> List2 <- c(List, 14)
> List2
[1]  2  4  8  10  12  14
```

If you want to permanently add this number to the original List, type the following:

```
> List = List2
> List
[1]  2  4  8  10  12  14
```

Now List contains number 14 as well.

Vectors can be of several types in R and it is important to check whether R has selected the correct type for you. Therefore, you should always check the structure of an object in R by using str():

```
> str(List)
num [1:6]  2  4  8  10  12  14
```

In this case, R tells us that our object called List is numeric (num) and thus consists of numbers, and that there is one dimension with numbers containing a total of 6 numbers ([1:6]). If you simply want to know whether an object is numeric or not, you can also formulate a question to R:

```
> is.numeric(List)
[1]  TRUE
```

In the example above, R has confirmed that List is indeed numeric by answering our question with TRUE. A vector can be of various types and this answer constitutes another important type: the logical type (consisting of the values TRUE and/or FALSE). We know our List is not made up of the values true and false, but we can check this to be sure:

```
> is.logical(List)
```

```
[1] FALSE
```

If you need help on a particular function, type ?function without the parentheses. So, for example, type ?is.logical. Based on this command, R provides information on logical vectors in the 'Plots and files' window (the Help tab) in the bottom-right corner of RStudio (also see Figure R.1 in 'Getting ready to start using R').

In R, we can use [] brackets to ask for specific information from a data frame or vector. Try the following:

```
> List[3]
```

```
[1]  8
```

By adding [3] you are asking R to provide you with the third element in the vector, which in this case is number 8.

Note that the first element of a vector can be found using the number 1 as opposed to other programming languages in which the first element is considered to be 0.

It can be useful to create *scripts* in R containing a series of commands that can be executed in one go. This script is saved with a .R extension, but it is basically a simple text file that contains the commands you could also enter in the R Console. Any line or combination of lines from a script can be executed by selecting the line(s) and pressing Ctrl+Enter/Return or pressing the run button (see Figure R.3).

You can add the following code into an R script by typing it in the Editor window (the upper window in Figure R.3):

```
# anything preceded by a '#'sign is a comment and
will be ignored by R.

11+114     # sum

118-116    # minus

15*3       # multiply

15/3       # divide

2^3        # power

9^0.5      # square root
```

Now select the entire text you just added in the Editor window and press the key combination Ctrl+Return or press the run button (➡) also highlighted

Figure R.3 Select the script and press Ctrl+Return or the run button to execute the code

in Figure R.3. You will see in the Console window, which should resemble the one in Figure R.3, that R has executed all lines that contain code. When the cursor is on a specific line and you press Ctrl+Return, it will just run that specific line.

The above used script shows you how to perform simple calculations in R (do note that you need brackets as you would in any equation with several elements). It also shows that you can add text to explain your script by starting a line with the # character. RStudio automatically prints this additional information in a separate colour (i.e. green in the Editor window), making it easy for you to see what in your script constitutes code and what consists of textual information. Adding explanations to your script is very useful for others who might want to copy your script, but also for yourself. You often forget why you have done something with your data in that particular way and we highly recommend to add such information in the scripts that you use for your analyses. If, for whatever reason, you later on decide to change one specific part of the analyses (e.g. by deleting one item) you only have to add one line and a short explanation and run the entire script again to see your new and improved results.

We will soon open a bigger data frame to practise working with these codes in more detail. First, we will install R Markdown (Allaire et al., 2018), a package that you will be using to create easy-to-read HTML files containing all your answers to the R practicals.

Part B: Installing packages – R Markdown

As with any research, your analyses and your results should be reproducible. Luckily, some programmers have come up with a great way to show others what you did: R Markdown (Allaire et al., 2018). R Markdown is a *package*, a combination of code written by smart R users that they bundled in a package that can be downloaded and used by others.[1] The R Markdown package was written to allow you to show your code and your output, write accompanying text, and subsequently turn it into an easy-to-read document (HTML, Word, or PDF). We recommend that you create HTML files using R Markdown for every practical.

As mentioned before, there are countless packages that you can use and R Markdown is one of these packages. To use a package, you have to install it and then call or load it. Enter the code below in the Console window. The first line of code will install the package and the second line will load the package in the current session. Please note that you only have to install a package once. Therefore, you should add this code to the Console and not to your script in the Editor window. While it is loading you will see a red stop sign in the top right corner of the Console. This means that it is still working. When it has finished running the code, you will see a new ">" appear in the Console:

```
> install.packages("rmarkdown")
> library("rmarkdown")
```

With the library command you should not get a 'response' or 'output' from R because you are just asking R to open a library and load the code in the background, not to give you any information back.

Now that you have loaded the code for the R Markdown package, you will be able to create a new R Markdown file by clicking on the ⊡ ▾ icon in the top left and then select 'R Markdown' from the list (also see Figure R.4 below) or via 'New File' in the 'File' menu.

You will be presented with a dialog box as presented in Figure R.5. If R mentions that this requires a newer version to be installed, click OK to continue.

---

1 There are many different packages to help you perform functions, do certain tests, and help you make better plots. Some of them will be discussed, but please see this link for an overview of all the packages currently available: https://cran.r-project.org/web/packages/available_packages_by_name.html

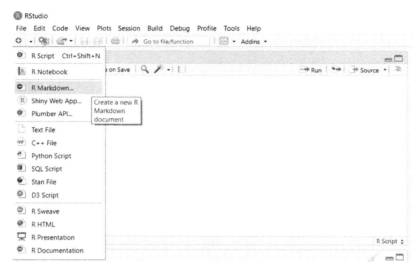

Figure R.4 Creating an R Markdown file (1)

Figure R.5 Creating an R Markdown file (2)

The dialog also visible in Figure R.5 provides you with the option to give the file a title (note that this is not the file name) and you can also specify the author of the document and the output type. Simply add your name under 'Author' and, as mentioned, we suggest using HTML for the output (PDF and Word are the other two available options). Do make sure that you save the RMD file, that is, the Markdown file, in the folder where you will perform your analyses from, otherwise you will have problems loading the data we will use later on. Click on 'File' and 'Save as' and save the file in a folder (e.g. R Practicals) where you will save all data and scripts for these practicals and name the file 'Prac1-yourinitials.rmd'.

Once we have created the file we see the output in the Editor that is also visible in R.6.

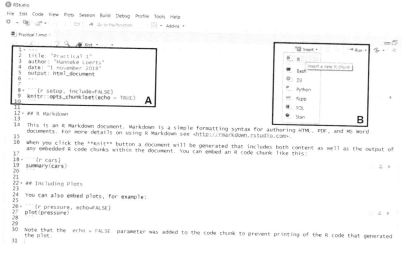

Figure R.6 Default R Markdown script with the header (box A) and a piece of code for the file to be made (marked by the square). Box B additionally shows how to create a new R chunk containing code

The header tells us the title, author, and date of the file (see box A in Figure R.6). Output tells us what form the output will be in, in this case HTML. Next we see a code to set some global options for the document and then, below box A in Figure R.6, a lot of text that can be deleted as we will create our own. There are three things important to remember when writing an R Markdown document:

1. # is used to indicate a header (## a smaller header and so on);

2. R code must be written between ```{r} and ``` as in the example below:

    ```{r}

    R code

    ```

    You do not necessarily have to type this: you can also click on 'Insert' to insert such a new R chunk (also see box B in Figure R.6).

3. 'Normal' text that you want in your Markdown, you can just write down.

Remove the text in the RMD file in the Editor window that is below the header and add 'Practical 1: test' as the header of the file (use ## Practical 1: test) and add a simple calculation below the header in an R chunk, for example:

    ```{r}

    20*10

    ```

Figure R.7 R Markdown script (left) and HTML output (right)

Finally, remember to save the RMD file (🖫) and to press 'knit' (🧶 **Knit**). This will call on the 'knitr' package (Xie, 2018), which will make sure all your code is executed and, together with the corresponding results, added to a first version of your HTML file. So, in Figure R.7 we see the RMD file (left) and the output in HTML in the viewer (right).

You can see that R Markdown turns your script into an easy-to-read HTML document, that can also be opened outside of RStudio, that contains the code as well as the answers. From now on, use R Markdown for all the practicals. For this practical you do not have to redo the assignments of Part A and you only have to include the code we will add from now on.

Part C: Importing and looking at data

You can download the data file 'Data-Practical1.csv' from the companion website. Make sure to save the file in the folder where you also saved your Markdown file, that is the file with the .rmd extension (e.g. the folder named 'R Practicals'). R by default works from the directory in which the program itself or, in our case, the RMD file is stored, and it is therefore crucial that you save all your files (data and scripts) in one folder!

1. STARTING THE REPORT

    a. This assignment will be added to the Markdown file containing your script and answers for Practical 1 that we just created, so add an informative header, for example 'Part C: Importing and Looking at Data' (remember to use ## to create a header).

    b. We will write code below the header, so you can start by typing ```{r} or by inserting a new R chunk by selecting the first option from the Insert drop-down list (🖫 Insert ▾ : also see Figure R.6).

    c. Let us first check if we are indeed working from the folder where we saved our scripts and data. You can get information on the current directory you are working in by typing getwd() in the R chunk (in the RMD file in the Editor window) as in Figure R.8, which is where you will type all your code from now on.

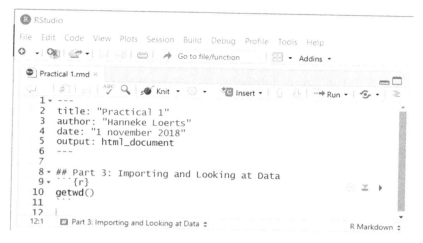

Figure R.8 R Markdown script with a line of code asking for the current working directory

If you run the chunk of code in Figure R.8, the directory you are currently working in will show up in the Console window as well as in your HTML output. Make sure this directory corresponds to the one where you saved the data that we will be working with.

2. OPENING AND INSPECTING A DATASET

You can open data files in many different formats in R, but many of them require packages. We will mostly use CSV (comma separated values) files, but you might sometimes come across other formats. In order to open an Excel file, for example, you would first have to install and load the 'readxl' package (Wickham & Bryan, 2018). This can be done as follows:

```
> install.packages("readxl")

> library("readxl")

> data <- read_excel("FileName.xlsx")
```

Note that you only have to install a package once through the Console. On the other hand, you will have to load a package every time you are going to use it (e.g. in your Markdown file).

It is also possible to import SPSS files in R. In order to do so, you need the 'memisc' package (Elff, 2018), and to import a SAV file you need the following line of code:

```
> data <- as.data.set(spss.system.file("FileName.sav"))
```

Please note that there are almost always several different packages available for doing what you want to do. Googling will usually help you make a well-informed decision.

While Excel and SPSS files require packages, .csv (comma separated values file) and .txt (tab-delimited text file) formats can be opened without installing packages and we would recommend that you use data in one of these formats. You can save a file as a .txt or .csv format from Word, Excel, or most other text editors you may be using.

a. The data file we want to open is a CSV file called 'Data-Practical1. csv'. We can do this by adding the following code in an R chunk (remember: without the ">"):

```
> Practical1 <- read.csv(file="Data-Practical1.csv",
head=TRUE,sep=";")
```

Here, we have created an object called 'Practical1' to include our file. The command to read a CSV file is read.csv and the arguments behind it simply refer to the actual name of the file, and to the fact that the first row contains labels (header names) and that all columns are separated by a semicolon.

Cannot open the file? Maybe you did not save it in the current working directory? Check what files are in your current working directory using the following code:

```
> dir()
```

If it is not in the list, locate the file on your computer and copy-paste it to the working directory.

b. Now that we have imported data into R, we need to check whether our data have been imported correctly. Using the head() function, we can see the first six/seven rows of our dataset. Alternatively, tail() will show us the last part of the dataset.

```
> head(Practical1)
```

```
> tail(Practical1)
```

If we want to see more than the first 7 lines, for example the first 10 lines, we can add the number of lines we would like to see as follows:

```
> head(Practical1, 10)
```

c. For any variable, or file, we can ask R what type of data it is.

```
> class(Practical1)
```

```
[1] "data.frame"
```

When data is stored in a data frame, this means it consists of rows and columns. You can use `dim()` to see the number of rows and columns the dataset has respectively (i.e. the *dimensions*). You can use `summary()` to get a better feel for the distribution of variables and to see whether there is any missing data (NA for 'not available' in R).

d. By using the functions mentioned above, check the number of rows and columns as well as whether the dataset has missing values and remember to add the code in your Markdown file.

This dataset has no missing data, which is good. The function `names()` will show you what variable names there are in your data. It will provide you with a character vector of the columns.

```
> names(Practical1)

[1] "participant" "age" "gender" "profsc"
```

We now have a better feel for the data and what it looks like, but we are still missing crucial information that is needed in order to fully interpret and analyse this dataset.

Use `str()` to look at the structure of the data:

```
> str(Practical1)
```

R will give you the following information:

```
'data.frame': 29 obs. of 4 variables:
$ participant: int 1 2 3 4 5 6 7 8 9 10 ...
$ age: int 16 20 24 22 18 14 15 17 19 21 ...
$ gender: int 1 2 1 2 1 2 1 2 1 2 ...
$ profsc: int 91 58 52 45 78 88 90 86 83 62 ...
```

R tells us that Practical1 is a data frame with 29 observations of 4 variables, and the variables are also listed. For each variable, R has specified the type of variable and listed the first 10 observations in the file. So, the first row of the file is Participant number 1, who is 16 and whose gender is '1' and who scored 91 on a proficiency test (remember that you can also use `head()` to read the first row horizontally).

3. DETERMINING VARIABLE TYPES AND ADDING LABELS

One problem with the current data frame is that R has read the file as containing only numbers, which is true, and it has therefore assumed that all variables are of the data type 'integer'. Integers are of the numeric type, which simply means that they are related to numbers. The only real difference between integer and numeric is that integer variables are whole values while numeric variables contain decimals. For this introductory course, it is not necessary to distinguish between numeric and integer values. Moreover, R makes sure your data type is stored correctly as either numeric or integer.

a. Now realize that not all variables in the data frame relate to actual numbers. We have used numbers to label different levels as for example for the variable *gender*. We have to tell R that *gender* does not relate to numbers, but that it is actually a factor, a nominal variable with numeric labels for the two levels. R needs to know where to find this variable and we use `Practical1$gender` to tell R that from the dataset Practical1 we want to use the variable *gender*.

```
> Practical1$gender <- as.factor(Practical1$gender)
```

The code above tells R to take the variable *gender* from the data frame 'Practical1' and regard it as a factor.

b. If you now use the `str()` code again, R will correctly report that *gender* is a factor with 2 levels: '1' and '2'. We currently do not know what the numbers '1' and '2' refer to, but this is crucial for an analysis comparing the genders and their proficiency scores.

```
> Practical1$gender <- factor(Practical1$gender,
> levels = c(1,2),
> labels = c("Female", "Male"))
```

The above function can be used to do everything we want in one go, as it tells R that we want to assign values to the variable *gender*, to make a factor of this variable, that it has the levels 1 and 2, and that these levels correspond to the labels Female and Male. In R we can create value labels using `factor()` and `ordered()`. Factor is used for nominal data whereas ordered is used for ordinal data. As *gender* is nominal, we will use `factor()`.

c. Before submitting this first practical, check whether all variables in the dataset are stored as the correct type. Use `str()` and, if necessary, turn variables into factors (`as.factor()`) or numeric variables (`as.numeric()`). After checking the data types, end your RMD file showing the structure of your final dataset:

```
> str(Practical1)
```

d. Run your code in the Console in the Markdown file and press 'knit' (Knit) to create an updated HTML file.

4. SAVING THE DATASET

Remember to also save your dataset, as it has been changed slightly. You can save the file in various formats, even in an Excel format, but then some information will be lost, such as the fact that we want the variable *gender* to be regarded as a factor and not, as is the default in R for numbers, as interval.

As we will use this dataset again in R during the next practical, we will save our file as one possible R format file (RDS) that will remember our changes using the following code:

```
> saveRDS(Practical1, file="Practical1.rds")
```

Please note that an RDS file can only be opened from R. Do you want to have a look at your data outside of R (and thus also without the properties we just added)? You can use write.csv() to create a CSV file of your data as follows:

```
> write.csv(Practical1, file="Practical1.csv")
```

Highly recommended tip

If you want more practice, we recommend using 'swirl' (Kross et al., 2017). This is an interactive package that lets you learn R. Simply enter the following commands and you are good to go:

```
> install.packages("swirl")
> library("swirl")
> swirl()
```

R PRACTICAL 2 DESCRIPTIVE STATISTICS (CHAPTER 3)

In this practical you will become familiar with some more functions of R. You will use the data that you also used during Practical 1 to perform some first analyses involving descriptive statistics. Please note that one of the implicit assignments in Practical 1 was to change all variables to the appropriate type (assignment C-3c). If you have not turned *participant* into a factor, please make sure to correct this before continuing to work on that dataset during this second practical.

Part A

1. CREATE A MARKDOWN FILE and OPEN THE DATA IN R

   a. Start a new Markdown file, name it Prac2-yourinitials.rmd, and save it in the folder where you want to work from (e.g. the 'R Practicals' folder we used for Practical 1). Remember that you need to save your Markdown in the folder where you also save(d) the data you will be using.

   b. Delete unnecessary text and add an informative heading for the sections and questions using #-signs (e.g. '## Part A' followed by '### 1. Open the data', '#### 1a' and so on), to return an output similar to the HTML one on the right in the viewer of Figure R.9.

   c. Open the RDS file we saved last time by using the following code:

   ```
   > Practical1 <- readRDS(file="Practical1.rds")
   ```

   As was also mentioned in Practical 1, please remember that you want both code and answers to be added to the RMD file for later use, so you will add everything in your RMD file (and not in the Console window!). In order to execute your line of code, you have to select it and run it by either pressing Ctrl+R, by clicking the run button (➡), or by pressing the run current chunk button next to your line of code (▶) (also see Figure R.9). They will all provide the same results, that is the answer to your code, so choose the one you find most convenient.

   d. Finally, remember to save the RMD file (🖫) and to press 'knit' (🔨 Knit) to create a PDF or HTML file. The knitted file should resemble the one in the viewer shown on the right of Figure R.9.

Figure R.9 R Markdown script (left) with the corresponding HTML output (right) after knitting the file. The script can be executed in various ways. You can select the code and press Ctrl+Return, you can click the run button ( ), or you can click on the 'run current chunk button' next to your line of code (▶). The output is obtained by pressing the knit button right above the script (Knit)

2. FIRST CALCULATIONS: DESCRIPTIVE STATISTICS

a. First, add an informative heading.

b. During this first step, we want to find the frequency of occurrence of each age. This can be done creating a `table()` for the variable *age*. Do note that R will need to know to which dataset the variable *age* belongs and we do that using the dollar sign $. So, in this case our dataset is called 'Practical1' and it contains *participant, age, gender* and *profsc* as variables. By writing 'Practical1$age', we are telling R that we want to work with the variable *age* from the file Practical 1.

So, use `table()` in combination with the above instructions and find out which age occurs most often. Do not forget to answer your question as text below your code in the Markdown file.

3. MORE DESCRIPTIVES: EXPLORING FREQUENCIES

a. Now we want to find the mean, the median, the range, and the standard deviation of the proficiency score in your data. The following functions can be used to calculate these:

```
> mean(File$VariableName)
```

```
> median(File$VariableName)
```

```
> range(File$VariableName)
```

```
> sd(File$VariableName)
```

Unfortunately, there is no built-in function to calculate modes in R. Therefore, one option is to use a function that tabulates the scores and subsequently takes the maximum score:

```
> which.max(tabulate(File$VariableName))
```

Table R.1 General guidelines for reporting decimals according to APA standards

Numbers	Round to	Example
Less than 0.001	As many decimals as needed	0.0003
0.001 – 0.1	3 decimals	0.027
0.1 – 10	2 decimals	2.52
10 – 100	1 decimal	16.7
> 100	Whole numbers	2137

You do not have to understand this formula at this point, but it is important to realize that you will repeatedly come across problems like these. We were definitely not the first to find out that R does not have a built-in mode-function and there is no need to reinvent the wheel. Often, you can find the code you need through a quick (or sometimes long and disappointing) Google search.

To make sure that you understood what you have done, briefly report on your findings in the Markdown file. Please keep in mind that we use a dot (and not a comma) to report decimals (e.g. 0.5) and that you do not always have to report all decimals, as can also be seen in Table R.1.

b. Also find and report the minimum age, the maximum age, the mean age, and the standard deviation. Minimum and maximum can be calculated as follows:

```
> min(File$VariableName)
```

```
> max(File$VariableName)
```

Or using:

```
> range(File$VariableName)
```

c. What is the most frequently occurring proficiency score?

4. GETTING TO KNOW THE DATA: RELATIONSHIPS

a. Imagine that the dataset concerns age of acquisition instead of age, and that a researcher who gathered these data is interested in finding out whether the age at which someone started learning an L2 is related to the proficiency they obtained in that language. A scatterplot is normally a good place to start examining such a question. Use the formula below to create such a scatterplot in which Variable1 will be plotted along the x-axis (horizontal) and Variable2 along the y-axis (vertical).

```
> plot(File$Variable1, File$Variable2)
```

Your labels are now not really nice, but you can easily change that using `xlab` and `ylab` as in the code below. Additionally, this formula adds a title above the graph using `main`.

```
> plot(File$Variable1, File$Variable2, xlab="label
x-axis", ylab="label y-axis", main="Title")
```

b. Type a caption **below** the scatterplot (e.g. Figure 1. Scatterplot showing the relationship between Age of Acquisition and Proficiency). Note that for APA-style papers, captions for figures go **below** the figure, but captions for tables go **above** the table!

The are some fancy, more complicated ways to add captions in R Markdown, but a simple way would be to add a line below the code for a plot with your caption. Putting text between double asterisks (`**text**`) will make it bold when you knit the file. If you want italics somewhere, simply put the text between single asterisks (`*text*`).

So, `**Figure X** Your caption goes here` will become the following in your knitted document:

Figure X Your caption goes here

c. At face value, do you think there is a relationship between the two variables?

5. GETTING TO KNOW THE DATA: COMPARING GROUPS

a. Now we want to find out the mean proficiency scores and the standard deviations for the male and the female subjects. There are multiple ways of getting to the answer to this question, but one easy-to-use function in R is the `aggregate()` function below.

```
> aggregate(Score~Factor, File, mean)
```

Using the above formula, you will get means for the Score (proficiency in this case) grouped by a Factor (gender in this case) as the tilde (~) basically means 'depends on'. In Chapter 4 of Part 1, we discuss this dependency relationship in more depth. Try to fill in the above formula and report on your results.

b. Which group has higher proficiency scores, the male or the female participants?

c. Which group scored more homogeneously? You can use the formula above to answer this question, but you need to change the value that will be reported by the formula.

d. Now create a boxplot of the proficiency scores of the female and male participants separately. We again use a formula where the dependent variable depends on the independent variable using the tilde-operator (~). Try to adapt the formula below to create the boxplot you want and remember that you have to use exactly those names that are used in the Practical1 file for your variables. You can use `str(File)` or `names(File)` to check the column names in your file.

```
> boxplot(Variable on the y-axis ~ Variable on
the x-axis, data=Your dataset, main="Title of your
boxplot", xlab="Label for the x-axis", ylab="Label
for the y-axis")
```

Add a clear and explanatory caption **below** your figure.

e. Compare your boxplot with the descriptive statistics. Can you find out how the boxplot is built up and what the different points of the boxplot signify? Explain this in your Markdown file (hint: there are 4 quartiles). You can also use Google to find out the answer.

Part B

1. ENTERING DATA MANUALLY

a. Enter the following 4 datasets in R, and provide the mean, the mode, the median, the range, and the standard deviation. As there is very little data in these datasets, you can enter them manually using the c command we also used in Practical 1 to create our vector called List. You can simply name the variables 'a', 'b', 'c', and 'd'.

    a. 3, 4, 5, 6, 7, 8, 9

    b. 6, 6, 6, 6, 6, 6, 6

    c. 4, 4, 4, 6, 7, 7, 10

    d. 1, 1, 1, 4, 9, 12, 14

You can use the formulas we used before (e.g. `mean(File$Varia-bleName)`), but you can also find packages that help you to report on several descriptive statistics for multiple variables at once (except for the mode again), such as the `describe(File$VariableName)` function from the 'psych' package (Revelle, 2018). If you choose this latter option, remember to install the package once (this can be done through the Console) and use the `library("psych")` code to load the package. Only after loading it will you be able to use the functions from the package, so the second line of code below should be added to your Markdown file:

```
> install.packages("psych")

> library("psych")
```

After installing and loading the package, the `describe(File$Var-iableName)` function will provide you with the most important descriptives for the variable you enter in the code, including information on the number of variables and participants, the most common measures of central tendency (mean, median, and mode), and measures for dispersion (*SD* and range).

   b. Do you agree with R's calculation of the mode for variable 'a'?

Part C

We will use a larger sample of data containing information on the motivation to learn French and the score on a French Proficiency test. The data can be downloaded either as a ready-to-use R data file (Practical2C.rds) with correct variable types and structures or as the original CSV file (Data-Practical2C.csv) in which variable types and labels still have to be added and altered. Please use the CSV file in case you are up for a challenge. In case you already had some difficulty, feel free to use the RDS file and continue with step 1b.

1. LOAD THE FILE INTO R

   a. Save the CSV file in the folder you are currently working in and load it using the code we also used in Practical 1. Check the structure and the data itself and make sure all variables are in the correct format and that the labels below are added to the levels of the variable *Motivation*. Note that you should choose between using `ordered()` or `factor()` here (see Practical 1 for examples and details). The labels for *Motivation* are:

     1=very low; 2=low; 3=neutral; 4=high; 5=very high

   b. Save the RDS file in the folder you are currently working in (if you have completed step 1a) and open it using the code we used before. Check the structure of the file (`str()`) and look at the data itself to get a feel for the data.

2. DESCRIPTIVE STATISTICS

   a. Find out the mean proficiency score, the median, and standard deviation for the group of students as a whole and then for the different motivation groups. In order to do this for the different motivation groups, we have to split up the file by *Motivation* and there are multiple ways to do that, but the simplest might be to use the aggregate formula we used before as well.

```
> aggregate(Score~Factor, File, mean)
```

Another option that we will use more in subsequent practicals (and that might be necessary here to find the modes) is to select data based on one level of a factor. You can, for example, select a high motivation group as follows:

```
> High <- Practical2C$Proficiency[Practical2C$
Motivation =="high"]
```

By using the above formula, you are asking R to create a subset called 'High' that consists of the variable *Proficiency* from the file Practical2C, but only the scores for the data points for which motivation equals (==) 'high'.

Not sure what the names of the levels were? Check them as follows:

```
> levels(Practical2C$Motivation)
```

Once you have calculated all the scores, it is important to also report them in an informative way. In order to create a table in R Markdown, you should copy, and potentially expand, the text below and then replace the x's by the actual values you calculated. Note that this should not be added in your Markdown file as code within an R chunk, but just as plain text.

```
value | Overall | very low | low | neutral | high |
very high

 - | - | - | - | - | - | -

mean | x | x | x | x | x | x

mode | x | x | x | x | x | x

median | x | x | x | x | x | x

sd | x | x | x | x | x | x
```

Now put an informative caption **above** the table.

b. Make a boxplot with the different motivation groups. Judging from the boxplot, do you think the groups will differ from one another? Report on your findings.

3. CHECKING THE NORMAL DISTRIBUTION

a. To check whether proficiency has a normal distribution, create a histogram using the following code:

```
> hist(FileName$Variable, prob=TRUE, xlab="Label
for x-axis")
```

If you were to use the above code without `prob=TRUE`, you would get a histogram with the raw frequencies that together add up to the total number of occurrences in the dataset. By adding the code, we make sure to plot probabilities instead of counts. Probability, or density plots, are often more useful when looking at distributions as they are unaffected by the number of bins or bars used.

b. Add a distribution curve to your histogram by adding the following line directly beneath your histogram function:

```
> curve(dnorm(x, mean=mean(FileName$VariableName),
sd=sd(FileName$VariableName)), add=TRUE)
```

By looking at the histogram, does the data seem to follow a normal distribution?

c. We also want the values for skewness and kurtosis to determine whether proficiency is normally distributed. We can use the 'psych' package and its `describe()` function to check those values. If you have not used this package before to calculate descriptives, please use `install.packages("psych")` in the Console once to install the package. Remember to load the package in your Markdown file using `library()` if you have not already done so.

Do the values for skewness and kurtosis deviate from zero and, if so, are they positive or negative? What does that tell you about the skewness and kurtosis? (Also try to link these values to the shape of the histogram you just created.)

d. Usually, you want to know whether your different groups are normally distributed by themselves. Carry out step 3a – 3c for the different motivation groups. *Hint: use the groups we created for motivation under 2a of Part C.*

R PRACTICAL 3 CALCULATIONS USING R (CHAPTER 4)

In this practical you will review some descriptive statistics and you will learn to get a first impression about the normality of a distribution. Finally, you will do some first 'real' statistics.

Part A

In the file 'Data-Practical3a.csv', you will find the results of the English Phonetics I exam of the student cohort 2000 in the English Department in Groningen. The scores are specified per question (Q1, Q2, etc.), and we are going to assume that these scores are measured on an *interval* scale. Since these are the real results, we have replaced the names by numbers for discretion. The questions below all refer to this file. Create one Markdown file containing all your answers and in which you also show and explain informative tables and graphs. We know that some would prefer to just copy-paste code and move on to the next question, but please always also answer the questions *based on* the output by reporting on it in the text you add in the Markdown.

1. IMPORTING DATA AND CREATING A MARKDOWN FILE

a. Download the data from the website and save the CSV file to the folder in which you will work.

b. Open RStudio and create a new Markdown file with an appropriate name and save it in the same folder as where you just saved the CSV file (we used 'R Practicals' previously).

c. Load the CSV file using the same technique you used in the previous practicals.

d. Check the data using functions such as `head()` and make sure that factors are factors and interval variables are interval variables using functions such as `str()` and, if needed, `as.factor()`, `as.numeric()` or `as.integer()`. Remember that we do not really differentiate between numeric and integer.

2. DESCRIPTIVES AND GRAPHS FOR GROUPS

a. In Practical 2, you calculated mean values etc. for different groups. You can use the `aggregate()` function to calculate each value separately for each group, but you can also create subsets of the data and use the `describe()` function from the 'psych' package (Revelle, 2018). We did that for the different motivation groups in Practical 2C (remember that the package will have to be loaded in this new Markdown as well). To show you that there are various ways to create subsets, we will use a slightly different formula here to create separate groups (but you can also adapt the one we used in Practical 2). This might initially seem confusing, but we want to show you different formulas for the same thing as we want you to understand that there are different ways to reach the same destination. Using subset(), you can select only that group that has the specific level you mention (below we create one for 1A) from your dataset:

```
> G1A <- subset(Practical3A, group == "1A")
```

Use the above formula to create a subset for each group.

Calculate the mean, max, min, range, and *SD* per group, using the *TOTAL* score and report in a table in your Markdown file all the scores in the same way as we did in Practical 2. Do not forget to add a caption above the table and answer the following questions in your report below the table: (1) Which group seems to have performed best? (2) And which group performed most homogeneously?

b. Which teacher (A/B) performed best? (Make sure that the variable *teacher* is a factor!)

c. Create a boxplot of the scores (based on *TOTAL*) for both teachers using the formula we used in Practical 2. Do not forget to name your boxplot and its axes.

3. CHECKING FOR NORMALITY

a. Create a histogram of *TOTAL* score with a normal distribution line and an informative title as you did in Practical 2.

b. Do these results approximately follow the normal distribution (at face value when looking at the histogram)?

4. USING *Z*-SCORES

a. Calculate and report on the *z*-scores of the *TOTAL* scores of the following students: 11, 33, 44, and 55. You can calculate *z*-scores in R by using scale(). So in our case it would be something like:

```
> scale(FileName$VariableName, center = TRUE,
scale = TRUE)
```

This calculates *z*-scores for the whole column and will also print all *z*-scores in your output. You can use this list and look for the correct students, but you can also add the *z*-scores to your existing dataset in a column called *z*-score, and subsequently create subsets as we did at the beginning of this practical to find the 4 students. You can create the new column as follows:

```
> FileName$zscore <- scale(FileName$
VariableName, center = TRUE, scale = TRUE)
```

5. PREPARING FOR INDUCTIVE STATISTICS

a. So far you have only done the descriptive statistics. What is your first impression about the difference between the groups of the two teachers?

b. We will now go through a first example of *hypothesis testing*. The question we want to answer is whether there is a difference between the total scores of the students of teacher A and the total scores of the students of teacher B. We are going to find out if your impressions in a. are correct. What is the null hypothesis belonging to the research question?

c. The statistical test we will carry out to test the null hypothesis is the independent samples *t*-test. 'Independent' refers to the fact that the two samples we took (from the two teachers) are not related (there are different students in each group). We will discuss this test later on in more detail; this is just to give you some first hands-on experience. The independent samples *t*-test that we will be using is a parametric test. We will thus first have to check for normality.

In Practical 2, we already saw that the closer to 0 the values of skewness and kurtosis are, the closer they are to the normal distribution. Apart from this, it would also be nice to know how close they are to a normal distribution, or, in other words, whether the values of skewness and kurtosis are close enough to the normal distribution. For this we will use the stat.desc() function from the package 'pastecs' (Grosjean & Ibanez, 2018) and we will calculate it for the *TOTAL* score. Make sure you install this package in your Console, and open it in your Markdown file using the library() function. Then fill in the following:

```
> stat.desc(FileName$VariableName, basic=FALSE,
norm=TRUE)
```

Apart from seeing the values for skewness and kurtosis you also see values for Skew.2SE and Kurt.2SE. These are the values of skewness and kurtosis divided by two times the standard error (*SE*) of the distribution (note that this is different from the *SE* of the mean). You do not have to know exactly how this works, but for samples that are quite small (up to say, 30), we can assume that values of Skew.2SE and

`Kurt.2SE` between -1 and 1 are close enough to a normal distribution (also see Field et al., 2012, p. 175). For samples that are a bit larger (say, between 30 and 200), it is fine if they stay within the -1.29 and 1.29 range. We have a sample of 130 students, so for the group as a whole it is fine if the values are between -1.29 and 1.29. What can you say about skewness and kurtosis now?

If we are interested in comparing groups, we should actually calculate these values for the groups (here: teachers) separately. Instead of making subsets, you can also use the following code:

```
> by(Filename$DependentVariable, FileName$
Independent  Variable,  stat.desc,  basic=FALSE,
norm=TRUE)
```

Can we say that the data of the two teachers are normally distributed?

6. CHECKING FOR NORMALITY USING A TEST

One of the assumptions of the *t*-test is that the data are distributed according to the normal distribution. You could of course simply use `stat.desc()`, as we have just done, and look at the `Skew.2SE` and the `Kurt.2SE` values. You may, however, want to know what the chance is that you go wrong in assuming the normal distribution. This can be established by applying the Shapiro-Wilk test. Remember that it is important that the distribution of each group is normal, rather than the distribution of the scores of the groups taken together.

a. We will thus want to test normality by comparing our group's distribution to the normal distribution. What is the null hypothesis for this comparison?

b. Note that we need to check the distribution of the different groups separately and we will use the Shapiro-Wilk test. You can adapt the following code for this:

```
> shapiro.test(File$Variable)
```

Do note that you will need to run this test for both teacher groups! With the above code, we are testing whether the distribution for each group is different from the normal distribution. If the significance value is (well) above .05, then you can assume that the data are normally distributed. In this case, do the data show a normal distribution?

Which method is best to check for normality?

We have created histograms, looked at skewness and kurtosis values, and performed a test to compare our data's distribution to the normal distribution, but which of these methods is best? The answer to this question very much depends on the sample size of your dataset.

It is always a good idea to start with visualizing your data, and a histogram of the data (per group!) can often be helpful to check whether their shapes approximately follow the bell-shaped curve of the normal distribution. While this method is the best option for rather large data-sets ($n > 200$), histograms are likely to look non-normal for small datasets with, for example, only 15 learners per group (also see Table R.2). A good second method would be to look at the values for skewness (i.e. the symmetry of the curve) and kurtosis (i.e. the pointedness) and check how much they deviate from zero. If you divide the value of skewness by the Standard Error (*SE*) of skewness, and the value of kurtosis by the *SE* of kurtosis, you will get a standardized value that is like a *z*-score, which is often more appropriate than the regular skewness and kurtosis values to evaluate normality (e.g. Field et al., 2012). In R we can calculate measures that represent skewness and kurtosis divided by twice the *SE* (`Skew.2SE` and `Kurt.2SE`). Generally, these scores should be below 1 to be considered normal (at least for small sample sizes). The easiest way to obtain these values in R is by using the `stat.desc()` function from the package 'pastecs' (Grosjean & Ibanez, 2018) as we did in assignment 5 above.

As you now know, you can also perform a Shapiro-Wilk for each group and assess whether these are non-significant to ascertain that your data are normally distributed. Note that the value and significance of Shapiro-Wilk is also provided by the `stat.desc` function used above as `normtest.W` and `normtest.p`, respectively. In general, it is best to use the Shapiro-Wilk to check for a normally distributed dataset. However, when sample sizes are large, the Shapiro-Wilk test is often too strict and it is very easy to get a significant value for this test. What is advised with samples larger than 200 is to have a good look at the histograms, for example (also see Table R.2).

It is always important to use various ways to check your data for normality and it should be clear now that the correct way of testing normality highly depends on your sample size. Table R.2 will give a rough guideline on how to check for normality with different sample sizes.

Table R.2 Rough guideline on how to check for normality

Check	Samples < 30	Samples > 30 and < 200	Samples > 200
Histogram	Good to check, but will probably not look normally distributed	Good to check	Very important to check because it will give you the best information
Skewness and kurtosis	-	Between -1 and 1	-
Skew.2SE and Kurt.2SE	Between -1 and 1	Between -1.29 and 1.29	-
Normality tests	Shapiro-Wilk	Shapiro-Wilk	-

7. CHECKING FOR EQUALITY OF VARIANCE

Another important assumption is that there is equality of variance between the groups. This means that the standard deviation in one group should not be drastically different from the standard deviation in another group. A good rule of thumb is usually to make sure that the largest standard deviation is not more than twice as big as the smallest standard deviation.

a. First, we will look at the standard deviations for the different groups. Use sd() to calculate the standard deviation for each group. What are the standard deviations for the two teacher groups? Do you think these groups are equal in their variance, using the rule of thumb?

b. Next, we will conduct Levene's test of Homogeneity. What would be the H_0 in this case?

c. We will need to install and call the 'car' package (Fox & Weisberg, 2011). Finally, we can conduct the test using the following code, where your dependent *TOTAL* score is now dependent on the different groups (the factor, that is, the teachers) in your dataset:

```
> leveneTest(Score ~ Factor, data=YourDataSet)
```

The *F* value seen in the R output is the outcome of the Levene test (similar to the ANOVAs *F*-value that will come back in later practicals) and the most important part for our purposes is expressed under Pr(>F). If this value, that is, the significance level, is smaller than .05, you can NOT assume equal variances. If it is bigger than .05, you can assume equal variances.

In this case, are your groups equal in variance?

8. PERFORMING THE *T*-TEST

Checking the assumptions first is important as they determine which type of test we can use. If your data are not normally distributed, you need to switch to a *Mann-Whitney* test, which is the non-parametric alternative to the parametric version of the independent samples *t*-test. If there is no equality of variance, you can still use the parametric *t*-test, but you will have to adjust the test a bit to account for the unequal variances (more details will follow below).

a. The *t*-test compares the scores of the two groups, so that you can estimate the significant difference between them, that is whether the null hypothesis should be rejected or not. In R we conduct a *t*-test using t.test() as in the code below.

```
> t.test(y ~ x, var.equal = TRUE/FALSE)
```

In the above formula, you will recognize the ~-operator to signify that there is a numeric (y) dependent variable or outcome of which the result may depend on a binary (x) variable, factor, or predictor. Which variable is the factor or predictor variable, that is the *independent*? And which one is the dependent variable?

The final part (var.equal = TRUE/FALSE) of the code can be added to specify equal variances. If Levene's test was significant, and equal variances cannot be assumed, the var.equal should be set to FALSE. If, however, equal variances can be assumed, you can add TRUE instead. If we leave it off completely then the default FALSE is used, which is mostly considered to be the more conservative and hence the better option anyway.

The output shows us some interesting numbers, but it also contains some information that is currently redundant. We see the *p*-value, which is the chance of incorrectly rejecting the null hypothesis (the chance of getting an alpha error!). If you added var.equal = FALSE, you will notice that the degrees of freedom (*df*) is a funny number because it is 127.08. Do not worry about this: it is due to the way it is calculated in R (using Welch's test for unequal variances). What is the chance of incorrectly rejecting the null hypothesis?

b. What is the conclusion you would draw with regard to the research question in 2b? Would you reject the H_0? What is the chance of incorrectly rejecting the H_0, and what does this mean? Is your conclusion about the H_0 in line with what you would expect from the descriptives?

Performing (different versions of) the *t*-test in R

You may sometimes also use a slightly different formula to perform exactly the same *t*-test:

```
> t.test(y1, y2, var.equal = TRUE/FALSE)
```

In this second version, the ~ is replaced by a comma and the choice of one or the other depends on the way in which your data is formatted. If your data has one column for the IV distinguishing groups and one column for the DV scores (the more common long format), then you should use the first version with the ~-operator. If, however, your data contains one column with all scores for group 1 and another column containing all scores for group 2 (also known as the wide format), such as y1 being the scores for teacher A and y2 containing the scores for teacher B, you should use a comma as in the second version instead.

We have now practised the most common version of the *t*-test, but you will only have to change the code slightly to perform one of the other versions. If your aim is to perform a paired samples *t*-test, the only difference when compared to the above codes would be the addition of `paired=TRUE` as in the following line of code:

```
> t.test(File$DV ~ File$IV, paired=TRUE)
```

For a one sample *t*-test, you would compare your variable to a theoretical mean μ (mu), which by default is 0 (but can be changed to any value by simply replacing the 0):

```
> t.test(File$VariableName, mu = 0)
```

The interpretation is almost identical for all three versions of the *t*-test.

Part B

The file 'Data-Practical3b.csv' contains the results of a vocabulary test (interval scores) for participants from two different motivation levels. The data result from an experiment in which motivation was a nominal independent variable and vocabulary score an interval dependent. Using all the tools and knowledge you have used so far, determine if there is a (significant) effect of *Motivation* on the vocabulary scores and report on it. Please make sure to turn the motivation variable into a factor first. Also: do not forget to look at the descriptives of your data, to plot the data, and to include your interpretation of the effect in the report.

R PRACTICAL 4

INDUCTIVE STATISTICS (CHAPTER 5)

In this practical we will take the next step in applying inductive statistics. You will do a simple means analysis and a correlation analysis. You will also learn how you should report the results of these statistical calculations. This practical contains two more advanced assignments on correlation for reliability.

Create a new Markdown file and add an appropriate heading for part A.

Part A: Reading and listening

1. Consider the following data (note that these data were already introduced in Activity 5.1). Eight students have participated in a reading test and a listening comprehension test. Reading ability and listening comprehension are operationalized by the variables R and L respectively. Both variables are measured on an interval scale. The results have been summarized in the table below.

Student	R	L
1	20	65
2	40	69
3	60	73
4	80	77
5	100	80
6	120	84
7	140	89
8	160	95

We will enter the above data in R manually using the long format, that is each row is one student, and you can follow the instructions below. So these are the steps you need to carry out:

- Create a variable called *Student* using the following code:

```
> Student <- seq(1,8)
```

In this code you create a sequence of numbers from 1 to 8.

- Enter the variables R and L as we did previously using `c()`.

- We will put these variables together in a data frame by using the following code:

```
> Practical4a = data.frame(Student,Reading,
Listening)
```

Make sure to check your file and make sure *Student* is a factor.

2. What would be H_0 if we wanted to test the relationship between reading and listening comprehension?

3. Why did we not ask you to calculate the mean and the *SD* for these two variables?

4. Make a plot of the results. In R we can do this using `plot()` as in the example code below:

```
> plot(x, y, xlab="label x-axis", ylab="label y-axis")
```

5. At face value, do you think reading and listening, as plotted in the graph, are related?

6. We want to know if we can conclude that reading skills and listening comprehension are significantly related. To determine this, you will have to calculate a Pearson *r* (or r_{xy}). Before you do this, however, you should realize that Pearson *r* is a parametric test that requires your data to be normally distributed. As the sample is very small, a histogram will probably not look normally distributed. For small samples ($n < 30$) it is better to look at skewness, kurtosis, and the Shapiro-Wilk (also see Practical 3A). Are the data approximately normally distributed?

7. If the assumption of normality has been met, please continue to perform the Pearson *r* using the following code:

```
> cor.test(Variable1, Variable2, method="pearson")
```

Note that, in case you want to perform a non-parametric correlation, you can fill in 'spearman' or 'kendall' for the method instead.

You should notice that the output of a correlation analysis is very similar to a *t*-test. Just as with a *t*-test, you can see a *t*-value. This might seem weird, but what R actually does, is compare the relationship of your variables to zero (the null hypothesis) and it uses a *t*-test for that with a corresponding *p*-value. Of course, the *p*-value does not tell us anything about the direction or strength of the relationship. For that, we have to look at the most important number at the bottom of our output and the 95% confidence interval (CI) of this estimate (also see Section 5.2.1). A correlation can be between -1 and 1 and the closer the correlation is to 0, the weaker the relationship is. Although the *r*-value already says something about the strength of the relationship, some people prefer to also calculate *r*-squared, which is simply obtained by squaring the *r*-value.

What is the value of r_{xy}? Is this a strong correlation? What is the chance of incorrectly rejecting your H_0? What do you decide? What is the effect size?

8. When reporting on results like these in scientific journals, there are particular rules and regulations on what and how to report. Here, we follow the most recent guidelines of the American Psychological Association, which states that we should report the value of the test statistic (*r* in this case), the degrees of freedom, the exact *p*-value (unless it is less than .001), and the size and direction of the effect (VandenBos, 2010). Based on this, write a sentence that you could include in the Results section of an article about the outcome of your test. It will be something like this (please choose an option or fill in the correct numbers between the {accolades}):

> 'A Pearson *r* correlation analysis showed that Reading Skills and Listening Skills were {significantly/not significantly} {positively/negatively} related (*r*({fill in the *df*}) = {fill in *r*-value}, *p* = {fill in the exact *p*-value or, if it is less than .001, *p* < .001}, two tailed, 95% CI [{fill in lower bound},{fill in upper bound}]).'

As you can see in the sentence, both the direction of the result AND the significance or *p*-value are reported. Note that the *r* is only for the Pearson *r* analysis. When you do a Spearman's Rho, you preferably use the Greek symbol ρ (or write out rho), and when you do a Kendall's Tau, you preferably use the Greek symbol τ (or write out tau). In Markdown, such symbols can be created by typing: ρ or τ.

Apart from the *r*-value and the *p*-value, you will see that there is another value mentioned in between brackets behind the *r*. This number refers to the degrees of freedom (*df*). In a correlation analysis, you can simply calculate the degrees of freedom by taking the number of participants -2. The lower and upper limits of the 95% confidence interval can be taken directly from the output.

Do not include entire R output in your results section. The results from the table are usually reported in the text, as in the above sentence. It is very helpful, however, to add the scatterplot to your report that you refer to in an additional sentence in which you also explicitly mention the direction of the effect. Conventionally, charts are included for significant results only.

*Note that most statistical notations have to be reported in italic. You can achieve this in Markdown by putting the letter that you want italicized *in between asterisks*. Also check this R Markdown Cheat Sheet (2014) for useful information on formatting in Markdown: https://www.rstudio.com/wp-content/uploads/2015/02/rmarkdown-cheatsheet.pdf*

Part B: Social class

A sociolinguistic researcher wants to find out if there is an association between the use of 'haven't got' versus 'don't have' and social class (two levels) (we saw this data already in Chapter 5.2.3 in Part 1). Social class is determined by asking people what they do for a living. The use of 'haven't got' or 'don't have' is determined by asking subjects to rephrase sentences (for instance: Jim is jobless). Note that the actual numbers in the dataset are slightly different from the ones discussed in Chapter 5!

Table R.3 Contingency table dividing the number of respondents according to social class and the use of 'don't have' and 'haven't got'

	low social class	high social class
haven't got	70	59
don't have	64	31

Questions:

1. List the variables included in this study and, for each variable, say what its function is (dependent, independent, etc.) and its type (nominal, ordinal, interval).

2. How would you formulate H_0 and H_a?

3. Which statistical test could be used?

Please note that there are two ways in which data can be entered for our analysis. The first and usually most common option also for other datasets is when the data are organized for each individual case. An example of this type of data organization would the format in Table R.4, which is generally referred to as long format (such as the data used in Part A of this practical).

The test we will be doing is also very easy to replicate afterwards, because it does not require the whole dataset; a contingency table as in Table R.3 with the total frequencies for each of the cells is enough.

4. The example code below shows exactly how to add the data in R using the contingency table format. You start by creating a data frame, using the cbind-function to combine rows and columns. Every c-element

Table R.4 Example of data in a long format

Participant	Variable 1	Variable 2
1	NO	YES
2	NO	NO
3	YES	NO
Etc.		

in the list represents a column, while every number within the c-element represents the value of a row for that specific column. Enter the data into R by using the following lines of code based on cbind() to put (or bind) numbers into columns:

```
> Table <- cbind(c(70,64),c(59,31))
```

If you simply type the name of your table, Table, to display it, you will see that the columns and rows do not have names yet. We can change that by adding the correct names in these codes:

```
> rownames(Table) <- c("Row1","Row2")
> colnames(Table) <- c("Column1","Column2")
```

Check whether your data are entered correctly.

5. Run the analysis by installing and loading the 'gmodels' package (Warnes et al., 2018) and entering the following code:

```
> CrossTable(Table, chisq=TRUE, expected=TRUE)¹
```

This will provide the chi-square value (chisq) and the expected values. The output contains a table with many versions for our cell frequencies, and below you will find the actual chi-square value (you do not need the one with Yates correction).

Although we are dealing with a non-parametric test, we do have to check some assumptions before conducting the actual test. One assumption is that every subject only contributes to one of the cells, which can normally be checked by comparing the number of subjects to the total of all cells. In this particular example, you can assume that this one has been met.

Secondly, as mentioned in Section 5.2.3, in a 2×2 table, none of the *expected* frequencies in the table should be lower than 5. Do note that in a larger table, the expected counts must be at least 1, and no more than 20% of the cells are allowed to be less than 5. If your expected cell frequencies are below 5, you should look at the outcome based on the Yates correction.

You should be able to find the expected values in the output provided by the above code. You will get quite a large output table, but note that the very first part explains what we can find in each cell, which includes the raw and expected counts. Has the assumption concerning the expected frequencies been met?

6. The actual results of the chi-square test can be found in the very bottom line of the output. Can you reject the null hypothesis?

---

1   You can also use R's built-in chisq.test(), but we chose CrossTable() as it provides more details on the expected counts and percentages as well.

7. What is the effect size? You can use `assocstats()` from the 'vcd' package (Meyer et al., 2017) and look for phi – φ (for variables with 2 levels) or Cramer's V (for variables with more than 2 levels). A value of .1 is considered a small effect, .3 a medium effect, and .5 a large effect.

8. A template for reporting the results of a chi-square would be (please choose an option or fill in the correct numbers between the {accolades}):

> 'A chi-square analysis revealed that the association between {variable 1} and {variable 2} was {significant/not significant}, $\chi2$({fill in the *df*}, *N*={fill in the total number of participants}) = {fill in $\chi2$-value}, *p* = {fill in the exact *p*-value or, if it is less than .001, *p* < .001}.'

In the case of significant results, do not forget to report on the direction of the association (e.g. men having a stronger preference for the colour blue). Also remember that, especially in case of significant results, you would want to report Phi (φ) or Cramer's V. You can create the chi-square symbol (and any other symbol) in Markdown using the following in your text χ^2.

Report on the results of this study in the way that it is conventionally done in APA research papers (using the above template) and add a bar graph to support your interpretation. You can use the following code to create a barplot (you can add any name for a colour):

```
> barplot(Table, beside = TRUE, col = c("colour1",
"colour2"), main = "Title", xlab = "Variable1",
ylab="Variable2")
```

You might also want to add a legend to explain the colours in your graph:

```
> legend("topright", fill = c("colour1", "colour2"),
c("reply1", "reply2"))
```

If you look up *barplot* in the help menu, what other way is there to add a legend to the barplot?

9. What happens if you remove `beside=TRUE` from the code (or change it to `beside=FALSE`)?

Part C: Gender and intelligence

A researcher wants to find out whether boys or girls are more intelligent. Eleven girls and eight boys (randomly selected) participated in an experiment in which scores were involved ranging 1–20 (interval).

Data:

Girls	Boys
17	16
16	15
14	13
19	19
18	15
17	14
16	13
15	12
16	
15	
19	

Answer the following questions in your Markdown file:

1. What are the dependent and independent variables and what kind of measures (nominal, ordinal, or interval/scale) are used for the variables?

2. How many levels does the independent variable have?

3. Formulate your statistical hypotheses (H_0 and H_a).

4. Which statistical test could be used? (Consult Table 8.1 in Chapter 8.)

5. Enter the data manually in R in a long format data frame using the same technique as used in Part A. Tip: do carefully consider this step – the two columns (Girls and Boys) in the data are not necessarily the variable columns in R. Remember that the columns should represent variables, not levels of variables! Once you have entered the data, do not forget to check whether all variables have the correct scale.

6. In a table, provide the following descriptive statistics for both groups: mean, minimum, maximum, standard deviation.

7. What are your first impressions about the difference between the boys and the girls?

8. Create a boxplot to visualize the results.

9. We will test the statistical significance of this experiment, but we first have to check the assumptions:

   - Check the distribution of the data by looking at the histogram,[2] the skewness and kurtosis values (using stat.desc), and by performing

---

[2] It is always good to plot a histogram of the data because it gives you a good impression of the spread of the scores. However, with samples that are smaller than, say, 30, the histogram is not the best way to check normality. For this, we really need to look at the values for Skew.2SE and Kurt.2SE, and the Shapiro-Wilk outcome (also see Practical 3A).

the Shapiro-Wilk like we did in the previous practical. Tip: if you forget which package to load, you can always type the function (e.g. `stat.desc`) in help and it will tell you which package it belongs to.

- Also test homogeneity of variance using Levene's test.
- Now run the test (see Practical 3 if you forgot how to do this).
- Carefully study the R output. The second line is the most important one as it states the values for t, the degrees of freedom (df) and the level of significance, that is the p-value. The degrees of freedom are related to sample size: for each group, this is the sample size minus one. These two values together form the value for degrees of freedom. What is the value of t? Which degrees of freedom are applied to this test? What is the level of significance? What is the 95% confidence interval? Can you reject H_0?

In addition to the values discussed above, the bottom line of the output shows the mean of each group (which we already knew) and the middle part of the output provides information on the 95% confidence interval of the difference between the two means. If the two outer ends of the spectrum are either both negative or both positive, then the chance of the difference being either negative or positive is relatively large. If the outer ends include a zero, that is if one value is negative and the other positive, then there is a chance that the difference might be 0. What do you observe in this example?

10. We are using an independent samples t-test. Why do you have to use this test rather than the one sample t-test or the paired samples t-test? (Explain this in your Markdown.)

11. As we explained in Chapter 4, it is important not only to look at the values of the test statistic and its corresponding p-values but also to look at effect sizes. Finding a significant difference does not automatically mean that this difference is meaningful or important. The effect size, as you will have deduced by its name, measures the size or magnitude of the effect (also see Chapter 5). Please note that there are various effect sizes, but we will use r^2 as it is used relatively often and is also relatively easy to understand. The formula for the effect size r^2, which was also discussed in more detail in Chapter 5 (Section 5.3.3), is:

$$r^2 = \frac{t^2}{t^2 + df}$$

You could choose to calculate r^2 by filling in the values on the basis of the output, but you can also make R do the work for you. There are several ways to do this, but we chose to calculate r-squared for our *t*-test using the procedure below. Following Field et al. (2012, p.385), we will store our *t*-test output as an object by using the following code (you can simply use your previously used *t*-test formula for this):

```
> test <- t.test(y ~ x, var.equal = TRUE/FALSE)
```

We then store both the value of the *t*-statistic, which is stored in our output as a [statistic], and our degrees of freedom, which is stored as a [parameter]. Use the following code to save those values as *t* and *df*:

```
> t <- test$statistic[[1]]

> df <- test$parameter[[1]]
```

We can then simply calculate r^2 by filling in the values we obtained with the above code:

```
> r2 <- t^2/(t^2+df)
```

You can now ask R to provide the r^2 value. Is it a small, medium, or large effect that we found?

As mentioned in Section 5.3.3 of Part 1, another well-known measure of effect size for the *t*-test is Cohen's *d*. You can run a simple test to check the effect size, by using the package 'effsize' (Torchiano, 2018) and running a so-called Cohen's *d* test:

```
> cohen.d(FileName$DependentVariable,
  FileName$IndependentVariable)
```

Note that the 'psych' package also has a cohen.d code, so when you load the 'effsize' package while 'psych' has already been loaded in the library, you will get the message: The following object is masked from 'package:psych': cohen.d. In this way, R gives priority to the package that was loaded last if there are overlapping functions.

Use *d* or r^2 to report on the effect size for this study? What would that mean for the number of participants you need to get enough power? See also Section 5.2.2 in Chapter 5 of Part 1.

12. Reporting on results of statistical studies has to be done according to fixed conventions. It is important to include descriptives per group as well as the important statistical values (*t*, *df*, *p*, r^2/d). Also note that statistical notations should be reported in italic (VandenBos, 2010) and that it is common practice to include a (reference to) a plot in your report. Below is the format that you should use for *t*-test results. Please choose an option or fill in the correct numbers between the {accolades}:

'An independent samples t-test revealed that, on average, the {boys/girls} showed a higher level of intelligence (M = {fill in the correct mean value}, SD = {fill in the correct SD-value}) than the {boys/girls} (M = {fill in mean}, SD = {fill in SD}). This difference was {significant/not significant}, t({fill in df}) = {fill in the value of t}, p = {fill in the value of p (or, if applicable p < .001)}, 95% CI [{fill in lower bound}, {fill in upper bound}]. This effect was of a {small/medium/large} size, r^2/d = {fill in value of r^2 or d}.'

13. What can you say about the meaningfulness of this outcome?

14. Is there any additional information you would like to have about this study?

What to do in case of violations of normality?

In case you want to compare the scores of two groups and the assumption of normality is violated, you should opt for a non-parametric Mann-Whitney U test, which is also known as the Wilcoxon rank-sum test. The code for this test would be:

```
> wilcox.test(DV~IV)
```

In case of a paired version and a violation of normality, you should use:

```
> wilcox.test(VAR1, VAR2, paired=TRUE)
```

Part D: Alpha – This assignment is slightly more advanced

In Chapter 5, we briefly discussed reliability, and stated that Cronbach's Alpha was a good measure to check for reliability of a test. The teachers from the data in Practical 3A are interested in the reliability of their exam. They have decided to use Cronbach's Alpha to check this.

1. Open the data for Practical 3A (you can re-use the code from Practical 3 for this).

2. Decide whether the 17-item phonetics test is reliable by carrying out Cronbach's Alpha. To do this in R we need the 'psych' package (that we also used before). We want to create a variable that contains all the 17 questions. This is done as follows:

```
> VariableName <- DataSet[, c(ColumnNumber-
FirstQuestion: ColumnNumberLastQuestion)]
```

Next we can run alpha on this variable by using:

```
> psych::alpha(VariableName)
```

The `psych::` part makes sure that R uses alpha from the 'psych' package. This is important because there is also an alpha function in the 'ggplot2' package (Wickham, 2016) which will have priority over the 'psych' package if that package was installed first. So just to make sure, add the package name when a function is present in multiple packages.

3. The output we get is quite big so let us work our way through it. The value of alpha at the top is Cronbach's Alpha, which tells us the overall reliability of the variable. As you can see there are two alphas, but you should look at the raw alpha. Do you think this is a reliable test?

4. Now we will check the individual items. The column `raw_alpha` in the table below the one we just discussed gives us the alpha statistic if we were to delete each item in turn. We basically want to find those values that are greater than the overall alpha value. Would removing any of the items substantially improve the reliability of the test?

5. The next table in our output provides us with more information about each item. The column labelled `r.drop` will tell us what the correlation would be between that particular item and the scale total if that particular item was not part of the scale total. So basically, this is a correlation such as the one we have seen in part B of this Practical, and you might recognize the r in the second/third column and look at that one. This regular r-value, however, is problematic because the item we are interested in is included in the scale total here. This means that, of course, there will be some kind of correlation because an item will always correlate with itself. In short: we have to look at `r.drop` as opposed to r.

But what does this statistic tell us and what should we look out for? Similar to 'normal' correlations, the higher the value of `r.drop`, the higher the correlation with the other items. And that is what we want: for the item to correlate with the overall score from the scale. So as a rule of thumb, `r.drop` values below .3 are problematic and the item should be removed (Field et al., 2012).

Which items should be removed because of problematic `r.drop` correlations?

R PRACTICAL 5 REGRESSION/ MISCELLANEOUS ASSIGNMENTS (CHAPTER 5/6)

This practical consists of three assignments, two containing tests that you have not yet performed and one that should be at least somewhat familiar to you.

Part A: Nativeness ratings and self-perceived L2 speaking skills

A researcher wants to find out if there is a relationship between a person's own perceived speaking skills in an L2 and their speaking skills as perceived by others. To investigate this, she asks participants to tell a story, and she records their voices. In a subsequent questionnaire, she asks them to rate their own speaking skills on a scale from 1 to 7. Later, she asks a group of 10 independent raters to listen to the speech samples and judge the nativeness of the speakers on the same scale from 1 to 7. For the analysis, she sums up all those scores.

Questions:

1. Add the data to a data frame.
2. What kind of measures (nominal, ordinal, interval) are used for the variables?
3. Formulate the relevant statistical hypotheses.
4. Is the relation linear? (Plot the data in a simple graph using plot(), but give the axes good names.)
5. Which statistical test could be used?
6. Apply the statistical test you chose. Can you reject H_0?
7. What is the effect size?
8. What can you say about the meaningfulness of this outcome?
9. Report on the results of this study in the way that it is conventionally done in research papers (see previous practical).

Self-rating	Nativeness rating
4	32
5	33
4	28
7	48
3	24
4	24
6	32
7	41
7	42
7	38
6	42
2	16
3	18
1	16
5	36
4	34

10. This part of the assignment is slightly more advanced. As you have read in Part 1, to get the power of 0.8 (1-β), we need about 28 participants to get a large effect. You now know how to find effect sizes, but you can also calculate power in R, by using the 'pwr' package (Champely, 2018). For the sake of the calculation, you can assume that the outcome of your statistical test was a parametric one, and you can fill in the observed statistic as if it were the parametric one.

```
> pwr.r.test(n = NumberofParticipants, r = r-statis-
tic(or the non-parametric equivalent), sig.level =
p-value of your outcome)
```

Is the power higher or lower than 0.8? What can you conclude about the meaningfulness of the data? Find out how many participants you would need to get a power of 0.8. Fill in pwr.r.test in the help menu on the bottom-right (where you also have the plots and files) to find out how to do this.

Part B: Age and writing scores

A researcher is interested in the writing scores of his guided writing class. He wants to know whether the age of his students affects their writing scores.

1. Download the data file from the website, save it, and inspect it.

2. What are the (independent and dependent) variables and what kind of measures (nominal, ordinal, interval) are used for the variables?

3. Formulate the relevant statistical hypotheses.

4. Plot the data in a scatterplot with the independent variable on the x-axis and the dependent variable on the y-axis. What do you see in the plot?

5. Which statistical test could be used to predict score on the basis of age?

6. Apply the statistical test you chose using the following code:

```
> model = lm(DV~IV, data=YourDataSet)
> summary(model)
```

Remember that R only provides information when you ask for it. You will thus have to ask for a summary() of the model to get the results. The summary() code will provide the regression coefficients and corresponding significance levels for the different coefficients. It also provides the effect size, an *F*-value, and the degrees of freedom for the model you built.

7. Can you reject H_0? If you have a problem interpreting the results, the explanation in Winter's tutorial (2013) might help.

8. What is the effect size?

9. Remember that this is not the end of the story; you have to check the assumptions! You should:

   a. Check whether the relationship is linear by plotting the data (you can assess this on the basis of the scatterplot you made before);

   b. Assess whether the residuals all deviate in a similar way from the model ('homoscedasticity'), for which you can use the following code to plot the fitted values on the x-axis and the residuals on the y-axis:

```
> plot(fitted(model), residuals(model)).
```

As discussed in Chapter 6 of Part 1, residuals are the differences between the observed values (the actual data) and the fitted values (as predicted by the model). A residuals plot, the one you created with the above code, is a plot in which the original scatterplot is slightly tilted and flipped and the model line would be the imaginary horizontal line at 0 (suggesting no deviation from the model). Homoscedasticity refers to the equality of the closeness across the entire regression line. We thus prefer not to see any odd patterns in this residual plot as we want the differences between the observed values and fitted values to vary constantly. In other words, if the plot does NOT show a particular pattern, this means all residuals vary more or less equally.

Although visual inspection is normally the best option to assess this assumption, you can also use the *Non-Constant Error Variance* test from the 'car' package (Fox & Weisberg, 2011) to assess homoscedasticity:

```
> ncvTest(model)
```

If the test is non-significant, homoscedasticity can generally be assumed.

c. Assess whether the residuals are normally distributed by creating a histogram or Q-Q plot of the residuals:

```
> qqnorm(residuals(model))
```

The above code plots the residuals of our model in a sorted order against data from a normal distribution. In other words, two sets of quantiles, the quantiles from our data and quantiles from a normal distribution, are plotted against one another. This is why this plot is referred to as a Q-Q or Quantile-Quantile plot. The dots should approximately follow a straight line if both of the plotted sets of quantiles come from the same distribution. You can additionally check normality of the residuals by using a Shapiro-Wilk test.

10. Report on the results of this study in the way that it is conventionally done in research papers. Mostly, you will see that researchers also report on the *F*-value to say something about how well the model accounts for the variation in the dependent variable and whether the model built was significant (also see Winter, 2013), but that is obviously not enough. According to Field et al. (2012), it is best to report the (unstandardized) coefficients, which are the estimated effects of the predictor variables, and all associated values in a table (including standardized betas). For now, we will use a (slightly simplified) table with the intercept, the regression coefficients ('estimates' in the R output), their standard errors, *t*-values, and *p*-values in your report. Note that this is basically the output you already obtained when asking for a model summary. You will often see (both in articles as well as in R output) that significance is denoted by asterisks with:

* for $p < .05$

** for $p < .01$

*** for $p < .001$

Table X Regression coefficients for the linear model of [fill in DV] as a function of [fill in IV]

	Estimate	SE	t-value	p-value
Intercept				
Factor				

Below you will find an example report that you can use:

'We constructed a linear model of {fill in DV} as a function of {fill in IV}. This model was significant (F({fill in the value of df1},{fill in df2}) = {fill in value of F}, p = {fill in the exact p-value or < .001}) and explained {fill in the R-squared value}% of the variance in the data (multiple R-squared). Regression coefficients are shown in Table X.'

As you can see, the first part of the report provides in-text information on the significance of the model and the variance explained (also see box D in Table 6.3). The second part and the information presented in the table can be taken from the Coefficients Table in the output (also see box C in Table 6.3). As always, you are additionally advised to explicitly mention the direction of the effect and what this means.

Part C: Instruction, age, and writing scores – This part is slightly more advanced

A researcher is inspired by the outcome of the study discussed in Part B of this practical and decides to partly replicate it. However, this researcher also wanted to study the effect of instruction. In addition to the effect of age, he compared the writing skills of two groups: a group that received guided writing and a group that received no guidance at all.

1. Download the data file from the website, save it, and inspect it.

2. What are the (independent and dependent) variables and what kind of measures (nominal, ordinal, interval) are used for the variables?

3. Formulate the relevant statistical hypotheses.

4. We could now create a regular scatterplot to visually examine the relationship between age and writing scores, and a boxplot could reveal the potential difference in scores on the basis of the group's instruction type. In analyses involving multiple independent or predictor variables, however, we normally also want to consider potential combined effects or interactions (see Chapter 7 for details). When you have one continuous and one categorical variable, the 'ggplot2' package (Wickham, 2016) provides a nice option to create a scatterplot with different coloured dots for each level of the independent categorical variable.

Plot the data in a scatterplot with different colours for the people in the different groups using the following code from the 'ggplot2' package (Wickham, 2016):

```
> qplot(Variable x-axis, Variable y-axis, colour =
grouping variable, data = YourDataSet)
```

What do you see in the plot?

5. Also make a boxplot to visualize the potential difference between the two instruction groups. What is your first impression of the difference?

6. Which statistical test could be used?

7. Apply the statistical test you chose for main effects only using the following code:

```
> model1 = lm(DV~IV1 + IV2, data=YourDataSet)

> summary(model1)
```

Take a look at the output and please note that the effect of a nominal/categorical predictor in a regression model is always more difficult to interpret than the effects of continuous variables. We have a variable with two levels ('guided' and 'none'), but only one level is shown in the output ('typenone'). This reveals that R used the guided writing group as a reference to compare the group who received no instruction to.
  Can you reject H_0?

8. We have not tested all potential effects yet. To add the interaction term, we can use the following code (remember to use a different name for this model, so you can compare the two):

```
> model2 = lm(DV~IV1 * IV2, data=YourDataSet)

> summary(model2)
```

The asterisk makes sure to test the interaction. For variables added in an interaction, the main effects are also always calculated, so we do not have to add those separately.
  Can you reject H_0?

9. As you know, interpreting interactions works best on the basis of a plot comparing the effect of one independent variable within the levels of the other independent variable. A useful package for this is the 'visreg' package (Breheny & Burchett, 2017). Install it, load it, and use the following code to plot the interaction:

```
> visreg(model2, xvar=IV1, by=IV2)
```

The `xvar` part will add IV1 on the x-axis and the `by=IV2` part will create separate graphs for the levels of the variable that you enter there.

10 What is the effect size?

11. One additional and very useful way to find out whether the addition of a variable, or in this case an interaction, makes your model better is to use ANOVAs to compare models that differ only with respect to one added variable (see for example Baayen, 2008, Chapter 6, p. 183 onwards). You could, for example, compare the model without the interaction to the model with the interaction with an ANOVA using the following code:

```
> anova(model1, model2)
```

The result of the ANOVA shows the RSS, the residual sum of squares, which refers to the amount of variance in the data that cannot be explained by the model. The lower the RSS value, the better the model is at explaining the variation in the dependent variable. What you really want to know, however, is whether the addition of a variable or interaction term significantly improves the model, which can be interpreted on the basis of the *p*-value. Is the interaction term a significant improvement or is it better to stick with the simpler model with only the main effects?

12. Remember that this is not the end of the story: we have to check the assumptions! You should:

a. Check whether the relationship is linear by plotting the data;

b. Assess whether the residuals all deviate in a similar way from the model ('homoscedasticity');

c. Assess whether the residuals are normally distributed by creating a histogram or Q-Q plot of the residuals. If you have forgotten how to do this, please check Practical 5B.

d. For multiple regression, it is additionally important to check (multi)collinearity. As explained in Section 6.4, this is generally best assessed using common sense. You could, however, also check (multi)collinearity in different ways depending on the measurement scales of your variables:

   i. If your IVs are interval, create a scatterplot and perform a Pearson *r*;

   ii. In case your IVs are nominal, create a barplot and perform a chi-square test;

   iii. In case you have one nominal and one interval variable, checking multicollinearity becomes a bit more problematic. We added some solutions to this in 'How To: Multiple Regression Analysis' on the companion website.

We would not want your IVs to correlate and so, in all the above situations, we would not want to obtain significant test results.

In addition to the above solution, you may also use a test for this using the code below from the 'car' package (Fox & Weisberg, 2011). Do make sure to leave out an interaction, however, as an interaction term always correlates highly with the separate factors as well.

```
> car::vif(model)
```

The general rule of thumb is that the VIF-scores should preferably not exceed 5, but definitely not exceed 10.

13. Now report on the results of this study in the way that it is conventionally done in research papers (also see Part B).

Note that, while the unstandardized coefficients (i.e. the estimates) that we obtained suffice for us, especially since we are including an interaction term, some journals suggest that you include the standardized coefficients in the report as well if the model only contains main effects. As mentioned in Section 6.3 of Part 1, checking and reporting on these standardized beta coefficients is especially useful in case of a multiple regression, as these values allow us to assess the relative importance of the different predictor variables. Fortunately, standardized beta coefficients can easily be obtained using the lm.beta() *function from the 'QuantPsyc' package (Fletcher, 2012).*

6 MORE ADVANCED GROUP COMPARISONS (CHAPTER 7)

In this practical you will carry out some special versions of the *t*-test and the ANOVA.

Part A: Exposure and vocabulary scores

In the Netherlands, children usually start with English classes in grade 5. Most children by then have already had some exposure to English through the media. A researcher wants to test a group of fifth-graders at the beginning of the year (pre-test) and test them again at the end of the year to see how much vocabulary they learn in a year (post-test). A group of 42 children participate in this experiment. Both the pre-test and the post-test consist of 20 similar multiple choice questions about the translation of nouns from English to Dutch. For each correct answer, the children can get 1 point. The data can be found on the website.

Questions:

1. Open and inspect the data.

2. What kind of measures (nominal, ordinal, interval) are used for the variables?

3. Formulate the relevant statistical hypotheses.

4. Create a table with descriptives and make a plot to visualize the data.

5. Which statistical test could be used to check whether there is a difference between the pre-test and the post-test? *Hint: the group of fifth-graders takes two tests. Therefore, these scores are paired!*

6. Apply the statistical test you chose. Do not forget to check assumptions first: in this case, a test of equality of variance is not necessary because the two samples are related. Can you reject H_0?

7. What is the effect size?

8. What can you say about the meaningfulness of this outcome?

9 Report on the results of this study in the way that it is conventionally done in research papers (see previous practicals).

Part B: Instruction and writing scores

The English Department wants to elaborate on the study discussed in Practical 5C and sets up a study to examine the effect of three different types of instruction on writing skills: no instruction, explanation in lectures only, and guided writing (GW). Thirty students are randomly assigned to each programme. The scores are results of a writing test, measured on an interval scale (0–100):

no instruction	lectures	GW
34	65	68
58	54	87
56	43	94
47	57	69
35	65	81
31	49	75
55	74	94
65	79	78
61	54	63
27	65	78

Questions:

1. List the variables in the study – if relevant, say which variables are dependent and which are independent.

2. What kind of measures (nominal, ordinal, interval) are used for the variables?

3. In the case of independent variables, how many levels does each independent variable have?

4. Add the data to a data frame in R. You can do this manually in R by following the steps below (or you can save the data as a CSV file first after entering it into Excel):

   a. Use seq() to enter a sequence with numbers for all participants;

   b. Remember that we advise adding one column for each variable, which means that you cannot import the data in the same format as it is presented above. We want to compare the scores people received and then conclude which type of instruction worked best. Therefore, your data should look something like this if you open it in Excel:

	A	B	C
1	Participant	Type	Score
2	1	0	34
3	2	0	58
4	3	0	56
5	4	0	47
6	5	0	35
7	6	0	31
8	7	0	55
9	8	0	65
10	9	0	61
11	10	0	27
12	11	1	65
13	12	1	54
14	13	1	43
15	14	1	57
16	15	1	65
17	16	1	49
18	17	1	74
19	18	1	79
20	19	1	54

Use the c-command that you used before to enter Type and Score as separate columns.

   c. Put all variables together in one data frame as you did in Practical 4A, and do not forget to check whether the data was entered correctly with labels added to the factor type when necessary.

5. Formulate the statistical hypotheses.

6. Which statistical test could be used?

7. Create a boxplot for your data; what do you see?

8. Provide a table with the following descriptive statistics for each group: mean, minimum, maximum, and standard deviation. In order to do so, you need to tell R to look at the scores for each type of instruction. You can create subsets, as you did in Practical 2, but you can also use the by() function (remember that R needs to know where to find your variables!):

```
> by(DependentVariable, IndependentVariable, describe)
```

The above code will provide you with all the values from the 'describe' function you also used before. If you prefer, you can also ask R to only provide a value such as the mean or the SD.

9. Next, we are going to assess the statistical significance of this experiment. Do not forget to check if the data are normally distributed. Also carry out Levene's test (see Practical 3). After all that, you can use the following code to conduct the actual test (also see Chapter 7) and it is best to save your test output as an object (here it is saved as 'Test'):

```
> Test = aov(DependentVariable ~ IndependentVariable,
data=YourDataSet)

> summary(Test)
```

After you save the test, you can simply check a summary of the output (`summary(Test)`) by entering the object name you chose, as in the second line of code above. Can you reject the H_0?

Now that we know whether the model is significant or not, we need to carry out some post-hoc contrasts. After all, we do want to know which of the groups differ significantly from which of the other groups. When there is homogeneity of variance, and the sample sizes are the same, Tukey's post-hoc test can be done. To use this test, you can simply type:

```
> TukeyHSD(Test)
```

The output table will help you to assess whether the groups differ significantly from each other. The column labelled `diff` provides the difference in means for the two groups.

What to do in case of violations of normality or homogeneity?

If you want to compare the scores of more than two groups and the assumption of normality is violated, you should opt for a non-parametric Kruskal-Wallis and the code for this test would be:

```
> kruskal.test(DV~IV)
```

In case of a violation of homogeneity of variance, a Welch's ANOVA can be performed instead:

```
> oneway.test(DV~IV)
```

10. What is the effect size? You can use the calculation in Chapter 7, but you can also use the following code where 'm1' is the name of the object containing the ANOVA output:

```
> summary.lm(m1)$r.squared
```

Do note that this is the r^2 value. To get the r value, you need to take the square root of this value. Note that in statistics papers, you might also see other effect sizes, such as eta-squared (η^2), omega-squared (ω^2) or Cohen's f. Eta-squared is exactly the same as r-squared, so when you read eta-squared you can just interpret it as you would interpret r^2. Omega-squared is said to be a bit more reliable, since eta-squared tends to be biased with small samples. Cohen's f, like Cohen's d, is a bit more difficult to interpret, but can be used to calculate power with the 'pwr' package that was used in Part A, question 10, of Practical 5. To check the power of our ANOVA study, however, we need the effect size Cohen's f and we can obtain that using the 'sjstats' package (Lüdecke, 2018). Once we have obtained that value, we can do a power analysis using the 'pwr' package (Champely, 2018). We have to fill in the number of groups (k), the number of participants per group (n), the value of Cohen's f (f), and the significance level (i.e. the p-value). Do remember to install and load the appropriate packages. If you are interested in performing this analysis, we recommend you have a look at the 'sjstats' package (Lüdecke, 2018) and the information on his website (Lüdecke, 2017): https://strengejacke.wordpress.com/2017/07/25/effect-siz e-statistics-for-anova-tables-rstats/.

11. What can you say about the meaningfulness of this outcome?

12. Report on the results of this study in the way that it is conventionally done in research papers using the following format for main effects:

'There was a significant effect of {fill in IV} on {fill in DV}, F({fill in $df1$}, {fill in $df2$}) = {fill in the value of F}, p ={fill in the exact p-value or < .001}. This effect was of a {small/medium/large} size, r^2/η^2= {fill in value of r^2 or eta-squared}.'

And the following format is an example of how you could report the actual group differences according to the post-hoc comparisons:

'A Tukey post-hoc analysis [or Bonferroni] revealed that group A (M = {fill in the correct mean value}, SD = {fill in the correct SD-value}) did score significantly higher than group B (M = {fill in mean}, SD = {fill in SD}), p = {fill in the exact p-value or < .001], 95% CI [{fill in lower bound}, {fill in upper bound}] and group C (M = {fill in mean}, SD = {fill in SD}), p = {fill in the exact p-value or < .001}, 95% CI [{fill in lower bound}, {fill in upper bound}]. No significant differences were found between group B and C, p = {fill in the exact p-value}.'

Note that the report always contains descriptives per group, the important statistical values (F, df, p, and η^2), as well as an explicit interpretation of the direction and size of the effect and a (reference to) a boxplot or a descriptives plot.

In the above example, we are reporting *SD* instead of *SE*. Which one to choose often also depends on the criteria of the journal in which you will publish your work.

Part C: Subtitles and vocabulary learning

A researcher interested in language learning wants to examine whether subtitles may help to increase the English L2 vocabulary knowledge of Dutch students. More specifically, she wants to compare low proficient and high proficient Dutch–English learners and examine the effects of subtitles in the L2, that is, English subtitles for English shows, compared to subtitles in the L1, that is, Dutch subtitles for English shows. In order to find an answer, a group of 30 low proficient and 30 high proficient learners of English are asked to watch one English movie every night for one week. In each group, half of them were exposed to the movies containing L1 subtitles and the other half viewed them with L2 subtitles. All participants perform a proficiency test before and after the experiment and their increase in score is used as the dependent variable. What are the effects of subtitle language and proficiency on the potential increase in vocabulary?

Questions:

1. Download the data from the website and open and inspect the data.

2. What are the variables, what are their functions, and what kind of measures (nominal, ordinal, interval) are used for the variables?

3. Formulate the relevant statistical hypotheses (note that you need one pair of hypotheses for every independent variable or combination of variables (i.e. potential interactions)!).

4. Which statistical test could be used?

5. Now before performing the test, we would like to create a table with descriptives and a plot to visualize the data. Remember that we are now not only interested in main effects, but also in interaction effects, that is combined effects of the two independent variables. You know how to retrieve the means for the two levels of each independent variable, but we would like to get the descriptives for every combination of the levels. In order to achieve this, you have to slightly adapt the by() code we used before to include a list() function that will split up our data into four groups based on the combination of our two independent variables. Use the following formula as a basis:

```
> by(DataFile$DV, list(DataFile$IV1, DataFile$IV2),
  describe)
```

6. The easiest way to put all four groups into one boxplot would be to use:

```
> boxplot(DataFile$DV ~ DataFile$IV1 + DataFile$IV2)
```

There is, however, another way to create a nice boxplot and for that we need the package 'ggplot2' (Wickham, 2016), which was also used to create most of the Figures in Part 1 of this book. So, we will install the package in the Console and load it in our Markdown file.

Now fill in the correct names and use the following function following the explanation above on where to put each variable (you do not have to fully understand it, but do give it a try!):

```
> ggplot(data = Datafile, aes(x = IV1, y = DV, fill
= IV2)) + geom _ boxplot(aes(fill = IV2), width = 1) +
theme _ bw()
```

For a first try this does look nice! However, this plot is not yet exactly what we want. First of all, let us alter the labels by adding the following directly after the formula for the graph:

```
> +ggtitle("Title")+labs(x="NameXAxis-IV1",y="NameYAxis
- DV", fill = "NameIV2")
```

Of course you can change colours, angles and much more – try experimenting with this yourself! And do not forget to add an informative caption!

7. Now it is almost time to apply the statistical test you chose, but do not forget to check assumptions first. One of these assumptions is homogeneity of variance and, since we are interested in an interaction between the language of the subtitles and the proficiency of the learners, we would want to compare the variances of the four groups. You can do so using the `interaction()` function from the 'car' package (Fox & Weisberg, 2011) as in the following code:

```
> LeveneTest(DataFile$DV, interaction(DataFile$IV1,
DataFile$IV2))
```

When checking assumptions for a factorial ANOVA, remember that you want to compare all the combinations of groups. The distribution, for example, should be approximately normal in each group or combination of groups. In order to do this, you could make clever use of the `list()` function to obtain all necessary values from the `stat.desc` function from the 'pastecs' package (Grosjean & Ibanez, 2018).

Before actually performing the statistical test, we have to add a small explanation on the different *F* tests available that we did not address in Chapter 7: Type I, II, III, and IV. These different types of tests have to do with the order in which variables are being added to the model, and whether this order is important or not. For our balanced design with only variables with no more than two levels, the difference is not crucial, but it might be good to be aware of the differences. Although there is no consensus on when to use which, we can give you the following, overly simplified, rules to work with:

- Type I: Is sequential and the order in which the variables are added can affect the results. Because of this, this type is often not used in cases where you have multiple main effects and interactions.

- Type II: Evaluates main effects while taking into account other main effects, but not interactions. Therefore, this type is only used to assess main effects.

- Type III: Is used when the effect of a variable or interaction needs to be evaluated by taking all other effects in the model into account, including interactions. The order is not important in the Type III test.

- Type IV: Is the same as Type III, but can be used when there is missing data.

As we are interested in a possible interaction, type III would be a logical choice. Type III is also the default in many other statistical packages (JASP, SAS, SPSS), but not in R. We therefore have to ask for type III ANOVAs explicitly and we will do so using the 'car' package (Fox & Weisberg, 2011). One important step for Type III ANOVAs is, however, that we have to make our contrasts orthogonal, which basically means that the sum of the two levels of the variable is 0. Normally, the numeric values of (dummy) variables are 0 and 1, but then they sum up to 1. We can change this by using the following code:

```
> contrasts(FileName$IV1) <- c(-1, 1)
> contrasts(FileName$IV2) <- c(-1, 1)
```

Note that contrasts are a little more complicated when you have variables with 3 levels. If you want or need to know more on why and how to do this, please read Levshina (2015, pp. 185–186) and/or Field et al. (2012, pp. 414–425).

We can now fit our ANOVA model using the code we used before and then use `Anova()` from the 'car' package to specifically ask for the Type III results:

```
> model = aov(DV ~ IV1*IV2, data=FileName)

> Anova(model, type="III")
```

Can you reject the different H_0s that you formulated before?

8. As mentioned in Chapter 7, most people would use omega-squared (ω^2) as an effect size measure for ANOVAs and we will do the same here. Luckily for us, the 'sjstats' package (Lüdecke, 2018) will easily provide the effect size for you, so install and load the package and use the following code:

```
> omega_sq(NameOfYourANOVAModel, partial = TRUE)
```

This code will provide us with the partial omega-squared values for all independent variables and the interaction separately. The code partial=TRUE provides the partial version of (ω^2), which partials out other effects and is hence the one we need when we have multiple independent variables as it assesses the effect sizes of each effect while partialling out the other effects.

The interpretation of (partial) ω^2 is as follows (Kirk, 1996; in Field et al., 2012):

- $\omega_p^2 = .01$ = small
- $\omega_p^2 = .06$ = medium
- $\omega_p^2 = .14$ = large

What is the effect size for the two main effects and the interaction?

9. What can you say about the meaningfulness of this outcome?

10. Report on the results of this study in the way that it is conventionally done in research papers. You can base your report on the example below.

'There was a significant main effect of {fill in IV1} on {fill in DV}, F({fill in df1}, {fill in df2}) = {fill in F-value}, p = {fill in exact p-value or < .001}. This effect was {small/medium/large}, ω_p^2 = {fill in value of partial omega-squared}.

There was also a significant main effect of {fill in IV2} on {fill in DV}, F({fill in df1}, {fill in df2}) = {fill in F-value}, p = {fill in exact p-value or < .001}. This effect was {small/medium/large}, ω_p^2 = {fill in value of partial omega-squared}.

There was a significant interaction effect between {fill in IV1} and {fill in IV2}, F({fill in df1}, {fill in df2}) = {fill in F-value}, p = {fill in exact p-value or < .001}. This effect was {small/medium/large},

ω_p^2 = {fill in value of partial omega-squared}. This interaction showed that {explain what the interaction means in your own words}. Specifically, the {DV} was higher for {fill in level 1 IV1} (M = {fill in the correct mean value}, SD = {fill in the correct SD-value}) than for {fill in level 2 IV1} (M = {fill in mean}, SD = {fill in SD}) in {fill in level 1 IV2}, but they differed in {fill in level 2 IV2} with higher scores for {fill in level 2 IV1} (M = {fill in mean}, SD = {fill in SD}) than for {fill in level 1 IV1} (M = {fill in mean}, SD = {fill in SD}) in {fill in level 1 IV2}.'

EXAM PRACTICE

In this practical you will practise an exam. Below, you will find a list with 8 problems (the same as those in Activity 8.1). Choose at least 2 of the following problems (you are welcome to do them all), and work these out in detail.

Include the following points in your answers to each of the problems below:

- List the variables in the study – if relevant, say which variables are dependent and which are independent.

- For each of the variables determine its scale (nominal, ordinal, interval).

- In the case of independent variables, how many levels does each independent variable have?

- Identify the appropriate perspective: assessing relationships, comparing means, predicting an outcome, or a combination of these; then choose the most appropriate statistical test.

- Formulate the relevant research hypotheses (H_0 and H_1/H_2).

- Report on the results of this study in the way that it is conventionally done in research papers. Your report of the outcome must include:

  ○ Descriptive statistics;

  ○ Value of the test-statistic;

  ○ Value of df;

  ○ Significance (the exact p-value or $< .001$) and the 95% CI, if possible;

  ○ Direction of the effect including, if applicable, descriptive statistics;

  ○ Effect sizes;

  ○ If applicable, also report on the assumptions, for example linearity, homogeneity of variance, and normality of the distribution;

  ○ Do not forget to illustrate your answer with tables and figures.

  ○ Reflect on the meaningfulness of the outcome.

a) A researcher wants to investigate if motivation affects the pronunciation of English by Dutch learners. To investigate the possible effect of motivation on pronunciation, she makes recordings of 24

Dutch learners of English pronouncing English sentences. She then measures the difference in vowel length before voiced and voiceless obstruents (e.g. tap vs. tab). A questionnaire has determined that 12 of these students are highly motivated and 12 students are not very motivated to pronounce English correctly. Tip: the dependent is the DIFFERENCE in vowel length between the two phonological contexts.

b) A researcher wants to find out whether the age at which one starts to learn a foreign language is related to language proficiency. To investigate this, she finds 20 Polish learners of French who have all been learning French for 10 years. The age of acquisition (AoA) of these learners ranges from 1 to 20, in such a way that each starting age is included precisely once. All learners take a 50-item French proficiency test; the proficiency score is based on the number of correct items.

c) To investigate the effect of input on second language learning, 60 randomly selected Japanese learners of Hebrew are divided into two groups: one experimental group of 30 is isolated in a dark room and exposed to Hebrew television 24 hours a day (thereby achieving maximum exposure to Hebrew); one control group of 30 is not exposed to Hebrew. After two months, both groups are submitted to a 100-item Hebrew proficiency test; the proficiency score is based on the number of correct items.

d) Another experimenter is also interested in Japanese learners of Hebrew, but for ethical reasons, chooses to focus on the effect of age and not on the effects of exposure. He also tests 60 Japanese learners of Hebrew and equally subdivides them into three age groups: 11–30 (AgeGroup 1), 31–50 (AgeGroup 2) and 51–70 (AgeGroup 3). Does age influence proficiency?

e) A researcher is interested in the effects of social reinforcement on toddlers' motor skills. In an experiment, 56 three-year-old children have to take marbles from a vase and put them into a box through a tiny hole. The number of marbles that have been put into the box is counted after four minutes. The children are randomly attributed to two groups. In a 10-minute learning period preceding the experiment, the children in the first group are encouraged by smiles and words of praise. The children in the second group are not encouraged.

f) In what way would the experiment in e) change if, in addition, the researcher wants to find out if social reinforcement equally affects the boys and girls in the experiment? Reconsider the number and type of variables accordingly, and decide on the type of analysis that would be required for this new situation.

g) To investigate the relation between active sports performance and stress a questionnaire is set up. The questionnaire determines if the participants are active sportswomen and sportsmen (Yes or No) and the degree of stress they experience in their daily lives (on a 3-point scale). The data can be found in the table below:

	Sports	
	YES	NO
stress1	20	19
stress2	24	17
stress3	28	14

h) Imagine that a researcher partly replicates the study in b) and adds another variable to his design: whether the participants have ever visited France ('yes' or 'no'). He wonders whether he can predict proficiency score based on a visit and/or starting age.

PART
2 -JASP

PRACTICALS IN JASP

GETTING READY TO START USING JASP

This section briefly explains why a student or researcher would want to use JASP (JASP Team, 2018) as opposed to, for example SPSS, and how to download and open the program. The most important components are also briefly discussed, and after this short introduction to JASP, you can start doing your first calculations in the program by following the instructions in Practical 1.

As JASP is often being updated, some features might be slightly different from what we present here. The version used for this book is JASP 0.10.2 (July 2019).

Why use JASP?

At the time of writing, JASP is still a relatively unfamiliar program to many. It was developed by researchers at the University of Amsterdam as an alternative to SPSS, but also as an alternative to R. As opposed to SPSS or other popular statistics programs with a user interface, JASP is free software that runs on Windows, Mac, and on Linux. Another difference with SPSS is that JASP offers Bayesian versions of the so-called frequentist statistical tests[1]. In comparison to R, JASP is much more user-friendly, since it has a user interface that resembles the SPSS user interface. The disadvantage of this is that the user is much more limited in the statistics that can be done. However, new features are being added all the time, giving the user more and more possibilities.

For absolute beginners in statistics who have little time to learn statistics and do not have to do very complicated analyses, we would recommend starting with JASP. For degree programmes that offer multiple statistics courses, the choice could be to start with JASP and switch to R when the basics have been mastered. All in all, it is a matter of choice, but R simply offers many more possibilities, which is why it has become so popular over the years.

Download and start using JASP

Go to the following website to download JASP: https://jasp-stats.org/download/. The JASP website also provides videos, GIFs, and blog posts explaining most of the functions the program offers. After installing, run the program. Upon opening the program, JASP will present a short text including a link that encourages you to open a data file and try out the program. Note that JASP can only open specific data files, the most

---

1   In spite of its relevance, Bayesian statistics goes beyond the scope of this book. See Chapter 4 in Part 1 for a short explanation.

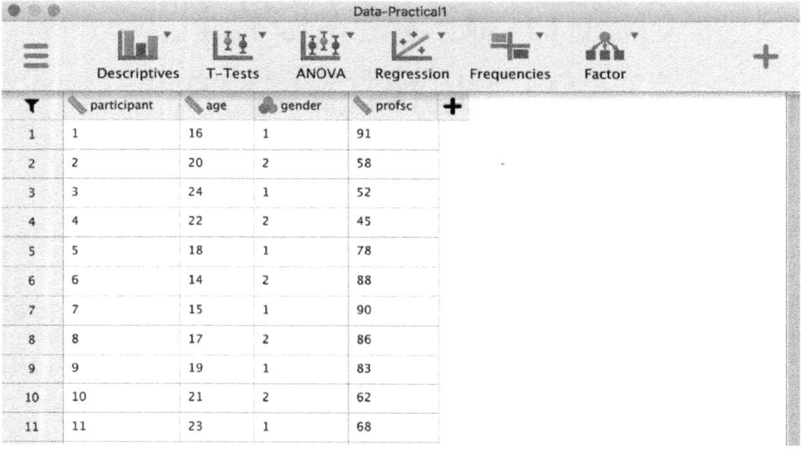
Data-Practical1
Descriptives
T-Tests
ANOVA
Regression
Frequencies
Factor
participant
age
gender
profsc
1 1 16 1 91
2 2 20 2 58
3 3 24 1 52
4 4 22 2 45
5 5 18 1 78
6 6 14 2 88
7 7 15 1 90
8 8 17 2 86
9 9 19 1 83
10 10 21 2 62
11 11 23 1 68

Figure J.1 Overview of JASP

common being .csv files (comma-separated values). Other extensions that JASP can handle are .txt (plain text files in the right format), .sav (SPSS data files), and .ods (OpenDocument Spreadsheet). Because JASP cannot run without a data file we will use the data file of the first practical that you can download from the companion website. To open the CSV file of Practical 1 click on the menu symbol ≡ in the top left of the screen, then go to *Open > Computer > Browse*, and select the folder where you saved the data file (Data-Practical1.csv). When you have done this your JASP screen should look something like the screenshot in Figure J.1.

If everything loaded correctly, you should see all four columns and 29 rows. There should not be extra empty columns or rows. If this is the case, you need to load the data in a spreadsheet program such as Excel and remove the empty columns and/or rows.

When you use the different functions that are displayed in the menu, your output will appear on the right. In other words, when you select a statistical test on the top of the screen (e.g. a *t*-test), and select the data you want to use, the results will be displayed on the right half of the window. Results can include descriptive statistics such as averages, medians etc., but also graphs and tables.

If you click on *Descriptives* in the top Menu, and select *Descriptive Statistics*, you will see a panel with options on top of the data, looking something like Figure J.2.

If you click on the arrow on the left side of this Options menu, you will go back to the data, and if you click on the arrow on the right side of the Descriptive Statistics Options, you will see only the Results or Output window (see Figure J.2). You can also drag the Options menu to the right if you click and hold one of the 3 dots that can be found in the top left, top right, bottom left, and bottom right of the menu, which will then reveal the data on the left again (see Figure J.3).

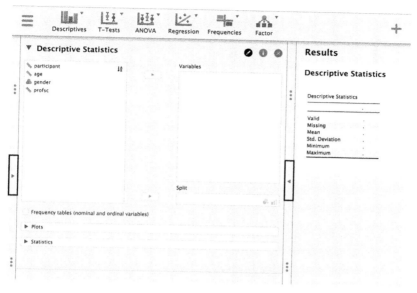

Figure J.2 Overview of JASP options and results window

Note that whenever you choose one of the analyses from the menu in JASP, this analysis will stay in your Output, unless you remove it. You can remove it either by clicking on the cross on the top right of the Options menu, or by hovering over the title of the output part and clicking on the little triangle arrow pointing down next to the title, and select *Remove*.

In the next section, Practical 1, we will use JASP to explore the data file further.

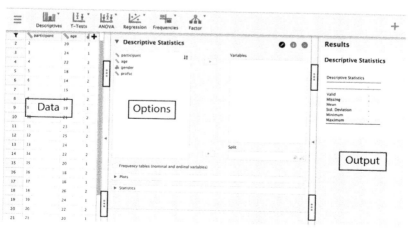

Figure J.3 Drag one of the three dots to move the options screen

JASP Practical 1 EXPLORING JASP AND ENTERING VARIABLES (CHAPTER 2)

In this practical you will become familiar with the statistical program JASP. You will practise defining variables, entering data via Excel, and opening and saving a dataset. You will also learn how to make an easy-to-read report in JASP. All this will prepare you for the statistical analyses you will be carrying out in the following practicals.

For this practical, we assume that you know how to open JASP. It is thus important that you have read, carried out, and understood 'Getting ready to start using JASP' before starting this practical.

Part A: Importing and looking at data

You can download the data file 'Data-Practical1.csv' from the companion website. Make sure to save the file in a folder where you can find it again. In JASP click on the menu symbol in the top left of the screen and go to *Open > Computer* and then click *Browse* to select your data file from your computer.

After you open the CSV data file you will see that there are four columns of data. These are the different variables. When you scroll down you will find that there are 29 rows, one for each participant.

1. STARTING THE REPORT

   a. You can make a report in JASP, in which you save all your notes and analyses. However, JASP does not allow you to start the report before you do any analyses. Therefore, we will start with an 'analysis' that we will remove again, in order for you to start the report.

   b. Click on *Descriptives > Descriptive Statistics*. You will see that an options window is superimposed on the data, with an empty table appearing as output on the right.

   c. To the right of *Results*, you will see an arrow pointing down ▼ when you hover over the word *Results*. Click on this arrow and select *Edit Title*. Choose a comprehensive title for your report of Practical 1A.

2. DETERMINING VARIABLE TYPES

One problem with the current data file is that JASP has decided on the basis of certain algorithms what the variable types are. It has read the *participant* variable as Interval, and the other variables as Nominal. We will now change these variables to their actual variable types.

a. In your 'report', click on the arrow next to your title again, and select *Add Note*. Now give the correct Variable Types for all 4 variables. We are going to assume that *profsc* was an interval variable.

b. Drag the Options and Output window to the right so that you see your data. When you click on the ruler left of the column header *participant*, you will get a dropdown menu. Select the correct variable type, and do the same for the other variables.

3. SETTING LABELS FOR NOMINAL VARIABLES

As you can see, the variable *gender* only has values of 1 and 2. You may realize that these values do not relate to actual numbers, but are instead labels for 'female' and 'male'. When we use numbers for nominal variables, we have to tell JASP that *gender* does not relate to numbers, but that it is actually referring to these two labels. By clicking on the word 'gender' you will be able to enter the labels under values, as can be seen in Figure J.4. In this dataset, the value 1 refers to 'female' and 2 to 'male'. You can change this by clicking on the number under label and typing in the correct label. The small symbol left of the word 'gender' is the symbol for a nominal variable.

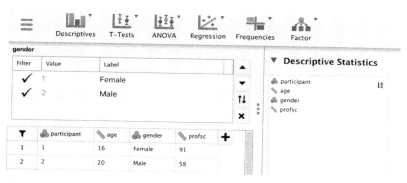

Figure J.4 Changing labels in JASP

4. SAVING THE JASP FILE

While working in JASP, do not forget to save your files. JASP files contain the data, the analyses, and now also your report in one file, which has the .jasp extension. Save your file as 'Pract1A-yourinitials.jasp'. This way, the changes you made to the labels and variables types will be saved together with the start of your report, so that you can always continue working on it.

Part B: Preparing a data file

In this part we will enter our data manually in Excel and save it as a CSV file. We will use this file again in Practical 2.

1. Open Excel or another spreadsheet program. Enter the following four interval datasets in Excel, adding A-D as variable names. You can enter them next to each other in one file.

   a. 3, 4, 5, 6, 7, 8, 9

   b. 6, 6, 6, 6, 6, 6, 6

   c. 4, 4, 4, 6, 7, 7, 10

   d. 1, 1, 1, 4, 9, 12, 14

2. Go to *File > Save as*, select or create the folder where you want to save it and under file format select .csv.

3. Save the file with the name 'Prac1B-yourinitials.jasp'.

4. You might get a message telling you that some features might be lost or a message asking you whether you want to keep the format. Just click *Yes*.

5. Now open the file in JASP just as you did in Part A, changing the variable types if necessary, change the title, and save the file as a JASP file.

JASP Practical 2

DESCRIPTIVE STATISTICS (CHAPTER 3)

In this practical you will become familiar with some more functions of JASP. You will use the data that you entered in the previous practical and do some first analyses involving descriptive statistics. You will use the JASP file to answer questions that will be asked later in this practical.

Part A

1. OPEN THE JASP FILE FROM PRACTICAL 1A

2. FIRST CALCULATIONS: DESCRIPTIVE STATISTICS

   a. During this first step, we want to find the descriptives for the variable *age*. You should still see the Descriptive Statistics Option menu in your JASP file, which should look like the screenshot in Figure J.5.

   b. Click on the variable *age* and move it to the *Variables* box on the right. You will see that the table in the right half of the screen suddenly gives you various statistics. In the options menu, to the right

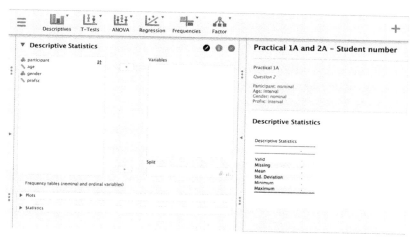

Figure J.5 Screenshot of the descriptives menu in JASP

of the title *Descriptive Statistics*, you can see three symbols, a pen, an *i* symbol, and an *x*. The *x* is to close the analysis and delete it from your file, the *i* is to get more information on the options in the menu, and the pen is to change the title. Click on the pen to change the title to 'Descriptive Statistics on Age'. To the left of the title, you will find a little arrow pointing down. Click on this to close the options menu.

c. What are the minimum age, the maximum age, the mean age, and the standard deviation? Report on your findings by adding a note to the JASP output. Also give your table a clear and explanatory caption **above** the table: 'Table 1. Descriptive statistics of the variable Age.'

d. The default selected descriptives are the mean, the standard deviation, and the minimum and the maximum values. If you want to add more, click on the *Output* table, and you will see that the *Descriptives* menu opens again. This is how you can always make changes to existing 'analyses' without having to redo everything. Now click on *Statistics* in the *Descriptives* menu to see more central tendency and dispersion measures to select from.

e. Which age occurs most often? Answer this question in your JASP report.

f. What does the little superscript a mean? *Hint: check the data file to help you find the complete answer to the previous question (manual counting).*

g. Close the options menu again by clicking on the arrow to the left of the title. Also make sure you regularly save your file by clicking Ctrl+s (Cmd+s on a Mac OS).

3. MORE DESCRIPTIVES

a. By opening a new *Descriptives* menu, find out the mean, the median, the mode, the range, and the standard deviation of the proficiency score in your data. Do not forget to change the title of your analysis to e.g. 'Descriptive Statistics on Proficiency'. Report on your findings in the JASP File. Please keep in mind that we use a dot (and not a comma) to report decimals (e.g. 0.5) and that we do not always have to report all decimals (use common sense!). JASP often uses 2 or 3 decimals by default. If you want to decide how many decimals JASP reports, you can change the decimals by going to the JASP menu and selecting *Preferences* > *Results* and checking the box that says *Fix the number of decimals*. As a general guideline you can use the information in Table J.1.

Table J.1 General guidelines for reporting decimals according to APA standards

Numbers	Round to	Example
Less than 0.001	As many decimals as needed	0.0003
0.001 – 0.1	3 decimals	0.027
0.1 – 10	2 decimals	2.52
10 – 100	1 decimal	16.7
> 100	Whole numbers	2137

4. GETTING TO KNOW THE DATA: RELATIONSHIPS

a. Imagine that the dataset concerns age of acquisition instead of age and that a researcher who gathered these data is interested in finding out whether the age at which someone started learning an L2 is related to the proficiency they obtained in that language. A scatterplot is normally a good place to start examining such a question.

b. While it is possible to make a scatterplot from the *Descriptives* menu, it is not the best option since it gives the scatterplot only as a combination with histograms. Therefore, we will make a plot by clicking on *Regression > Correlation Matrix*. You do not need to do anything with the table (you can even deselect the *Pearson* option). Instead, move both the *age* and the *profsc* variable to the right and click on *Correlation matrix* under *Plots*.

c. Add a clear and explanatory caption to your figure. Note that captions to figures go **below** the figure according to APA guidelines. For tables, the captions go **above** the table.

d. At face value, do you think there is a relationship between the two variables?

5. GETTING TO KNOW THE DATA: COMPARING GROUPS

a. Now we want to find out the mean proficiency scores and the standard deviations for the male and the female participants. Go to *Descriptives > Descriptive Statistics* again, and this time move *profsc* to the *Variables* box and *gender* to the *Split* box. The Split box makes sure that all the Descriptive Statistics are calculated for each group separately.

b. Which group has higher proficiency scores, the male or the female participants? Report this in your JASP file.

c. Which group scored more homogeneously?

d. Under *Plots*, click on *Display boxplots*. You should now get a boxplot for the female and the male participants separately. You can make it a coloured one, by selecting *Color*. Again, add an explanatory caption. You can add the caption below the figure when you click on the arrow next to the main title of this analysis and select *Add notes*.

e. Compare your boxplot with the descriptive statistics. Can you find out how the boxplot is built up and what the different points of the boxplot signify? Explain this in your JASP file (hint: there are 4 quartiles). You can also use Google to find out the answer.

f. After you have reported on your findings in the JASP report, save the JASP file.

Part B

1. Open the data file that you made in Practical 1B.

2. Provide the mean, the mode, the median, the range, and the standard deviation of each of the four datasets.

3. Report your findings in the JASP file by adding comments and adding a caption (above the table).

4. Do you agree with JASP's calculation of the mode for variable *A*?

Part C

We will use a large sample of data containing information on the motivation to learn French and the score on a French Proficiency test. The data to this part can be found on the website. The file is called 'Data-Practical2C.csv'.

1. OPEN THE FILE IN JASP

   Check the variable types and the data itself and make sure the labels are added to the levels of the variable *Motivation*. Do remember that we are now dealing with an ordinal variable. The labels for *Motivation* are:

   1 = very low; 2 = low; 3 = neutral; 4 = high; 5 = very high

2. DESCRIPTIVE STATISTICS

   a. Find out the mean proficiency score, the median, mode, and standard deviation for the group of students as a whole and then for the different motivation groups. As in the previous parts, report on the answers in the JASP file.

   b. Make a boxplot with the different motivation groups. Judging from the boxplot, do you think the groups will differ from one another? Report on your findings.

3. CHECKING THE NORMAL DISTRIBUTION

a. To check whether proficiency has a normal distribution, first create a histogram for the whole group together by going to *Descriptives* > *Descriptive Statistics* again, selecting *Proficiency* (and not adding *Motivation* to the Split box). Then click on *Plots* and select both *Distribution Plots* and *Display density*. When the *Display density* is selected, the histograms will plot probabilities that together add up to 1 instead of the raw frequencies that together add up to the total number of occurrences in the dataset. A curve is automatically added as well. When leaving *Display density* unticked, the histograms will show the absolute values of the data. When selecting *Display density*, the y-axis changes into *density* with the total of the bars amounting to 1. It does not really matter which one you choose, but if you want to compare different distributions, it is sometimes easier to compare them when they have the same scale.

b. By looking at the histogram, do the data seem to follow a normal distribution?

c. We also want the values for skewness and kurtosis to determine whether proficiency is normally distributed. Under *Statistics* > *Distribution* in the *Descriptive Statistics* menu, select *Skewness* and *Kurtosis*. Do these values deviate from zero and, if so, are they positive or negative? What does that tell you about the skewness and kurtosis? (Also try to link these values to the shape of the histogram you just created.)

d. Usually, you want to know whether your different groups are normally distributed by themselves. Carry out steps 3a–3c again for the different motivation groups.

CALCULATIONS USING
3 JASP (CHAPTER 4)

In this practical you will review some descriptive statistics and you will learn to get a first impression about the normality of a distribution. Finally, you will do some first 'real' statistics.

Part A

1. IMPORTING DATA AND CREATING THE JASP FILE

a. In the file 'Data-Practical3a.csv', you will find the results of the English Phonetics I exam of the student cohort 2000 in the English Department in Groningen. The scores are specified per question (Q1, Q2, etc.), and we are going to assume that these scores are measured on an *interval* scale. Since these are the real results, we have replaced the names by numbers for discretion. The questions below all refer to this file. Create a JASP file containing all your answers, in which you also show and explain informative tables and graphs. We know that some would prefer to just follow instructions and move on to the next question, but please always also answer the questions *based* on the output by reporting on it in the notes you add in the JASP file.

b. After you have opened the file in JASP, check the data and the variables.

2. DESCRIPTIVES AND GRAPHS FOR GROUPS

a. In Practical 2, you calculated mean values etc. for different groups. Check how to do this if you have forgotten. The students were in different groups (1A, 1B, etc.). Calculate the mean, maximum, minimum, range, and *SD* per group, using the *TOTAL* score. Also have a look at the quartiles. Selecting *Quartiles* will give you values for the dataset if it is split up in four equal groups. These quartiles also represent the four parts of the boxplot.

Do not forget to add a caption above the table and answer the following questions in your report below the table: (1) Which group seems to have performed best? (2) Which group performed most homogeneously? (3) And which teacher (A/B) performed best?

   b. Create a boxplot of the scores (based on *TOTAL*) for both teachers. Do not forget to add a caption.

3. CHECKING FOR NORMALITY

   a. Create a histogram of the *TOTAL* score with a normal distribution line and an informative caption as you did in Practical 2.

   b. Do these results approximately follow the normal distribution (at face value when looking at the histogram)?

4. USING *Z*-SCORES

   a. JASP allows you to calculate and add a new variable, by clicking on the plus-symbol that can be found next to the last column of your dataset. We are going to calculate *z*-scores of the *TOTAL* score by creating such a formula. Click on the plus symbol, name your new variable 'z-scores', and drag and drop the following to the formula window:

- TOTAL

- -

- mean

- TOTAL

- /

- σy

- TOTAL

It should now read: $(\text{TOTAL} - \text{mean(TOTAL)})/\sigma y\ \text{TOTAL}$. After you click on *Compute column*, a new column should appear in your data file.

   b. Report on the *z*-scores of the following students: 11, 33, 44, and 55.

5. INDUCTIVE STATISTICS

   a. So far you have only done the descriptive statistics. What is your first impression about the difference between the groups of the two teachers?

   b. We will now go through a first example of *hypothesis testing*. The question we want to answer is whether there is a difference between the total scores of the students of teacher A and the total scores of the students of teacher B. We are going to find out if your impressions in a. are correct. What is the null hypothesis belonging to the research question?

c. The statistical test we will carry out to test the null hypothesis is the *t*-test. We will discuss this test later on in more detail; this is just to give you some first hands-on experience. The test we want to use is the independent samples *t*-test. That is because the two samples we took (from the two teachers) are not related (there are different students in each group). Which variable is the grouping variable, that is, the *independent*? And which one is the dependent variable?

d. The independent samples *t*-test that we will be using is a parametric test. We will thus first have to check for normality. In Practical 2, we already saw that the closer to 0 the values of skewness and kurtosis are, the closer they are to the normal distribution. Apart from this, it would also be nice to know how close they are to a normal distribution, or in other words when the values of skewness and kurtosis are close enough to the normal distribution. For this, we will have to make our own calculation.

Go to *Descriptives > Descriptive Statistics* and add the independent variable in the *Split* box and the dependent variable in the *Variables* box. Select the *Skewness* and *Kurtosis* boxes under *Statistics > Distribution*.

In the table you will not only get the values for skewness and kurtosis, but also the Standard Errors of skewness and kurtosis. We are going to divide the skewness and kurtosis values by their standard errors. You do not have to know exactly how this works, but this is as if you are calculating a *z*-score for the skewness and kurtosis values. For samples that are quite small (say, up to 30), we can assume that the outcome of skewness/$SE_{skewness}$ and kurtosis/$SE_{kurtosis}$ that are between –1.96 and 1.96 are close enough to a normal distribution (also see Field et al., 2012, p. 175). For samples that are a bit larger (say, between 30 and 200), it is fine if they stay within the –2.58 and 2.58 range. We have a sample of 130 students, so for this group it is fine if the values are between –2.58 and 2.58. What can you say about skewness and kurtosis now? Can we say that the data of the two teachers are normally distributed?

e. The *t*-test compares the scores of the two groups, so that you can estimate the difference between them, that is whether the null hypothesis can be rejected or accepted. In JASP, we conduct a *t*-test by going to *T-Tests > Independent Samples T-Test*. Add the dependent variable and the independent variable to their respective boxes.

f. You do not need to change anything under *Hypothesis*, but what do you think the different options here are meant for?

g. Under *Additional Statistics*, tick the option *Descriptives* and *Descriptives plots*. What is your first impression about the difference between the groups of the two teachers?

6. TESTING EQUALITY OF VARIANCE

We are going to stay in the menu of the Independent Samples *t*-test, but before we look at the results of the *t*-test, there are a few more steps we want to take.

a. One of the assumptions is that there is equality of variance between the groups. This means that the standard deviation in one group should not be drastically different from the standard deviation in another group. A good rule of thumb is usually to make sure that the largest standard deviation is not more than twice as big as the smallest standard deviation. First look at the different standard deviations of the groups of both teachers. What are the standard deviations for the two teacher groups? And what is the smallest? Do you think these groups are equal in their variance?

b. Under *Assumption Checks* you can tick *Test equality of variances*. In your output file, you will now see a table labelled *Test of Equality of Variances (Levene's)*. The null hypothesis here would be that the groups are similar in variance.

   The *F* value seen in the JASP output is the outcome of the Levene test (similar to the ANOVA's *F*-value that will come back in later practicals) and the most important part for our purposes is expressed under *p*. If this value, that is the significance level, is smaller than .05, you can NOT assume equal variances. If it is bigger than .05, you can assume equal variances.

   In this case, are your groups equal in variance?

c. If there is no equality of variance, you will need to change the *Student* test under *Tests* to *Welch*, which is the test that is used for unequal variances. However, if there is equality of variance, you do not need to change anything under *Tests*.

7. CHECKING FOR NORMALITY WITH A NORMALITY TEST

Another assumption of the *t*-test is that the data are distributed according to the normal distribution. You could of course simply look at the skewness and the kurtosis as we did earlier. If skewness and kurtosis is close to 0, or at least with *z*-scores between −1.96 and 1.96 (or 2.58 in this case), you can assume that the distribution is approximately normal. However, you may want to know what the chance is that you go wrong in assuming the normal distribution. This can be established by applying the Shapiro-Wilk test. It is important that the distribution of each group is normal, rather than the distribution of the scores of the groups taken together. Note: when sample sizes are very small (smaller than 20) or very large (larger than 200), it is sometimes said that this test is not so reliable.

a. We will thus want to test normality by comparing our group's distribution to the normal distribution. What is the null hypothesis for this comparison?

b. Under *Assumption Checks* now also tick *Normality*. There should now be a table in your output that says *Test of Normality (Shapiro-Wilk)*.

    If the significance value is above .05, then you can assume that the data are normally distributed. In this case, do the data show a normal distribution?

c. If the data are not normally distributed, you need to change the *Student* or *Welch* test under *Tests* to *Mann-Whitney*, which is the non-parametric alternative to the parametric version of the independent samples *t*-test. If the data are normally distributed, you do not need to change anything.

Which method is best to check for normality?

We have created histograms, looked at skewness and kurtosis values, and performed a test to compare our data's distribution to the normal distribution, but which of these methods is best? The answer to this question very much depends on the sample size of your dataset.

It is always a good idea to start with visualizing your data, and a histogram of the data (per group!) can often be helpful to check whether their shapes approximately follow the bell-shaped curve of the normal distribution. While this method is the best option for rather large datasets ($n > 200$), histograms are likely to look non-normal for small datasets with, for example, only 15 learners per group (also see Table J.2). A good second method would be to look at the values for skewness (i.e. the symmetry of the curve) and kurtosis (i.e. the pointedness) and check how much they deviate from zero. If you divide the value of skewness by the Standard Error (*SE*) of skewness, and the value of kurtosis by the *SE* of kurtosis (both of which can be found in the JASP output, as in assignment 5 of this practical), you will get a standardized value that is like a *z*-score, which is often more appropriate than the regular skewness and kurtosis values to evaluate normality (e.g. Field et al., 2012). Generally, this *z*-score should be between -1.96 and 1.96 to be considered normal. The easiest way to obtain these values is by using a calculator to divide the skewness value by the *SE* of skewness and the kurtosis value by the *SE* of kurtosis, as we did in assignment 5 above:

$$z\text{-}score \ of \ Skewness = \frac{Skewness}{SE \ of \ Skewness} \qquad z\text{-}score \ of \ Kurtosis = \frac{Kurtosis}{SE \ of \ Kurtosis}$$

As you now know, you can also perform a Shapiro-Wilk for each group and make sure that these are non-significant to ascertain that your data are normally distributed. In general, it is best to use the Shapiro-Wilk to check for a normally distributed dataset. However, when sample sizes

Table J.2 Rough guideline on how to check for normality

Check	Samples < 30	Samples > 30 and < 200	Samples > 200
Histogram	Good to check, but will probably not look normally distributed	Good to check	Very important to check because it will give you the best information
Skewness and kurtosis	-	Between −1 and 1	-
Skewness and kurtosis divided by their Standard Errors	Between −1.96 and 1.96	Between −2.58 and 2.58	-
Normality tests	Shapiro-Wilk	Shapiro-Wilk	-

are large, the Shapiro-Wilk test is often too strict, and it is very easy to get a significant value for this test. What is advised with samples larger than 200 is to have a good look at the histograms, for example (also see Table J.2).

It is always important to use various ways to check your data for normality and it should be clear now that the correct way of testing normality highly depends on your sample size. Table J.2 will give a rough guideline on how to check for normality with different sample sizes.

8. INDUCTIVE STATISTICS

a. Now that we have checked the assumptions, we can look at the outcomes of the t-test. You will find this information in the first table of this analysis (under Independent Samples T-test in your output). The output shows us some interesting numbers, but it also contains some information that is currently redundant. For now, we will first focus on the significance value or the p-value of the t-test. We see the p-value which indicates the chance of incorrectly rejecting the null hypothesis (the chance of getting an alpha error!).

b. What is the chance of incorrectly rejecting the null hypothesis concerning the two teachers?

c. What is the conclusion you would draw with regard to the research question in 2a? Would you reject the H_0? What is the chance that we go wrong in our decision to reject H_0 (the α-error)? Is your conclusion about the H_0 in line with what you would expect from the descriptives?

We have now practised the most common version of the t-test, but you will only have to click on one of the other options in the T-Test menu of JASP to perform one of the other versions. If your aim is to perform a paired samples *t*-test, the only difference when compared to the above information is that you would have one group of participants who have two scores, so the scores would be next to each other in two columns instead of in one column.

For a one sample *t*-test, you would compare your variable to a theoretical mean μ (mu), which by default is 0 (but can be changed to any value by simply replacing the 0 under *Test value* in JASP).

The interpretation is almost identical for all three versions of the *t*-test.

After you have reported on everything, make sure you save your JASP file.

Part B

The file 'Data-Practical3b.csv' contains the results of a vocabulary test (interval scores) for participants from two different motivation levels. The data result from an experiment in which motivation was a nominal independent variable and vocabulary score an interval dependent. Using all the tools and knowledge you have used so far, determine if there is a (significant) effect of motivation on the vocabulary scores and report on it. Please make sure to turn the *Motivation* variable into a factor first. Also: do not forget to look at the descriptives of your data, to plot the data, and to include your interpretation of the effect in the report.

JASP Practical
4

JASP Practical

INDUCTIVE STATISTICS (CHAPTER 5)

In this practical you will take the next step in applying inductive statistics. You will do a simple means analysis and a correlation analysis. You will also learn how you should report the results of these statistical calculations. This practical contains two more advanced assignments on correlation for reliability.

Part A: Reading and listening

1. Consider the following data (note that these data were already introduced in Activity 5.1). Eight students have participated in a reading test and a listening comprehension test. Reading ability and listening comprehension are operationalized by the variables R and L respectively. Both variables are measured on an interval scale. The results have been summarized in the table below. Enter the values manually in Excel, save the file as a CSV format, and open it in JASP.

2. What would H_0 be if we wanted to test the relationship between reading and listening comprehension?

3. Why did we not ask you to calculate the mean and the SD for these two variables?

4. Make a scatterplot of the results. You did this in Practical 2, so check back if you have forgotten how to do this.

5. At face value, do you think reading and listening, as plotted in the graph, are related?

Student	R	L
1	20	65
2	40	69
3	60	73
4	80	77
5	100	80
6	120	84
7	140	89
8	160	95

6. We want to know if we can conclude that reading skills and listening comprehension are significantly related. To determine this, you will have to calculate a Pearson r (or r_{xy}). Before you do this, however, you should realize that Pearson r is a parametric test that requires your data to be normally distributed. You can run the Shapiro-Wilk test in the *Descriptive Statistics* menu under *Descriptives*. Are the data approximately normally distributed?

7. For the actual correlation test, go to *Regression > Correlation Matrix*. If the assumption of normality was met, you can keep the *Pearson* checked under *Correlation Coefficients*. This is the parametric correlation test. The Spearman's rho and the Kendall's tau are non-parametric versions. Move the variables to the right, and also select *Confidence intervals*.

   The *p*-value in the table gives us the significance value. Of course, the *p*-value does not tell us anything about the direction or strength of the relationship. For that, we have to look at the *Pearson's r* and the 95% confidence interval (CI) of this estimate (also see Section 5.2.1). The *Pearson's r* represents the strength of the correlation. A correlation can be between –1 and 1 and the closer the correlation is to 0, the weaker the relationship is. Although the *r*-value already says something about the strength of the relationship, some people prefer to also calculate *r*-squared, which is simply obtained by squaring the *r*-value.
   What is the value of r_{xy}? Is this a strong correlation? What is the chance of incorrectly rejecting your H_0? What do you decide? What is the effect size?

8. The degrees of freedom (*df*) in a correlation are the total number of values minus 2. What are the degrees of freedom here?

9. When reporting on results like these in scientific journals, there are particular rules and regulations on what and how to report. Here, we follow the most recent guidelines of the American Psychological Association, which state that we should report the value of the test statistic (*r* in this case), the degrees of freedom, the exact *p*-value (unless it is less than .001), and the size and direction of the effect (VandenBos, 2010). Based on this, write a sentence that you could include in the Results section of an article about the outcome of your test. It will be something like this (please choose an option or fill in the correct numbers between the {accolades}):

   'A Pearson *r* correlation analysis showed that Reading Skills and Listening Skills were {significantly/not significantly} {positively/negatively} related (*r*({fill in the df}) = {fill in *r*-value}, *p* = {fill in the exact *p*-value or, if it is less than .001, *p* < .001}, two-tailed, 95% CI [{fill in lower bound}, {fill in upper bound}]).'

As you can see in the sentence, both the direction of the result AND the significance or *p*-value are reported. Note that the *r* is only for the

Pearson *r* analysis. When you do a Spearman's rho, you preferably use the Greek symbol ρ (or write out rho), and when you do a Kendall's tau, you preferably use the Greek symbol τ (or write out tau).

Apart from the *r*-value and the *p*-value, you will see that there is another value mentioned in between brackets behind the *r*. This number refers to the degrees of freedom. In a correlation analysis, you can simply calculate the degrees of freedom by taking the number of participants minus 2. The lower and upper limits of the 95% Confidence Interval can be taken directly from the output.

Whenever you are reporting on statistics in a research paper, it is not very common to include entire JASP outputs in your results section apart from the scatterplot. The results from the table are usually reported in the text, as in the above sentence. Conventionally, charts are included for significant results only.

Note that statistical notations have to be in italic. When you add notes in your JASP report, there is the option of making text italic.

Part B: Social class

A sociolinguistic researcher wants to find out if there is an association between the use of 'haven't got' versus 'don't have' and social class (two levels) (we saw this data already in Chapter 5.2.3 in Part 1). Social class is determined by asking people what they do for a living. The use of 'haven't got' or 'don't have' is determined by asking subjects to rephrase sentences (for instance: Jim is jobless). Note that the actual numbers in the dataset are slightly different from the ones discussed in Chapter 5!
Questions:

1. List the variables included in this study and, for each variable, say what its function is (dependent, independent, etc.) and its type (nominal, ordinal, interval).

2. How would you formulate H_0 and H_a?

3. Which statistical test could be used?

4. There are two ways in which data can be entered for our analysis. The first and usually most common option also for other datasets is when the data

Table J.3 Contingency table dividing the number of respondents according to social class and the use of 'don't have' and 'haven't got'

	low social class	high social class
haven't got	70	59
don't have	64	31

Table J.4 Example of data in a long format

Participant	Variable 1	Variable 2
1	NO	YES
2	NO	NO
3	YES	NO
Etc.		

are organized for each individual case. An example of this type of data organization would be the format in Table J.4, which is generally referred to as long format (such as the data used in Part A of this practical).

The second option is when you only have the total frequencies for each of the cells in the contingency table, such as the one in Table J.3.

For this practical, we will use the raw data in the long format. These can be found in the file 'Prac4B_data.csv'. The data file consists of values of 1s and 2s. For *social class*, 1 is high and 2 is low social class. For the *reply*, 1 is 'haven't got' and 2 is 'don't have'. Open the file in JASP.

5. Go to *Frequencies > Contingency Tables* and move one variable to *Rows* and the other to *Columns*. To check the expected values, select *Expected* under *Cells*. Under *Statistics*, you want to deselect the χ^2 (chi-square) symbol, since we are not interested in that yet.

Although we are dealing with a non-parametric test, we do have to check some assumptions before conducting the actual test. One assumption is that every subject only contributes to one of the cells, which can normally be checked by comparing the number of subjects to the total of all cells. In this particular example, you can assume that this one has been met.

Secondly, as mentioned in Section 5.2.3, in a 2x2 table, none of the *expected* frequencies in the table should be lower than 5. Do note that in a larger table, the expected counts must be at least 1, and no more than 20% of the cells are allowed to be less than 5. If your expected cell frequencies are below 5, you should look at the outcome based on the χ^2 *continuity correction,* which is also known as the Yates correction. With samples smaller than about 30, it is advised to use the *Likelihood ratio* test.

You should be able to find the expected values in the output provided. Has this assumption been met?

6. Go to *Frequencies > Contingency Tables* again, and move the variables again. At this point we want to make sure that the χ^2 symbol is selected and that *Expected* is deselected. It is also useful to select the different *Percentages* (*Row, Column,* and *Total*), as these will give us the relative frequencies in each cell.

The actual results of the chi-square test can be found in the second table of the output. Can you reject the null hypothesis?

7. What is the effect size? Click on *Phi and Cramer's V* under *Statistics*. Phi (φ) is used for variables with 2 levels and Cramer's V for variables with more than 2 levels. A value of .1 is considered a small effect, .3 a medium effect, and .5 a large effect.

8. In other statistics programs it is sometimes possible to visualize the results of a chi-square analysis in a barplot. In JASP this is not quite possible (yet), but it is possible to make two histograms under *Descriptive Statistics*, one for *social class* and one for *reply*. Try to make these histograms. Which values in the contingency table do the bars in these histograms correspond to?

9. A template for reporting the results of a chi-square would be (please choose an option or fill in the correct numbers between the {accolades}):

> 'A chi-square analysis revealed that the association between {variable 1} and {variable 2} was {significant/not significant}, χ^2({fill in the *df*}, N={fill in the total number of participants}) = {fill in χ^2-value}, *p* = {fill in the exact *p*-value or, if it is less than .001, *p* < .001}.'

In the case of significant results, do not forget to report on the direction of the association (e.g. men having a stronger preference for the colour blue). Also remember that, especially in the case of significant results, you would want to report Phi (φ) or Cramer's V.

Report on the results of this study in the way that it is conventionally done in APA research papers.

Part C: Gender and intelligence

A researcher wants to find out whether boys or girls are more intelligent. Eleven girls and eight boys (randomly selected) participated in an experiment in which the range of scores was 1–20 (interval).

Data:

Girls	Boys
17	16
16	15
14	13
19	19
18	15
17	14
16	13
15	12
16	
15	
19	

Answer the following questions in your JASP file, but carefully consider the first four questions before you enter the data in a spreadsheet and open them in JASP:

1. What are the dependent and independent variables and what kind of measures (nominal, ordinal, or interval/scale) are used for the variables?

2. How many levels does the independent variable have?

3. Formulate your statistical hypotheses (H_0 and H_a).

4. Which statistical test could be used? (Consult Table 8.1 in Chapter 8.)

5. Taking the previous questions in consideration, enter the data in Excel using the format you used before. Tip: the two columns (Girls and Boys) in the data are not necessarily the variable columns in R. Remember that columns should represent variables, not levels of variables! Once you have entered the data, do not forget to check whether all variables have the correct scale.

6. Provide the following descriptive statistics for both groups: means, minimum, maximum, standard deviations.

7. What are your first impressions about the difference between the boys and the girls?

8. Create a boxplot to visualize the results.

9. We will test the statistical significance of this experiment, but we first have to check the assumptions:

    a. Check the distribution of the data by looking at the histogram,[1] and the skewness and kurtosis values, and by performing the Shapiro-Wilk as we did in the previous practical.

    b. Also test homogeneity of variance using Levene's test.

    c. Now run the test (see Practical 3 if you have forgotten how to do this).

    d. Carefully study the first table in the JASP output. This contains the values for t, the degrees of freedom (df) and the level of significance, that is, the p-value. The degrees of freedom are related to the sample size: for each group, this is the sample size minus one. These two values together form the value for degrees of freedom. What is the value of t? Which degrees of freedom are applied to this test? What is the level of significance? Can you reject H_0?

---

[1] It is always good to plot a histogram of the data because it gives you a good impression of the spread of the scores. However, with samples that are smaller than, say, 30, the histogram is not the best way to check normality. For this, we really need to look at the values for skewness and kurtosis, and the Shapiro-Wilk outcome (also see Practical 3A).

e. In the Independent Samples *t*-test menu, go to *Additional Statistics* and tick the box for *Location parameter* and *Confidence Interval*. This will add information on the 95% Confidence Interval of the difference between the two means. If the two outer ends of the spectrum are either both negative or both positive, then the chance of the difference being either negative or positive is relatively large. If the outer ends include a zero, that is if one value is negative and the other positive, then there is a chance that the difference might be 0. What do you observe in this example?

f. You can also click on *Descriptives* and *Descriptive Plots* in the Independent Samples *t*-test menu. The first will give you a table with the independent variable and its levels, the number of participants (*N*), the mean, and the *SD*. In the descriptives, you will also see the 'standard error of the mean' (*SE*). This measure gives information about the error in generalizing the results from the sample to the population. Obviously, this error is smaller when the sample is larger, which is expressed by the formula:

$$SE = \frac{\sigma}{\sqrt{N}}$$

Do note that we can often only use the *SD* of the sample as we do not know the standard deviation of the population (σ).

g. The descriptive plots option will generate a line graph with error bars that represent the 95% Confidence Intervals.

10. We are using an independent samples *t*-test. Why do you have to use this test rather than the one sample *t*-test or the paired samples *t*-test? (Explain this in your JASP file.)

11. As we explained in Chapter 4, it is important not only to look at the values of the test statistic and its corresponding *p*-values but also to look at effect sizes. Finding a significant difference does not automatically mean that this difference is meaningful or important. The effect size, as you will have deduced by its name, measures the size or magnitude of the effect (also see Chapter 5). Please note that there are various effect sizes, but we will use r^2 as it is used relatively often and is also relatively easy to understand. The formula for the effect size r^2, which was also discussed in more detail in Chapter 5 (Section 5.3.3), is:

$$r^2 = \frac{t^2}{t^2 + df}$$

Calculate r^2 using a calculator or Excel and report the value in your JASP file.

12. As mentioned in Section 5.3.3 of Part 1, another well-known measure of effect size for the *t*-test is Cohen's *d*. The advantage of using this one is that it is automatically calculated in JASP, namely after selecting the *Effect Size* option under *Additional Statistics* in the Independent Samples *t*-test menu. Report the value of *Cohen's d* in your JASP file.

13. You have now reported two effect size values. What would these mean for the number of participants you need to get enough power? See also Section 5.2.2 in Chapter 5 of Part 1.

14. Reporting on results of statistical studies has to be done according to fixed conventions. It is important to include descriptives per group, as well as the important statistical values (*t, df, p, r^2/d*). Also note that statistical notations should be reported in italic (VandenBos, 2010) and that it is common practice to include a (reference to a) plot in your report. Below is the format that you should use for *t*-test results. Please choose an option or fill in the correct numbers between the {accolades}):

> 'An independent samples *t*-test revealed that, on average, the {boys/girls} showed a higher level of intelligence (*M* = {fill in the correct mean value}, *SD* = {fill in the correct *SD*-value}) than the {boys/girls} (*M* = {fill in mean}, *SD* = {fill in *SD*}). This difference was {significant/not significant}, *t*({fill in *df*}) = {fill in the value of *t*}, *p* = {fill in the value of *p* (or, if applicable *p* < .001)}, 95% CI [{fill in lower bound}, {fill in upper bound}]. This effect was of a {small/medium/large} size, r^2/d = {fill in value of r^2 or *d*}.'

Instead of the *SD*, the *SE* may also be reported. According to APA guidelines, the exact value of *p* has to be provided when the value is bigger than .001, but in this case we do not know the exact value, because we only have three decimal places.

15. What can you say about the meaningfulness of this outcome?

16. Is there any additional information you would like to have about this study?

What to do in case of violations of normality?

If the groups do not meet the assumptions, you can do a non-parametric test to compare your groups. If the data do not show equality of variance, you can solve this by choosing Welch's *t*-test instead of Student. When the data are not normally distributed or when your data are ordinal, you can do a Mann-Whitney *U* test. You can find these tests in the same menu. Instead of a *t*, you report the *U* for this test.

Part D: Alpha – This assignment is slightly more advanced

In Chapter 5, we briefly discussed reliability, and stated that Cronbach's Alpha was a good measure to check for reliability of a test. The teachers from the data in Practical 3A are interested in the reliability of their exam. They have decided to use Cronbach's Alpha to check this.

1. Open the data for Practical 3A (you can re-use the JASP file from Practical 3 for this).

2. Decide whether the 17-item phonetics test is reliable by carrying out Cronbach's Alpha. To do this in JASP, go to *Descriptives > Reliability Analysis*. Select all 17 questions and move them to the right. Under *Scale Statistics*, select *Cronbach's α*. Use the *unstandardized* one. Do you think this is a reliable test?

3. Now check the individual items. Under *Individual Item Statistics*, select *Cronbach's α (if item dropped)*. This gives the alpha statistic if we were to delete each item in turn. We basically want to find those values that are greater than the overall alpha value. Would removing any of the items substantially improve the reliability of the test?

4. Under *Individual Item Statistics*, you can also select *Item-rest correlation*. This column will tell us what the correlation would be between that particular item and the scale total if that particular item was not part of the scale total. So basically this is a correlation such as the one we have seen in part A of this Practical.

But what does this statistic tell us and what should we look out for? Similar to 'normal' correlations, the higher the value of the item-rest correlation, the higher the correlation with the other items. And that is what we want: for the item to correlate with the overall score from the scale. So as a rule of thumb, the item-rest values below .3 are problematic and the items should be removed (Field et al., 2012).

Which items should be removed because of problematic item-rest correlations?

JASP Practical

5

REGRESSION/ MISCELLANEOUS ASSIGNMENTS (CHAPTER 5/6)

This practical consists of two assignments, one containing a test that you have not yet performed and one that should be at least somewhat familiar to you.

Part A: Nativeness ratings and self-perceived L2 speaking skills

A researcher wants to find out if there is a relationship between a person's own perceived speaking skills in an L2 and their speaking skills as perceived by others. To investigate this, she asks participants to tell a story and records their voices. In a subsequent questionnaire, she asks them to rate their own speaking skills on a scale from 1 to 7. Later, she asks a group of 10 independent raters to listen to the speech samples and judge the nativeness of the speakers on the same scale from 1 to 7. For the analysis, she sums up all those scores.

Questions:

1. Add the data to a spreadsheet and open it in JASP.

2. What kind of measures (nominal, ordinal, interval) are used for the variables?

3. Formulate the relevant statistical hypotheses.

4. Is the relation linear? (Plot the data in a simple scatterplot.)

5. Which statistical test could be used?

6. Apply the statistical test you chose. Can you reject H_0?

7. What is the effect size?

8. What can you say about the meaningfulness of this outcome?

Self-rating	Nativeness rating
4	32
5	33
4	28
7	48
3	24
4	24
6	32
7	41
7	42
7	38
6	42
2	16
3	18
1	16
5	36
4	34

9. Report on the results of this study in the way that it is conventionally done in research papers (see previous practical).

10. This part of the assignment is slightly more advanced. As you have read in Part 1, to get the power of 0.8 (1- β), we need about 28 participants to get a large effect. You now know how to find effect sizes, but you can also calculate power. This is currently not possible in JASP itself, but can be done in various ways. One option is to download a program called G*Power (Faul et al., 2007; also see http://www.gpower.hhu.de), which allows you to calculate the power by filling in the test statistic, the p-value and the N. There are also online websites that offer this as well (e.g. https://www.anzmtg.org/stats/PowerCalculator/PowerCorrelation). Another possibility is to do this in R. How this can be done is explained in R Practical 5A.

Part B: Age and writing scores

A researcher is interested in the writing scores of his guided writing class. He wants to know whether the age of his students affects their writing scores.

1. Download the data file from the website, save it, open it in JASP, and inspect it.

2. What are the (independent and dependent) variables and what kind of measures (nominal, ordinal, interval) are used for the variables?

3. Formulate the relevant statistical hypotheses.

4. Plot the data in a scatterplot with the independent variable on the x-axis and the dependent variable on the y-axis. What do you see in the plot?

5. Which statistical test could be used to predict score on the basis of age?

6. Apply the statistical test you chose by going to *Regression > Linear Regression*, and adding the variables to their respective boxes. The most important part of the output is to be found in the *Coefficients* table, which will provide estimates of the intercept and slope AND the accompanying standard error values. You will also find *t*-values and the corresponding *p*-values. The *Model Summary* gives the effect size. The *F*-value and the degrees of freedom for the model you built can be found in the *ANOVA* table. This table actually gives the same results as if you were to analyse the same data with a so-called ANCOVA (Analysis of Covariance).

7. Can you reject H_0? If you have a problem interpreting the results, the explanation in Winter's tutorial (2013) might help.

8. What is the effect size?

9. Remember that this is not the end of the story; you have to check the assumptions! You should:

   a. Check whether the relationship is linear by plotting the data (you can assess this on the basis of the scatterplot you made before);

   b. Assess whether the residuals all deviate in a similar way from the model ('homoscedasticity') by going to *Plots* and selecting the *Residuals vs. predicted* option.

      As discussed in Chapter 6 of Part 1, residuals are the differences between the observed values (the actual data) and the fitted values (as predicted by the model). A residuals plot is a plot in which the original scatterplot is slightly tilted and flipped and the model line would be the horizontal line at 0 (suggesting no deviation from the model). Homoscedasticity refers to the equality of the closeness across the entire regression line. We prefer not to see any odd patterns in this residual plot as we want the differences between the observed values and fitted values to vary constantly. In other words, if the plot does NOT show a particular pattern, this means that all residuals vary more or less equally.

   c. Assess whether the residuals are normally distributed by creating a histogram or a Q-Q plot of the residuals, two options below the residual plots option. For the histogram, it is best to tick *Standardized residuals*, as this will probably give you a better picture. The Q-Q plot will also plot the standardized residuals. In such a Q-Q plot, two sets of quantiles, the quantiles from our data and quantiles from a normal distribution, are plotted against one another. This is why this plot is referred to as a Q-Q or Quantile-Quantile plot. The dots should approximately follow a straight line if both of the plotted sets of quantiles come from the same distribution. If the histogram shows a normal distribution and if the Q-Q plot overall reveals a straight line, we can assume normality.

10. Report on the results of this study in the way that it is conventionally done in research papers. Mostly, you will see that researchers also report on the F-value to say something about how well the model accounts for the variation in the dependent variable and whether the model built was significant (also see Winter, 2013), but that is obviously not enough. According to Field et al. (2012), it is best to report the standardized (or beta) coefficients, which are the estimated effects of the predictor variables, and all associated values in a table. In other words, in a research report, it is common to add a table with the intercept, the regression coefficients (Unstandardized in the JASP output), their standard errors, the standardized betas, t-values, and p-values. Note that this is basically the output you have already obtained with the Coefficients table. You will also often see that significance is denoted by asterisks with:

* for $p < .05$

** for $p < .01$

*** for $p < .001$

Below you will find an example report and table that you can use:

'We constructed a linear model of {fill in DV} as a function of {fill in IV}. This model was significant (F({fill in the value of df1},{fill in df2}) = {fill in value of F}, p = {fill in the exact p-value or < .001}) and explained {fill in the R-squared value}% of the variance in the data (R-squared). Regression coefficients are shown in Table X.'

As you can see, the first part of the report provides in-text information on the significance of the model and the variance explained (also see the first table in Table 6.4). The second part can be taken from the Coefficients table in the output (see also the third table in Table 6.4). As always, it is important to explicitly mention the direction of the effect (a positive effect for age) and what this means. If you prefer, you could also add the coefficients and p-values in the text as follows: 'We found that as {predictor variable} increased, the {dependent variable} also increased significantly (β = {fill in Standardized β}, p = {fill in the exact p-value or < .001}).'

Table X Regression coefficients for the linear model of [fill in DV] as a function of [fill in IV]

	Estimate	SE	t-value	p-value
Intercept				
Factor				

6 MORE ADVANCED GROUP COMPARISONS (CHAPTER 7)

In this practical you will carry out some special versions of the *t*-test and the ANOVA.

Part A: Exposure and vocabulary scores

In the Netherlands, children usually start with English classes in grade 5. Most children by then have already had some exposure to English through the media. A researcher wanted to test a group of fifth-graders at the beginning of the year (pre-test) and test them again at the end of the year to see how much vocabulary they learn in a year (post-test). A group of 42 children participated in this experiment. Both the pre-test and the post-test consisted of 20 similar multiple choice questions about the translation of nouns from English to Dutch. For each correct answer, the children could get 1 point. The data can be found on the website.

Questions:

1. Open and inspect the data.

2. What kind of measures (nominal, ordinal, interval) are used for the variables?

3. Formulate the relevant statistical hypotheses.

4. Create a table with descriptives and make a plot to visualize the data.

5. Which statistical test could be used to check whether there is a difference between the pre-test and the post-test? *Hint: the group of fifth-graders takes two tests. Therefore, these scores are paired!*

6. Apply the statistical test you chose. Do not forget to check assumptions first: in this case, a test of equality of variance is not necessary because the two samples are related. Can you reject H_0?

7. What is the effect size?

8. What can you say about the meaningfulness of this outcome?

9. Report on the results of this study in the way that it is conventionally done in research papers (see previous practicals).

Part B: Instruction and writing scores

The English Department wants to determine the effect of different types of instruction on writing skills: no instruction, explanation in lectures only, and guided writing (GW). Thirty students are randomly assigned to each programme. The scores are results of a writing test, measured on an interval scale (0–100):

no instruction	lectures	GW
34	65	68
58	54	87
56	43	94
47	57	69
35	65	81
31	49	75
55	74	94
65	79	78
61	54	63
27	65	78

Questions:

1. Put the data in Excel, save it as a CSV file, and open it in JASP. Remember that we advise you to add one column for each variable, which means that we cannot import the data in the same format as it is presented above. We want to compare the scores people received and then conclude which type of instruction worked best. Therefore, your data should look something like this:

	A	B	C
1	Participant	Type	Score
2	1	0	34
3	2	0	58
4	3	0	56
5	4	0	47
6	5	0	35
7	6	0	31
8	7	0	55
9	8	0	65
10	9	0	61
11	10	0	27
12	11	1	65
13	12	1	54
14	13	1	43
15	14	1	57
16	15	1	65
17	16	1	49
18	17	1	74
19	18	1	79
20	19	1	54

2. List the variables in the study – if relevant, say which variables are dependent and which are independent.

3. What kind of measures (nominal, ordinal, interval) are used for the variables?

4. In case of independent variables, how many levels does each independent variable have?

5. Formulate the statistical hypotheses.

6. Which statistical test could be used?

7. Create a boxplot for your data. What do you see?

8. Provide the following descriptive statistics for each group: mean, minimum, maximum, standard deviation.

9. Check the normality with skewness and kurtosis divided by their standard errors. A Shapiro-Wilk test of Normality is not really possible to carry out in JASP with nominal variables with more than two levels. An ANOVA can handle slight deviations from normality quite well, especially if the design is balanced, so we can assume here that we can continue with the ANOVA. The ANOVA does also have an option to check the Q-Q plot of the residuals. When the residuals in this plot are more or less on a straight line, normality can be assumed. If there is no normal distribution, you can always decide to run a non-parametric version of the ANOVA, which is the Kruskal-Wallis.

10. Next, we are going to assess the statistical significance of this experiment. Go to *ANOVA > ANOVA*, and add the independent and dependent variables to the specific boxes on the right. Do not forget to check for

Equality of Variance under *Assumption Checks* and selecting *Homogeneity tests*. In case of violations of homogeneity, you can ask for a Welch's correction to your ANOVA by selecting *Welch* under *Homogeneity corrections*. After this, check the output of the ANOVA table. Can you reject the H_0?

Now that we know whether the model is significant or not, we need to carry out some post hoc contrasts. After all, we do want to know which of the groups differ significantly from which of the other groups. When there is homogeneity of variance, and the sample sizes are the same, Tukey's post-hoc test can be done. To use this test, simply go to *Post Hoc Tests* and move the independent variable to the right. Also select the *95% Confidence Interval*. The output table will help you to assess whether the groups differ significantly from each other.

11. What is the effect size? You can calculate the value of r^2 manually with the formula used in Chapter 7, but JASP can also calculate effect sizes for you, such as eta-squared (η^2) or omega-squared (ω^2). These are effect sizes for ANOVAs that are often reported in statistics papers. Eta-squared is exactly the same as r-squared, so when you read eta-squared you can just interpret it as you would interpret r^2. Omega-squared is said to be a bit more reliable, since eta-squared tends to be biased with small samples. You can find out the values for eta-squared or omega-squared by going to *Additional Options* and selecting *Estimates of effect size* under *Display*.

12. What can you say about the meaningfulness of this outcome?

13. Report on the results of this study in the way it is conventionally done in research papers using the following format for main effects:

> 'There was a significant effect of {fill in IV} on {fill in DV}, $F(\{\text{fill in } df1\}, \{\text{fill in } df2\}) = \{\text{fill in the value of } F\}$, $p = \{\text{fill in the exact } p\text{-value or} < .001\}$. This effect was of a {small/medium/large} size, $r^2 / \eta^2 = \{\text{fill in value of } r^2 \text{ or eta-squared}\}$.'

And the following format is an example of how you could report the actual group differences according to the post hoc comparisons:

> 'A Tukey post-hoc analysis [or Bonferroni] revealed that group A ($M = \{\text{fill in the correct mean value}\}$, $SD = \{\text{fill in the correct SD-value}\}$) did score significantly higher than group B ($M = \{\text{fill in mean}\}$, $SD = \{\text{fill in SD}\}$), $p = \{\text{fill in the exact } p\text{-value or} < .001\}$], 95% CI [{fill in lower bound}, {fill in upper bound}] and group C ($M = \{\text{fill in mean}\}$, $SD = \{\text{fill in SD}\}$), $p = \{\text{fill in the exact}$

> *p*-value or < .001}, 95% CI [{fill in lower bound}, {fill in upper bound}]. No significant differences were found between group B and C , *p* = {fill in the exact *p*-value}.'

Note that the report always contains descriptives per group, the important statistical values (F, df, p, and η^2), as well as an explicit interpretation of the direction and size of the effect. Additionally, we always advise including a (reference to) a plot.

In the above example, we are reporting *SD* instead of *SE*. Which one to choose often also depends on the criteria of the journal in which you will publish your work.

Part C: Subtitles and Vocabulary Learning

A researcher interested in language learning wants to examine whether subtitles may help to increase the English L2 vocabulary knowledge of Dutch students. More specifically, she wants to compare low-proficient and high-proficient Dutch–English learners and examine the effects of subtitles in the L2, that is, English subtitles for English shows, compared to subtitles in the L1, that is, Dutch subtitles for English shows. In order to find an answer, a group of 30 low-proficient and 30 high-proficient learners of English are asked to watch one English film every night for one week. In each group, half of them are exposed to the film containing L1 subtitles and the other half viewed them with L2 subtitles. All participants perform a proficiency test before and after the experiment, and their increase in score is used as the dependent variable. What are the effects of subtitle language and proficiency on the potential increase in vocabulary?

Questions:

1. Download the data from the website and open and inspect the data.

2. What are the variables, what are their functions, and what kind of measures (nominal, ordinal, interval) are used for the variables?

3. Formulate the relevant statistical hypotheses (note that you need one pair of hypotheses for every independent variable or combination of variables (i.e., potential interactions)!).

4. Which statistical test could be used?

5. Now before performing the test, we would like to create a table with descriptives and a plot to visualize the data. Remember that we are now not only interested in main effects, but also in interaction effects, that is, combined effects of the two independent variables. You know how to make boxplots and how to retrieve the means for the two levels of each independent variable

in the *Descriptive Statistics* menu, but we would like to get the means and the standard deviations for every combination of the levels.

a. To make a boxplot with all four groups, you need to make a new column with a combination of the two independent variables. The other option would be to filter one independent variable (e.g. *Proficiency*), using the filter option that is visible to the left of the *Proficiency* column. You then enter the other independent variable (e.g. *Subtitles*) in the *Split* box. This option should work but does not let you save the results per in JASP version 0.10.2. In that case, you would have to create a column in Excel with a combination of the two independent variables (e.g. LowL1, LowL2, and so on).

b. You can also go to ANOVA and click *Descriptive statistics* under *Additional Options*. You can also make a plot for the interaction under *Descriptives Plots*, by choosing, for example, *Proficiency* on the horizontal axis and separate lines for the *Subtitles*.

6. Now it is almost time to apply the statistical test you chose, but do not forget to check assumptions first! When checking assumptions for a factorial ANOVA, remember that you want to compare all the combinations of groups. The distribution, for example, should be approximately normal in each group or combination of groups. The newly created column should be of help here.

7. Before actually performing the statistical test, we have to add a small explanation on the different *F* tests available that we did not address in Chapter 7: Type I, II, III, and IV. These different types of tests have to do with the order in which variables are being added to the model, and whether this order is important or not. For our balanced design with only variables with no more than two levels, the difference is not crucial, but it might be good to be aware of the differences. Although there is no consensus on when to use which, we can give you the following, overly simplified, rules to work with:

- Type I: Is sequential and the order in which the variables are added can affect the results. Because of this, this type is often not used in cases where you have multiple main effects and interactions.

- Type II: Evaluates main effects while taking into account other main effects, but not interactions. Therefore, this type is only used to assess main effects.

- Type III: Is used when the effect of a variable or interaction needs to be evaluated by taking all other effects in the model into account, including interactions. The order is not important in the Type III test.

- Type IV: Is the same as Type III, but can be used when there is missing data.

As we are interested in a possible interaction, Type III would be a logical choice. Type III is also the default in most statistical programs, among which JASP. So we will not change anything here. Can you reject the different H_0's that you formulated before?

8. As mentioned in Chapter 7, most people would use omega-squared (ω^2) as an effect size measure for ANOVAs. This is because ω^2 is actually an adjustment of η^2 to predict the effect size in the population instead of only in the sample. However, for a two-way ANOVA, we would prefer to calculate the partial effect size. JASP does calculate the partial η^2, but not the partial version of the ω^2. We will select both the partial η^2 and the ω^2 under *Additional Options*.

The interpretation of (partial) η^2 is identical to the interpretation of r^2 (Field et al., 2012):

- .01 = small

- .09 = medium

- .25 = large

The interpretation of (partial) ω^2 is as follows (Kirk, 1996; in Field et al., 2012):

- $\omega_p^2 = .01$ = small

- $\omega_p^2 = .06$ = medium

- $\omega_p^2 = .14$ = large

What is the effect size for the two main effects and the interaction?

9. What can you say about the meaningfulness of this outcome?

10. Report on the results of this study in the way it is conventionally done in research papers. You can base your report on the example below.

There was a significant main effect of {fill in IV1} on {fill in DV}, F({fill in $df1$}, {fill in $df2$}) = {fill in F-value}, p = {fill in exact p-value or < .001}. This effect was {small/medium/large}, $\{\omega^2/\eta_p^2\}$ = {fill in value of omega-squared or partial eta-squared}.

There was also a significant main effect of {fill in IV2} on {fill in DV}, F({fill in $df1$}, {fill in $df2$}) = {fill in F-value}, p = {fill in exact p-value or < .001}. This effect was {small/medium/large}, $\{\omega^2/\eta_p^2\}$ = {fill in value of omega-squared or partial eta-squared}.

There was a significant interaction effect between {fill in IV1} and {fill in IV2}, F({fill in $df1$}, {fill in $df2$}) = {fill in F-value}, p = {fill in exact p-value or < .001}. This effect was {small/medium/large}, $\{\omega^2/\eta_p^2\}$ = {fill in value of omega-squared or partial eta-squared}. This interaction showed that {explain what the interaction means in your own words}. Specifically, the {DV} was higher for {fill in level 1 IV1} (M = {fill in the correct mean value}, SD = {fill in the correct SD-value}) than for {fill in level 2 IV1} (M = {fill in mean}, SD = {fill in SD}) in {fill in level 1 IV2}, but they differed in {fill in level 2 IV2} with higher scores for {fill in level 2 IV1} (M = {fill in mean}, SD = {fill in SD}) than for {fill in level 1 IV1} (M = {fill in mean}, SD = {fill in SD}) in {fill in level 1 IV2}.

EXAM PRACTICE
7

In this practical you will practise an exam. Below, you will find a list with 7 problems (the same as those in Activity 8.1). Choose at least 2 of the following problems (you are welcome to do them all), and work these out in detail.

Include the following points in your answers to each of the problems below:

- List the variables in the study – if relevant, say which variables are dependent and which are independent.

- For each of the variables, determine its scale (nominal, ordinal, interval).

- In the case of independent variables, how many levels does each independent variable have?

- Identify the appropriate perspective: assessing relationships, comparing means, predicting an outcome, or a combination of these; then choose the most appropriate statistical test.

- Formulate the relevant research hypotheses (H_0 and H_1/H_2).

- Report on the results of this study in the way that it is conventionally done in research papers. Your report of the outcome must include:

  o Descriptive statistics;

  o Value of the test-statistic;

  o Value of df;

  o Significance (the exact p-value or $< .001$) and the 95% CI if possible;

  o Direction of the effect including, if applicable, descriptive statistics;

  o Effect sizes;

  o If applicable, also report on the assumptions, for example linearity, homogeneity of variance, and normality of the distribution;

  o Do not forget to illustrate your answer with tables and figures.

  o Reflect on the meaningfulness of the outcome.

a) A researcher wants to investigate if motivation affects the pronunciation of English by Dutch learners. To investigate the possible effect of motivation on pronunciation, she makes recordings of 24 Dutch learners of English pronouncing English sentences. She then measures the difference in vowel length before voiced and voiceless obstruents (e.g. tap vs. tab). A questionnaire has determined that 12 of these students are highly motivated and 12 students are not very motivated to pronounce English correctly. Tip: the dependent is the DIFFERENCE in vowel length between the two phonological contexts.

b) A researcher wants to find out whether the age at which one starts to learn a foreign language is related to language proficiency. To investigate this, she finds 20 Polish learners of French who have all been learning French for 10 years. The age of acquisition (AoA) of these learners ranges from 1 to 20, in such a way that each starting age is included precisely once. All learners take a 50-item French proficiency test; the proficiency score is based on the number of correct items.

c) To investigate the effect of input on second language learning, 60 randomly selected Japanese learners of Hebrew are divided into two groups: one experimental group of 30 is isolated in a dark room and exposed to Hebrew television 24 hours a day (thereby achieving maximum exposure to Hebrew); one control group of 30 is not exposed to Hebrew. After two months, both groups are submitted to a 100-item Hebrew proficiency test; the proficiency score is based on the number of correct items.

d) Another experimenter is also interested in Japanese learners of Hebrew, but for ethical reasons, chooses to focus on the effect of age and not on the effects of exposure. He also tests 60 Japanese learners of Hebrew and equally subdivides them into three age groups: 11–30 (AgeGroup 1), 31–50 (AgeGroup 2), and 51–70 (AgeGroup 3). Does age influence proficiency?

e) A researcher is interested in the effects of social reinforcement on toddlers' motor skills. In an experiment, 56 three-year-old children have to take marbles from a vase and put them into a box through a tiny hole. The number of marbles that have been put into the box after four minutes is counted. The children are randomly attributed to two groups. In a ten-minute learning period preceding the experiment, the children in the first group are encouraged by smiles and words of praise. The children in the second group are not encouraged.

f) In what way would the experiment in e) change if, in addition, the researcher wanted to find out if social reinforcement equally affects the boys and girls in the experiment? Reconsider the number and type of variables accordingly, and decide on the type of analysis that would be required for this new situation.

g) To investigate the relation between active sports performance and stress, a questionnaire is set up. The questionnaire determines if the participants are active sportswomen and sportsmen (Yes or No) and the degree of stress they experience in their daily lives (on a 3-point scale). The data can be found in the table below:

	Sports	
	YES	NO
stress1	20	19
stress2	24	17
stress3	28	14

REFERENCES

Abutalebi, J. and P. A. Della Rosa (2008) 'Imaging Technologies' in L. Wei and M. G. Moyer (eds) *The Blackwell guide to research methods in bilingualism and multilingualism* (Oxford: Blackwell) pp. 132–57. 10.1002/9781444301120.ch8.

Allaire, J. J., Y. Xie, J. McPherson, J. Luraschi, K. Ushey, A. Atkins, H. Wickham, J. Cheng, W. Chang, and R. Iannone (2018) Rmarkdown: Dynamic Documents for R (version 1.10) [Computer software]. Available from https://CRAN.R-project.org/package=rmarkdown

APA Manual (2010) – please see VandenBos, G. R. (ed.).

Baayen, R. (2008) *Analyzing linguistic data: A practical introduction to statistics using R* (Cambridge: Cambridge University Press) 10.1017/CBO9780511801686.

Becker, A. and M. Carroll (1997) *The acquisition of spatial relations in a second language* (Amsterdam: John Benjamins).

Breheny, P. and W. Burchett (2017) 'Visualization of regression models using visreg', *The R Journal*, 9(2): 56–71.

Brown, J. S. and T. S. Rodgers (2002) *Doing second language research* (Oxford: Oxford University Press).

Champely, S. (2018) pwr: Basic Functions for Power Analysis (version 1.2-2) [Computer software]. Available from https://CRAN.R-project.org/package=pwr

Cohen, J. (1992) 'A power primer', *Psychological Bulletin*, 112(1): 155–59.

Cohen, J. (1994) 'The earth is round (p *American Psychologist*, 49: 997–1003.

De Bot, K. and M. Gullberg (eds.) (2010) *Gestures in language development* (Amsterdam, Philadelphia: John Benjamins).

De Bot, K., W. Lowie and M. Verspoor (2007) 'A dynamic systems theory approach to second language acquisition', *Bilingualism: Language and Cognition*, 10(1): 7–21.

Elff, M. (2018) memisc: Management of Survey Data and Presentation of Analysis Results (version 0.99.14.12) [Computer software]. Available from https://CRAN.R-project.org/package=memisc

Evans, J. D. (1996) *Straightforward statistics for the behavioral sciences* (Pacific Grove: Brooks/Cole).

Faul, F., E. Erdfelder, A. -G. Lang and A. Buchner (2007) 'G*Power 3: A flexible statistical power analysis program for the social, behavioral, and biomedical sciences', *Behavior Research Methods*, 39: 175–91.

Field, A. (2009) *Discovering statistics using SPSS* (3rd ed.) (London: Sage).

Field, A., J. Miles and Z. Field (2012) *Discovering statistics using R* (London: Sage).

Fletcher, T. D. (2012) QuantPsyc: Quantitative Psychology Tools. (version 1.5) [Computer software]. Available from https://CRAN.R-project.org/package=QuantPsyc

Fox, J. and S. Weisberg (2011) *An R companion to applied regression* (2nd ed.) (Thousand Oaks, CA: Sage).

Grendel, M. (1993) *Verlies en herstel van lexicale kennis* (Nijmegen: Nijmegen University Press).

Grosjean, P. and F. Ibanez (2018) pastecs: Package for Analysis of Space-Time Ecological Series (version 1.3.21)[Computer software]. Available at https://CRAN.R-project.org/package=pastecs

Hansen, L., E. S. Kim and Y. Taura (2010) 'L2 vocabulary loss and relearning: The difference a decade makes'. Paper presented at the AAAL Annual Conference, Atlanta, 6 March 2010.

Hendriks, B. C. (2002) *More on Dutch English ... please?: A study of request performance by Dutch native speakers, English native speakers and Dutch learners of English* (Nijmegen: Nijmegen University Press).

Ioannidis, J. P. A. (2005) 'Why most published research findings are false', *PLoS Medicine*, 2(8): e124. Retrieved from http://www.plosmedicine.org/article/info:doi/10.1371/journal.pmed.0020124.

JASP Team (2018) JASP (Version 0.9)[Computer software]. Available at https://jasp-stats.org/

Kirk, R. (1996) 'Practical significance: A concept whose time has come', *Educational and Psychological Measurement*, 56: 746–59. 10.1177/0013164496056005002.

Klein, W. (1989) 'Introspection into what? Review of C. Faerch and G. Kasper (eds.) in "Introspection in second language research 1987"', *Contemporary Psychology: A Journal of Reviews*, 34: 1119–20.

Klein, W. and C. Perdue (1992) *Utterance structure: Developing grammars again* (Amsterdam: John Benjamins).

Kross, S., N. Carchedi, B. Bauer and G. Grdina (2017) swirl: Learn R, in R (version 2.4.3) [Computer software]. Available at https://CRAN.R-project.org/package=swirl

Levshina, N. (2015) *How to do linguistics with R: Data exploration and statistical analysis* (Amsterdam: John Benjamins).

Lowie, W. and B. Seton (2013) *Essential statistics for applied linguistics* (Basingstoke: Palgrave Macmillan).

Lüdecke, D. (25 July 2017) Effect Size Statistics for Anova Tables #rstats. (Last accessed 25 July.) Retrieved from: https://strengejacke.wordpress.com/2017/07/25/effect-size-statistics-for-anova-tables-rstats/

Lüdecke, D. (2018) sjstats: Statistical Functions for Regression Models (version 0.17.1) [Computer software]. Available at http://doi.org/10.5281/zenodo.1284472

Mackey, A. and S. M. Gass (2005) *Second language research: Methodology and design* (New York/London: Routledge).

Mackey, A. and S.M. Gass (2016) *Second language research: Methodology and design (2nd edition)* London/New York: Roudledge.

Meyer, D., A. Zeileis and K. Hornik (2017) vcd: Visualizing Categorical Data. (version 1.4-4) [Computer software].

Mohamed, A. (2018) 'Exposure frequency in L2 reading: An eye-movement perspective of incidental vocabulary learning', *Studies in Second Language Acquisition*, 40(2): 269–93.

Open Science Collaboration (2015) 'Estimating the reproducibility of psychological science', *Science*, 349. 10.1126/science.aac4716.

R Core Team (2018. R: A language and environment for statistical computing (version 3.5.1) [Computer software]. Available at https://www.R-project.org/

R Markdown Cheat Sheet (August 2014) Retrieved from https://www.rstudio.com/wp-content/uploads/2015/02/rmarkdown-cheatsheet.pdf

Revelle, W. (2018) psych: Procedures for Psychological, Psychometric, and Personality Research (version 1.8.4) [Computer software]. Available at https://CRAN.R-project.org/package=psych

RStudio Team (2016) RStudio: Integrated Development for R. RStudio (version 1.1.456)[Computer software]. Available at http://www.rstudio.com/

Torchiano, M. (2018) effsize: Efficient Effect Size Computation (version 0.7.1) [Computer software]. Available at https://CRAN.R-project.org/package=effsize

Van Lier, L. (2004) *The ecology and semiotics of language learning: A sociocultural perspective* (Boston, MA: Kluwer).

VandenBos, G. R. (ed.) (2010) *Publication manual of the American Psychological Association* (6th ed.) (Washington, DC: American Psychological Association).

Verspoor, M., K. De Bot and W. Lowie (eds.) (2011) *A dynamic approach to second language development: Methods and techniques* (vol. 29) (Amsterdam: John Benjamins).

Warnes, G. R., B. Bolker, T. Lumley and R. C. Johnson (2018) gmodels: Various R Programming Tools for Model Fitting (version 2.18.1) [Computer software]. Available at https://CRAN.R-project.org/package=gmodels

Warren, P., F. Boers, G. Grimshaw and A. Siyanova-Chanturia (2018) 'The effect of gloss type on learners' intake of new words during reading: Evidence from eye-tracking', *Studies in Second Language Acquisition*, 40(4): 883–906.

Webb, S. and E. Kagimoto (2011) 'Learning Collocations: Do the number of collocates, position of the node word, and synonymy affect learning?', *Applied Linguistics*, 32(3): 259–76.

Weltens, B. (1989) *The attrition of French as a foreign language* (Dordrecht: De Gruyter Mouton).

Wickham, H. (2016) *ggplot2: Elegant graphics for data analysis* (2nd ed.) (New York: Springer).

Wickham, H. and J. Bryan (2018) readxl: Read Excel Files (version 1.1.0) [Computer software]. Available at https://CRAN.R-project.org/package=readxl

Wieling, M. (2018) 'Analyzing dynamic phonetic data using generalized additive mixed modeling: A tutorial focusing on articulatory differences between L1 and L2 speakers of English', *Journal of Phonetics*, 70: 86–116. https://doi.org/10.1016/j.wocn.2018.03.002.

Winter, B. (2013) *Linear models and linear mixed effects models in R with linguistic applications.* (Last accessed 26 August.) Retrieved from http://arxiv.org/pdf/1308.5499.pdf

Winter, B. and M. Wieling (2016) 'How to analyze linguistic change using mixed models, growth curve analysis and generalized additive modeling', *Journal of Language Evolution*, 1(1): 7–18.

Wong, W. and K. Ito (2018) 'The effects of processing instruction and traditional instruction on L2 online processing of the causative construction in French: An eye-tracking study', *Studies in Second Language Acquisition* 40(2): 241–68.

Xie, Y. (2018) knitr: A General-Purpose Package for Dynamic Report Generation in R. R package version 1.20. [Computer software]. Available at https://cran.r-project.org/web/packages/knitr/index.html

INDEX

PACKAGES USED IN PART 2-R

FUNCTIONS USED IN PART 2-R